Telemachus Thomas Timayenis

The Modern Greek: its pronunciation and relations to ancient

Greek, with an appendix on rules of accentuation, etc

Telemachus Thomas Timayenis

The Modern Greek: its pronunciation and relations to ancient Greek, with an appendix on rules of accentuation, etc

ISBN/EAN: 9783337157432

Printed in Europe, USA, Canada, Australia, Japan

Cover: Foto ©Paul-Georg Meister /pixelio.de

More available books at **www.hansebooks.com**

THE

MODERN GREEK:

ITS

PRONUNCIATION AND RELATIONS TO ANCIENT GREEK,

WITH AN

APPENDIX ON THE RULES OF ACCENTUATION,

ETC.

BY

T. T. TIMAYENIS,

OF THE SPRINGFIELD COLLEGIATE INSTITUTE.

NEW YORK:

D. APPLETON AND COMPANY, 549 & 551 BROADWAY.

SPRINGFIELD, MASS. :

J. D. GILL, 260 MAIN STREET.

1877.

UNIVERSITY PRESS: WELCH, BIGELOW, & CO.,
CAMBRIDGE.

TO THE

REV. M. C. STEBBINS, A.M.,

PRINCIPAL OF THE SPRINGFIELD COLLEGIATE INSTITUTE,

This Volume

IS MOST RESPECTFULLY DEDICATED,

AS A TOKEN OF ADMIRATION

FOR DISTINGUISHED ABILITIES SUCCESSFULLY DEVOTED TO THE PROMOTION OF CLASSICAL
LEARNING IN THIS COUNTRY,

AND A MEMORIAL OF FRIENDSHIP

WHICH HAS EXISTED UNBROKEN DURING MANY YEARS OF ALMOST
DAILY INTERCOURSE.

THE AUTHOR.

PREFACE.

———•◦•———

IN preparing this volume, I have made frequent use of the "Ἱστορία τῆς Ἑλληνικῆς Γλώσσης," by the late Professor D. Mavrophredes (Smyrna, 1871). Important aid has also been received from Professor Geldart's work on "The Modern Greek Language in its Relation to Ancient Greek." Other works which I have advantageously consulted are, Anastasius Georgiades' "Tractatus de Elementorum Græcorum Pronunciatione," Gr. et Lat., Paris, 1812; "Eclaircissements tirés des Langues sémitiques sur quelques points de la Pronunciation Grecque"; Professor Clyde's "Romaic Greek"; Sophocles' "Romaic Greek Grammar" and "Glossary of Later and Byzantine Greek." Frequent references have been made also to the works of ancient and modern Greek authors, especially to those that have touched upon the subject of Greek pronunciation. But my obligations are much greater to Konstantinus Oekonomos, whose work, "Περὶ προφορᾶς τῆς Ἑλληνικῆς Γλώσσης," St. Petersburg, 1829, has been constantly by me.

The subject of Greek pronunciation has been often discussed by scholars since the time of Erasmus, who was the first to propagate that new system of pronunciation known as the Erasmian system. Scholars to-day,

generally speaking, although more or less convinced of
the fact that the Erasmian system of Greek pronunciation is quite at variance with the nature of Grecian
phraseology, with the testimony of ancient authors, and
established principles of history and logic, yet tolerate
this pronunciation because "they do not see that any
good will result to students by adopting the pronunciation now prevalent in Greece." They say, "We
study Greek for the culture it imparts; we do not care
which is the true pronunciation"! Now, we study the
"queen of languages," the language of infinite flexibility
and of unequalled vigor, the language which speaks to
the ear like French, to the mind like English, — the
language which possesses a literature enshrining works
"not only of imperishable interest, but also of imperishable importance for the development of human thought";
we study the language without which human knowledge
would appear like the year without spring, or like the
day without its bright sun; and yet we say, "We do not
care how we pronounce such a language"!

Now, we believe with the Rev. F. W. Farrar, that
the reasons why we spend so long a time in acquiring the
mastery of the Greek are, because the Greek is one of
the most delicate and perfect instruments for the expression of thought which was ever elaborated by the mind
of man, and because it is therefore admirably adapted,
both by its points of resemblance to our own and other
modern languages, and by its points of difference from
them, to give us the idea or fundamental conception of
all Grammar; that is, of those laws which regulate the
use of the forms by which we express our thoughts.
Again, the Greek being a "synthetic language," many of
its advantages lie in its compactness, precision, and

beauty of form. Now, suppose we grant that the advantages we seek to obtain from the study of the Greek
cannot be increased by a change of pronunciation; yet,
we claim, that by adopting the pronunciation prevalent in
Greece, Grecian philology would receive a new impetus.
Scholars in this country and elsewhere, would be better
able to judge of the literary productions of the modern
Greeks; they would better observe how many idioms and
peculiarities of language prevalent among the ancient
authors, still remain unchanged in the language of the
modern Greeks; and, finally, the study of modern language would become easier to the young student, because the euphony, grace, and variety of sound and
harmony of the pronunciation of the modern Greeks,
have in a greater or less degree been wrought into all
the modern languages. Hence, their pronunciation is
comparatively an easy matter to attain, if one is thoroughly drilled in the sounds which the modern Greeks
give to the vocal elements of their language. On the
other hand, the Erasmian system, an author remarks,
" causes its adherents to lose all delicacy, euphony, and
accuracy of expression or sound."

The appendix " on accentuation," although it may
seem foreign to a work of this kind, has been added at
the request of many instructors. It is to be hoped that
by means of the rules which are there given, the study
of this difficult branch of knowledge will become easier
and more interesting to the young student. A few other
grammatical rules have been added, which seem to me
are not given fully, either in Professor Goodwin's or
Hadley's Grammar. Professor Zelf's and Professor
Gennadius' Grammars have been consulted in the prep-
aration of these rules. Scholars are wont to confound

Romaic with Modern Greek, and this sad mistake, it seems to me, is mainly to be attributed to that statement of Professor Sophocles, who in the preface of his *Romaic Grammar* says, " Romaic, or, as it is often called, Modern Greek." Now, Professor Clyde asserts that " this glaring mistake has influenced the opinions of many British scholars, and proves most conclusively that " Professor Sophocles has confounded things which differ." But not only Professor Clyde, but Professor Geldart also remarks, " Sophocles' works, especially his Grammar, require to be used with caution. For the headings ' Ancient ' and ' Modern ' which he places over his various paradigms, should be read, in nearly every case, ' Language of Polite Society ' and ' Language of the Common People ' or ' Cultivated ' and ' Vernacular '; for the so-called ancient forms never died out, but may nearly all be found in the more cultivated modern Greek . . . Again, in other ways truth is sacrificed by Professor Sophocles to system, as when he gives τοῦ πατέρα, τοῦ ἄνδρα, as the modern Greek for τοῦ πατρός, τοῦ ἀνδρός. These forms occur no doubt, but the classical forms are more common even in the vernacular." . . .

But the reason why Professor Sophocles, a Greek himself, and a scholar of so distinguished a reputation, has committed so serious a mistake is to be attributed to the fact that he left Greece many years ago, when quite a young man, and when education in Greece was in a sad condition. Hence, Professor Sophocles is familiar with the vernacular Greek of his times, — which in fact might be called " Romaic Greek," — but since the emancipation of Greece and the establishment of the University and other schools of learning " Romaic Greek " has entirely disappeared, and in its stead the modern Greek, which is the newest phase of the old Greek, has resumed its place.

It is not my purpose now, nor is this the place, to state fully the distinction there exists between Romaic and Modern Greek. Suffice it to say, that this difference cannot be better indicated in brief, than by that which exists between " broad Scotch " and " good English." Professor Clyde says " there are phrases in one unknown to the other, like the famous ' neffow o' glawr,' which all the English of George IV. and his boasted knowledge of Scotch to boot, were not able to explain."

There remains for me the pleasant duty of tendering my warmest thanks, first of all, to the Rev. M. C. Stebbins, principal of the Springfield Collegiate Institute, without whose valuable assistance I doubt much if this volume would have ever seen the light. Not only has his kind and valuable service aided much in the construction of the plan and the development of the work, but also all the proofs have passed under his critical eye. Should this work ever accomplish the mission for which the author sends it out into the world, its success will mainly be due to his broad and thoughtful scholarship.

To Professor W. S. Tyler, D. D., of Amherst College, to Professor E. Anagnos of Boston, and to all others who have honored this work with their favorable notice, I beg to return my thanks. Last, but not least, I must tender my thanks to a personal and esteemed friend, S. Holman Esq., for the very kind encouragement I have received while this work was yet in embryo.

With the valuable assistance of such a scholar as the Rev. M. C. Stebbins, my task might well have been executed far better than it is. But such as it is, I commit it very humbly to the judgment of the public; but with a comfortable degree of confidence that its deficiencies will be charitably regarded by those who are best qualified to appreciate the difficulties necessarily attendant upon the discussion of the topics herein treated.

T. T. TIMAYENIS.

SPRINGFIELD COLLEGIATE INSTITUTE,
    SPRINGFIELD, MASS., September 1, 1877.

CONTENTS.

PART I.

PART II.

APPENDIX.

PART I.

CHAPTER I.

ON THE PRONUNCIATION OF THE GREEK LANGUAGE.

'Ελλὰς μέν ἐστι μία, πόλεις δὲ πλείονες·
σὺ μὲν ἀττικίζεις, ἡνίκ' ἂν φωνὴν λέγῃς
αὐτοῦ τιν', οἱ δ' Ἕλληνες ἑλληνίζομεν.
(Ποσείδιππος ὁ κωμικὸς παρὰ Δικαιάρχῳ, ἀποσπ. 26.)

THE pronunciation of the Greek language that is prevalent in Greece, bids fair to find its way into the schools and universities of the Old World and the New. Scholars everywhere, after much discussion, are coming to the conclusion "that the pronunciation of the modern Greeks, even if it is not identical with the ancient, must have a closer resemblance to the old than that of the Western nations." It is high time, therefore, that scholars should adopt in this country, and in fact wherever the Greek language is studied, the pronunciation prevalent in Greece, which, as we will endeavor to prove, must have a closer resemblance to the old than any other pronunciation now in use. Why it is that so little attention is paid in this country to the way the modern Greeks pronounce their language we will notice hereafter. But it is worth while to consider how eager we are to acquire a correct pronunciation when we study a foreign language, and how careless in pronouncing "the language" in which the loftiest and deepest thoughts were expressed.

Perhaps the idea prevails that after the fall of Greece, which dates from the war of the Peloponnesus, "Greece not only saw her greatness fall, but her spoken language also pass into oblivion." How mistaken, indeed, he must be, who supposes that the traditional language of the Greeks is a thing of the past, is evident from what follows. It may be true, that after Greece had become a Roman province she saw, with liberty, the arts, sciences, and literature fall into decadence. It may be true that there were no more such statesmen and great captains as Themistocles, Miltiades, Leonidas, Pausanias, Aristides, and Cimon; no more great orators like Pericles, Isocrates, Demosthenes, and Æschines; no more poets like Sophocles, Euripides, and Pindar; no more historians like Herodotus, Thucydides, Xenophon, Ctesias, and Polybius; no more philosophers like Pythagoras, Socrates, Plato, and Aristotle; no more sculptors like Phidias and Praxiteles; no more painters like Apelles, and Zeuxis, and Parrhasius, yet the

Greeks never lost their language. In spite of the invasions of the Goths, of the Bulgarians, of the Arabs, and of the Turks, the Greek language, I repeat, never ceased to be spoken by the descendants of the ancient Hellenes. Now, let not the reader do me the injustice to suppose that I am unduly influenced by *patriotism* in my statements. My object is to present facts, — to deal with facts, and to present them in their true light. If there are any defects in the pronunciation of the modern Greeks, I will not hesitate to point them out.

There is perhaps no nation in the history of the world which has suffered so many invasions, from so many different races; yet, far from yielding to the direful influences bearing upon her, she has succeeded in preserving many of the virtues of her illustrious ancestors, together with the language, with so little change, — a change less than that between the English of Chaucer and the English of to-day.

It is wonderful that the Greeks were able to preserve their language under the many vicissitudes which the nation had to pass through, especially while under the Turkish yoke. It is perhaps this that causes many to disbelieve the fact that the Greek is as really a living language as it was in the days of Homer. To bear in mind the various means the Turks adopted to

kill, so to speak, the Greek language, — the cruelty
and barbarity they exercised over the conquered
people, — might perhaps prepare one to believe
that "it was buried in a quiet grave and had given
place to a degenerate scion, or had at best sunk
into the dotage of a second childhood."

And yet, nothing is more true than the statement, that the Greek is as truly a living language as it was in the days of Homer.   To
express my sentiments, I can do no better than to
use the words of an English writer, who says on
this subject, "That it is a strange and unparal-
leled fact that one of the oldest known languages
in the world, a language in which the loftiest and
deepest thoughts of the greatest poets, the wisest
thinkers, the noblest, holiest, and best of teachers,
have, directly or indirectly, found their utterance
in the far-off ages of a hoar antiquity, should at
this day be the living speech of millions throughout the East of Europe, and various parts of Asia
Minor and Africa; that it should have survived
the fall of empires, and risen again and again
from the ruins of beleaguered cities, deluged, but
never drowned, by floods of invading barbarians,
Romans, Celts, Slaves, Goths and Vandals,
Avars, Huns, Franks, and Turks; often the language of the vanquished, yet never of the dead;
with features seared by years and service, yet
still essentially the same, — instinct with the fire

of life, and beautiful with the memory of the past."

Professor A. N. Arnold says, "The language of Greece has undergone no *revolution* since the time of the Attic historians, philosophers, orators, and poets. Through all the successive invasions and conquests of the country, by the Romans, the Goths, the Huns, the Sclavonians, the Crusaders, the Venetians, and the Turks, the basis of the population and the substance of the language have survived unchanged. There has never been a period when there were not some who wrote Greek with a fair approach to Attic purity. . . . . Since the time of Homer, the Greek has never been a dead language. Western Europe by that libel only proclaimed her own ignorance and shame. If there has been a time when even Athenians spoke a wretched patois, there were even at that time educated men and women in Constantinople who spoke and wrote the language in a style which would have been quite intelligible, not only to Plutarch and Pausanias, but also to Pericles and Plato."

CHAPTER II.

At the first appearance of the Turkish suprem-- acy in Greece, hundreds of families fled to the West of Europe, bearing with them that very system of pronunciation which not only the Greeks still use, but which learned Europe universally allowed until the time of Erasmus.

The Erasmian system of Greek pronunciation was proposed about the beginning of the sixteenth century. Hume informs us that the new system was vigorously opposed; it also divided the Grecians themselves (at Oxford) into parties. The penalties inflicted for adopting the new pronunciation were no less than whipping, degradation, and expulsion; and the Bishop declared that, rather than permit the new pronunciation of the Greek, it were better that the language itself were totally banished the universities. (History of England, Ch. XXXIII., A. D. 1547.)

At present many seem to be satisfied that it is best for every one to pronounce Greek after the analogy of his own vernacular tongue. This

of course gives rise to as many modes of reading
Greek as there are modern languages in Europe.
And it is worthy of notice that "no system of
Greek pronunciation conflicts oftener with the
direct testimony of the ancient grammarians, as
well as with the established principles of the
Greek language, than that which takes the English for its basis." Professor Sophocles attributes
it to the fact that in no other European language
is the same letter or combination of letters oftener
employed to denote more than one sound or no
sound at all. However, some maintain that an
Englishman, for instance, learns Greek more
easily by attempting to pronounce it as if it were
English. This cannot be true, for "English
orthoepy is confessedly complicated and discour-
aging, even when it confines itself to its own
language."

Now, the general uniformity of modern Greek
pronunciation, wherever the language is spoken,
is very strong argument for its antiquity, and
against its being a corruption resulting from con-
tact with other languages. In the Spanish dialect we clearly trace the influence of Arabic, in
Italian of Teutonic, in French of Celtic sounds;
in Greek, on the other hand, though the countries
where it is spoken are as widely distant and the
foreign influences to which it has been subject as
diverse, we find generally the same traditional

pronunciation among learned and unlearned alike. In Egypt, in Asia Minor, on the shores of the Euxine, in Constantinople, in Athens, in Crete, in the Ægean, the pronunciation presents the greatest harmony in respect to those letters on which the whole controversy turns.

CHAPTER III.

LOCAL PECULIARITIES.

THE same local peculiarities which existed in the different sections of ancient Greece are prevalent in those sections to-day. The Spartan of to-day, like the Spartan of old, uses the same short, cutting, laconic expressions. He is inclined to an active life of warfare, differing in this respect from the modern Athenian, who possesses the same elegance in his bearing and expression as the Athenian of old. It may not be out of place to remark that many of the superstitious notions of the ancients are still prevalent, especially among the common people of Asia Minor. For instance, according to Herodotus, when Xerxes was marching to invade Greece. . . . . εὖρε πλατάνιστον τὴν κάλλεος εἴνεκα δωρησάμενος κόσμῳ χρυσέῳ καὶ μελεδωνῷ ἀθανάτῳ ἀνδρὶ ἐπιτρέψας. . . . . Now, it is curious to notice that this custom of hanging trinkets to "Oriental planes" (platani) is still prevalent in Asia Minor. The people hang trinkets to such of the plane-trees as happen to strike their fancy. It is a custom with the people of that country, for which I doubt whether they themselves can account. It is simply a custom handed down from generation to generation, and from which neither time nor any other influence has been able to dissuade them.

Again, the same strong hold religion had upon the great mass of the people is still prevalent, especially in some of the islands of the Archipelago, such as Icaria, Rhodes, and the interior of Asia Minor. Mr. Alexander S. Murray in his manual of mythology enumerates many of the superstitious notions of the ancient Greeks, and, in fact, it is astonishing to consider that neither time nor Christianity itself could dissuade the people from many of those religious notions. Now, it is a well-known fact, that it was in the firm belief of his interests being the special care of a deity, that the husbandman sowed his seed and watched the vicissitudes of its growth; that the sailor and trader intrusted life and property to the capricious sea. To-day, the husbandman of Asia Minor sows his seed under the firm belief that St. George or St. James will watch over his interests and will bring to him an abundant harvest. The sailor and the trader intrust life and property to St. Nicolas, who, by the way, is the patron of all seafaring people. In the city of Smyrna, in a parish called "Άνω Μαχαλᾶς,"— "the upper parish," — there is a sort of a cavern called "ἡ Κρυφὴ Παναγιά," — the secret virgin. This "secret virgin" is considered the patron of mechanics, and her place is daily thronged by all classes of workingmen, who, in offering a part of their scanty earnings to her, earnestly pray that she may not cease to exercise her influence over their respective callings. Now, it is a fact, that in ancient times the mechanic traced the skill and handicraft, which grew unconsciously upon him by the practice, to the direct influence of a God. I knew of a poet in Asia Minor, by the name of George Kanares (Γεώργιος Κανάρης) who, a few years ago, wrote an interesting poem and dedicated it to his patron saint, St. Eusthathios! In Mr. Murray's mythology, we notice that artists ascribed the mysterious evolution of their ideas, and poets the inspiration of their song, to "a supreme cause." . Everywhere in nature was felt the presence of august, invisible beings, — in the sky, with its luminaries and clouds; on the sea, with its fickle, changeful movements; on the earth, with its lofty peaks, its plains and rivers. To-day, old women in the East pretend to cure all sorts of diseases during full moon, and by the influence of certain invisible beings who inhabit certain stars. Old women pretend to cure pimples on the face by rubbing mud on it during full moon. Again, the deities of the ancients were represented as immortal, and, being immortal, they were next, as a con-

sequence, supposed to be omnipotent and omnis-
cient.   Their physical strength was extraordinary,
the earth shaking sometimes under their tread.
St. George to-day is represented as riding on a
fiery steed, with a spear in his hand with which
he killed a fiery dragon lying at the feet of his
horse.   Mythology teaches us that there were
tales of personal visits and adventures of the Gods
among men, taking part in battles and appearing
in dreams.   Now, the greater part of those pecul-
iar-looking barracks — the so-called churches —
that are seen nestled on top of hills and scattered
hither and thither, in the interior of Asia Minor,
were erected because some devout Christian declared that such a saint appeared to him ordering
the erection of a church to his memory!   In praying it was a custom of the ancients to lift their
hands and turn the face towards the east.   This is
still the practice of the ignorant classes in Asia Minor.   Here is a specimen of what seems to have
been the usual form of praying among the ancient
Greeks: "Zeus, our Lord, give unto us whatever
is good, whether we ask it of thee or not; whatever is evil keep far from us, even if we ask it of
thee."   The peasant in the East to-day, in praying, will lift his hands and turn his face towards
the east, and will say in a low tone, as appears to
have been the ancient custom, "My God, our
Lord, I pray to thee, give us whatever is good, and
keep far from us whatever is evil, even if we ask

it of thee." This is a very common form of
prayer, which was handed down, as it seems, from
generation to generation. Pythagoras, the philosopher, taught his followers to pray with a loud
voice; but loud prayers do not appear to have
been customary.

Sneezing was regarded as something divine;
and Xenophon informs us, that, on one occasion,
a soldier happening to sneeze, all those present,
with one accord, bowed to the God. "Τοῦτο δὲ λέ-
γοντος αὐτοῦ πτάρνυταί τις· ἀκούσαντες δ' οἱ στρατιῶται πάντες μιᾷ ὁρμῇ προσεκύνησαν τὸν θεὸν." . . .
To-day, if any one happens to sneeze after nine
o'clock in the evening, the peasants of Asia Minor
are wont to pour wine on the ground. Finally,
we must not forget to mention, as a proof of the
wide-spread religious feeling of the ancient
Greeks, the national festivals or games, such as
the *Olympian*, *Pythian*, *Nemean*, and *Isthmian*,
maintained in honor of certain Gods. To-day,
likewise, the peasant of the East, in celebrating
the feast of his patron saint, suspends all business
and celebrates the day with festivals and dancing,
cordial invitations being extended to both friends
and foes, — a custom which was in existence
among the ancient Greeks, because it is well
known that they used to suspend whatever war
might be going on between separate states, and to
permit visitors to pass unmolested, even through
hostile territories.

This tendency to polytheism is certainly a remnant of the religion of the ancient Greeks. Although Christianity has shed its light in Asia Minor and on the islands of the Archipelago, the people are addicted to those superstitious notions, and they will never be abandoned so long as the barbarous Turk holds sway over those countries. In the Kingdom of Greece the people are enlightened, and free from most of the superstitious notions of their brethren in the East.

Let us not, however, forget that the inhabitants of Asia Minor are praiseworthy in retaining the language of their illustrious ancestors. I have alluded to the "local peculiarities" which are still prevalent, in order to show that the Greeks are a remarkably conservative race. Although the Turks prohibited, under penalty of death, the Greek language to be spoken or taught anywhere in Greece Proper or in Asia Minor; although a war of extermination was carried on by them, not only against the people, but against the renowned monuments of antiquity; although all teachers, when pointed out, were instantly murdered, and the silence which reigned in that country — once the home of the hero and the statesman — resembled the silence of an old cemetery, the Greeks succeeded in keeping up their schools, and thus kept their language, in spite of their oppressors.

CHAPTER IV.

MISTAKEN NOTIONS CONCERNING THE MODERN GREEK PRONUNCIATION.

One cause that makes scholars so averse to the adoption of the modern Greek pronunciation is the belief that the Greeks must have lost their language, owing mainly to the invasions of so many barbarous tribes, to which Greece for centuries submitted, until the year 1821, when the War of Independence was proclaimed, which terminated in throwing off the Turkish yoke. But how erroneous this idea! An English writer says "that it seems hardly too much to say that our conduct in this regard shows a kind of literary ingratitude, which ought to shock our moral sense. Greece has, in various ages, preserved to us the succession of culture, when the rest of the earth was overrun with savages. For us it has held the citadel of civilization against the barbarism of the world, and now the danger is over we have forgotten our benefactor, and trouble ourselves little how it fares with him." The case reminds us of the words of the Preacher: "There was a little city, and few men within it; and there

came a great king against it, and besieged it, and
built great bulwarks against it. Now there was
found in it a poor wise man, and he by his wisdom delivered the city; yet no man remembered
that same poor man." . . . .

Why forget that during the time when Turkey
held control over Greece, and when Greece
seemed dead to the rest of the world; when the
Turks, I repeat, had prohibited, under penalty
of death, the Greek language to be spoken anywhere within their domain, often some remote
church among the defiles of the mountains, and
far from the Turks, used to serve as a school,
where the Greek language was taught and
spoken? Why forget that the Greeks had subterranean schools in Constantinople, the very
capital of Turkey, where, under learned Greek
professors, the Greek language was by night
taught to thousands of Greeks? Now, in those
supernatural efforts, so to speak, on the part of the
Greeks, lies the whole mystery of their success
in preserving their language. No! Not for a
moment has the Greek forgot who were his ancestors; not for a moment has he thought of giving
up his language. Time, and the invasions of barbarians, had no effect whatever to change or
demoralize either the people or the language.
Idiomatic expressions, peculiarities of language,
so common among the ancient Greek authors, are

to be heard, even to-day, in the different sections of Greece. Foreign words are rigorously excluded; and even in the public press the names of foreign newspapers, sometimes also of foreign places, are subjected to translation. Thus, the Times is known as ὁ Χρόνος, the New York Herald, as ὁ Κῆρυξ τῆς Νέας Ὑόρκης, etc.; and whereas it would sound ridiculous to call " Le palais des Tuileries" the palace of the Tileworks, it is actually translated by the "'Ανάκτορα τῶν Κεραμείων" in modern Greek.

It may be well here to state that it is from the ancient grammarians we learn the pronunciation of the Greek language. Moreover, a scholar affirms that Dionysius of Halicarnassus, by referring the Greek alphabetical sounds to their proper organs, has, as it were, embalmed them for our use. So that, knowing these facts, we can assert that the modern Greek pronunciation has a closer resemblance to the ancient Greek than any other existing pronunciation.

Again, this is evident from the clearness and distinctness with which the educated classes especially pronounce. It is evident from the striking similarity which exists in pronouncing Greek in all the countries where the modern Greek pronunciation is prevalent. In Greece, in Asia Minor, in Egypt, on the islands, one and the same pronunciation exists. It is again evident

from the purity of style with which the papers
are edited in Greece. It is evident from the fact
that the Greek historians, such as Xenophon and
Herodotus, are the delight of every Greek who
reads them as understandingly as the average
American does the history of his own country.
Take the last paragraph of the Olympian Oration,
delivered by Professor Philippos Ioannou, on the
second anniversary of the modern Olympiads,
A. D., 1870. The subject of the oration is, "The
Intellectual Progress of the Greek Nation from
the War of Independence to the Present Time."
In the closing paragraph Professor Arnold states :
"Embracing about a page and a half of closely
printed octavo, there are about fifty verbs, every
one of which is found in Liddell and Scott's
ancient Greek lexicon. . . . . Of seventy-five or
eighty nouns, all but one are found in the above-
named lexicon, and this one is simply a modifica-
tion of a well known root, familiar to Greek
scholars, and represented by several cognate
words (παγιωτής). . . . . Of about fifty adjectives,
all but one are found in the lexicon, and of this
one the corresponding adverb is found. Indeed,
the adjective itself is found in Pickering's lexicon.
All the nouns and adjectives, without the slightest
exception, are declined as in the ancient grammars. Among eight or ten different pronouns,
personal, relative, demonstrative, and compound,

occurring in all about twenty-four times, there is
only one instance of departure from ancient
usage. Of ten adverbs, the only one not belonging to the ancient language is the negative δὲν
(contraction for οὐδέν) instead of οὐ or οὐκ. This
modern form is used twice, and the ancient form,
οὐχί, also occurs twice. So slight is the difference
between the Greek language of B. C. 400 and
that of A. D. 1870." Now, is this not a proof
that the language must be essentially the same?
And does not identity of language necessarily
imply identity of *sound?* How is it that the
people of Athens recently filled the ancient
theatre of Bacchus to overflowing, to witness the
representation of Antigone in ancient Greek?
How is it that the Athenian heart, ever finely
susceptible to the sentiments of humanity, gave
evidence by many a tear that the people who
witnessed it were imbued with the spirit of the
tragedy, and felt in their very hearts the pathos
of the piece? To what do you attribute all this?
To what can it be attributed but to the fact that
the "ancient Greek" is to-day essentially the
living language of the modern Greeks? What
more need be said in favor of adopting the modern
Greek pronunciation, which alone is the true pronunciation of the Greek language?

The Rev. John Groves, a distinguished Greek
scholar, asserts that "We have, after an examina-

tion made with no little labor, formed a decided opinion that the pronunciation of the Greeks has undergone very little change for 'TWO THOUSAND YEARS.'   The written language itself has been preserved in greater purity, during an equal extent of years, than any of the European languages of the same stock."   He is inclined to believe, with an intelligent traveller in Greece, that the "contemporary of William of Malmesbury or of Froissart would find more difficulty in conversing with his modern countrymen than any Athenian of the purer ages with his."

Bishop Horsley remarks that it may reasonably be supposed that the pronunciation of the Greek language, even in the time of Eustathius, which flourished in the beginning of the thirteenth century, much more resembled the pronunciation of the best ages than anything we can substitute for it now; certainly much more than our BARBAROUS recitation of Greek, CORRUPTED by our bad way of sounding it.   To the same effect is the opinion of a well-known English author, who has bestowed as much attention upon the subject of pronunciation generally as "any writer of our age."   There seems, says Mr. Midford, no reasonable ground for doubting that the present polite pronunciation of Constantinople approaches nearer to the speech of the ancient Greeks than that of any other moderns, with any advantage the

study can give, and that in order to obtain the
nearest possible approximation to the ancient
Greek pronunciation we can do no other way so
well as to adopt the Constantinopolitan.

Furthermore, the University of Cambridge in
England has candidly acknowledged that the
English are almost singular in the erroneous and
vitiated pronunciation of the Greek language.
And, in a well-known literary journal, a writer
has remarked, in strong language: "It is, I believe, an undisputed fact, that our pronunciation
of Greek bears not the slightest resemblance to
that of the ancients. . . . . A remedy should be
found. . . . . Great attention ought to be paid to
the pronunciation of the modern Greeks, ...
which must obviously approximate more to the
standard of the ancients than the method prevalent in England and elsewhere."

Again, it is an undisputed fact, that by studying the Greek as a living language, and by
adopting the modern Greek pronunciation, many
idioms of modern Greek may be employed in
a manner hitherto unlooked for, in the criticism
of documents of doubtful age, as, for example, the
Gospel of St. John, — with a view of determining
the period at which they were written.

Professor Geldart asserts that the relation between accent and quantity in poetry can never be
fully nor fairly judged by any one who is not

familiar with the sound of Greek read accentually, a familiarity which can hardly be acquired apart from a practical acquaintance with Greek as a living, spoken language.

Furthermore, "the pronunciation of Greek, and the interchange of certain letters within the limits of the Greek language, is a sealed mystery to those who are ignorant of the sounds which the Greeks of the present day give to the letters of their alphabet and their several combinations."

Finally, as exactly the same letters appear to be interchangeable in ancient and modern Greek, we hold it to be in itself the strongest proof of the general identity of modern and ancient Greek pronunciation. But we will notice this point hereafter. We will now proceed to discuss the subject concerning the neglect of the modern Greek pronunciation.

CHAPTER V.

AFTER the foregoing considerations, the reader may be curious to know why scholars are so loath to adopt the pronunciation prevalent in Greece. For, in fact, how can the Western nations ever suppose that their pronunciation is correct, when they pronounce the Greek, which is the living language of millions of people, according to the sound of their respective languages? Is this not a regrettable confusion? Now, would it not be better to have for the Greek one uniform pronunciation, such as we have for every other spoken language?

The reasons for this neglect are many and various. With learned men of the old school it is due, very probably, "to a certain antiquarian bent of mind, amounting to a positive prejudice against everything modern." Professor Geldart is certainly right, when he says, that with such scholars the fact that a language is dead, is, of itself, the best reason for studying it, — forgetting that "a living dog is better than a dead lion."

To such, the discovery that the Greek is as really a living language as it was in the days of Homer, can hardly be expected to prove welcome. The manner of life which such persons lead is not inaptly expressed in the words of Southey : —

> " My days among the dead are passed.
>   Around me I behold,
>   Where'er these casual eyes are cast,
>   The mighty minds of old :
>   My never-failing friends are they,
>   With whom I converse night and day."

The remaining reasons for this neglect, Professor Geldart attributes to "the political insignificance of the nation; the obscurity of its literature; the small practical use of the language; and last, but perhaps not the least, the prevalence of the Erasmian system of pronunciation."

CHAPTER VI.

" ŒDIPUS. Where are we now, my dear Antigone ?
    Knowest thou the place ?
    ANTIGONE. Far as my eyes can reach I see a city
    With lofty turrets crowned ; and if I err not,
    This place is sacred ; by the laurel shade,
    Olive and vine thick planted, and the songs
    Of nightingale sweet warbling through the year."

THE political insignificance of Greece cannot be
of very long duration. A people which has made
such rapid strides in education as the Greek nation,
since its independence was established, must "be
worth something, after all." Professor Felton
said, in reference to the University of Athens,
"That many of its professors would do honor to
any university of Europe"; and it is not saying
too much when I say that the University of
Athens is acknowledged to-day as one of the very
best universities of Europe. General education
is widely spread in Greece, and no nation sur-
passes the modern Greeks "in general informa-
tion." But in order that the reader may fully
understand the astonishing progress the Greeks

have made in the sciences, arts, and literature, that is to say, in civilization, since 1832, the year when Greece was declared an independent kingdom, it is necessary that I preface my remarks by a brief description of the country before the occurrence of that memorable event.

> " Before I farther in the tale do pass,
>   It seemeth me accordant unto reason
>   To tell you all, the condition
>   Of each of them, so as it seemeth me,
>   And who they were, and of what degree,
>   And eke in what array they all were in."

In 1821 a general war against the Turks was declared, and, after a war of seven years — a most cruel and atrocious war — the Greeks succeeded in obtaining their liberty. Education during those years, and previous to 1821, was indeed in a sad condition. The Turks would permit the Greeks to have churches, but they would not permit them to have any "regular schools." The Greeks accordingly turned many of their churches into school-houses, and here is a faithful description of one of those "schools" by a Greek who attended one of them: "The rich were wont to attend the subterranean schools established in Constantinople, Smyrna, and other cities. These schools were generally taught by able and scholarly men, who had studied in Germany. The poor attended the schools held in the church.

The school was kept at the entrance of the church, and our teacher was the priest, a man of not extensive acquirements. We went at about eight o'clock in the morning, and were ranged in two lines in the porch, one on each side of the door. The children sat on sheepskins spread on the floor with the wool up, the floor being swept very clean. Sometimes we were ranged round against the wall, without distinction of age or class, brothers being generally placed together, and the girls in another group. The exercises began at eight o'clock, by all standing, while a prayer was repeated by the teacher. Then we all said the Creed. The priest then repeated the psalm beginning 'Eléeson me o Theós,' which is much used by us in ancient Greek, of which I understood the meaning when a little boy. It needed not a translation. When this was done, the boys began to read, one at a time going with his book to the master, who corrected any errors. There were two classes, — one in an alphabet book, called 'philláda' (leaves); the other in the Psalter, or the 'Apostles.' The 'Apostles' contained the Acts and all the Epistles. Both the Psalter and the 'Apostles' were in ancient Greek. Each scholar had a few lines to read, which he studied as a lesson at his seat. We never studied mathematics, as we did afterwards, in the school of Oekonomos in Smyrna. This

school of Ockonomos was what I may term a
'private school.' A few such schools were to be
found in Asia Minor at that time. But they were
generally placed under the protection of some
European power, and thus they were left unmolested. To this day, the Evangelical College
in Smyrna, though a Greek institution, endowed
by a Greek, is under the protection of England.
After dinner we learned to write. Three or four
small sheets of paper sewed together, without a
cover, served for each of the older boys, who
used to write with large crow-quills. These quills
were very durable. The shepherds supplied us
from the birds they killed. The pens were
mended by the master. We sat on sheepskins,
as I mentioned, spread on the floor, and placed
the paper on our knees with our inkstands beside
us. The master gave a copy of the alphabet
alone to each learner, and afterwards a line or
more, written always in a small hand. All the
exercise of the afternoon, for two or three hours,
was in writing. Before the close of school-hours,
the writing was shown to the master, who punished the negligent by feruling their hands.
Great offences were punished by bastinado on the
feet. This was performed after the Turkish manner, by lifting the feet up. In ours and the neigh-
boring villages of poor Greeks, the boys carried
every week ten paras (two and a half cents), or

bread, olives, eggs, cheese, wine, to feed the master. This was the regular price. There was no danger of being starved. Each was informed whether to carry a loaf of bread or a piece of cheese this week, which was generally different from the last and the next week. At the rates established then, I suppose the master received about the *value* of four dollars per month for teaching thirty boys. There was no such thing as boarding, so that the expense of living cannot be estimated as in the United States; but everything was cheap. Beef was two and a half cents a pound; veal or lamb, four cents; goat's flesh, two cents. Flour was four cents a pound."

Such was the state of education in those years of bitter slavery. The monasteries, especially those on Mount Olympus, afforded instruction to those who wished to learn, but generally speaking it was "religious instruction," and those attending, for the most part, were preparing for the ministry. Shortly after the release from the Turkish yoke, the courts of England, France, and Russia, being desirous to give to Greece a fresh proof of their friendly (?) disposition, took upon themselves the responsibility of directing the internal affairs of the kingdom, and of framing a constitution for the nation. The Greeks were opposed to the friendly wishes of the Powers; they were opposed to the form of government the Powers wished to establish over them; they were unwilling to have foreigners direct the destinies of their nation; so that, after the lapse of ten years (since 1832), "The Minerva," a Greek paper then published in Athens, asserted in strong language, "After the lapse of more than ten years, and an expenditure of thirty millions of dollars, the interests of the country are so completely neglected, that to this moment (1842), Greece is left with the greatest part of her domain uncultivated; with her forts filled with mud; with many of her rich plains and valleys in a state of progressive desolation; with some few schools and seminaries of learning, supported principally by private contribution, and denied the benefit of a vigilant superintendence; with churches more fit for stables than for temples of religion; with suppressed monasteries; with a clergy in rags; with a navy inferior to the one in the days of Capodistria; with a population small enough, and yet diminishing by constant emigration to Turkey; with many and rich uniforms, but without a manufacturing establishment; with plenty of commercial treaties, but with a commerce poorer and more insignificant than ever; with a bank which promises wonders, but with no resources and public credit."

The above picture of Greece is by no means an exaggeration of the actual state of things at

the time. The budget for 1843 showed a revenue
of 15,669,795 drachmas, against an expenditure
of 18,666,582 drachmas, which it was feared
would be increased to more than 6,000,000 drach- .
mas, inasmuch as it was thought that the government would hardly realize more than 12,000,000
drachmas from the revenue of the realm. The
causes of these misfortunes must be attributed
to the fact that the Powers were determined to
establish in Greece an "absolute monarchy,"
and the Greeks, on the other hand, wished to
have a constitutional government. Others laid
the blame upon the Bavarians, upon those "who"
— to use the language of " The Minerva " —
" disbanded the veterans of Greece, and gave
the bread of her liberators to worthless merce-
naries, who led to the slaughter-house the heroes
of her revolution, and exiled in foreign missions
the best of her statesmen; who shackled the
press, burdened the people with taxes, wasted the
loan and the revenue, gave the national lands to
strangers, weakened the interests of her protect-
ors, dampened the sympathies of her friends,
disregarded the Protocols, despised the advice
of kings, persecuted the constitution, and introduced into the country that system of government which must be stigmatized as ' absolute
and despotic.' "

Others maintain, and perhaps with justice, that

the real causes are to be sought in the memorable
treaty of the 7th of May, 1832, between the
Minister of Bavaria on one side and the Plenipotentiaries of England, France, and Russia on
the other. By virtue of this memorable state
paper, the sovereignty of Greece was conferred
upon King Otho, and it was further agreed, between the contracting parties, that his Majesty,
being then a minor, should proceed to his kingdom, under the tutelage of THREE Regents, not
one of whom was to be a Greek, who, besides a
a loan of sixty millions of francs, were to have a
mercenary army of four thousand men!

The history of the last fifty years, a Greek
asserts, has recorded many wrongs, many acts of
oppression and injustice; but neither the history
of the present, nor the annals of ancient and
modern times, can afford us a more terrible example of national vassalage than that which we
see in the case of Greece, and which portrays in
such vivid colors the beauties of an exotic policy,
which Mr. Macaulay has justly characterized as
the worst species of slavery. Mr. Perdicaris
remarks that the sacrifices of Greece, the full
hecatombs which she laid on the altar of liberty,
the deep sympathy which her suffering and heroic
courage created in the minds of the civilized
communities of the world, are still fresh in our
memory, and we can hardly dissipate our blush,

or smother our indignation, when, with such
glorious antecedents, we find such wretched consequences; when in the place of that substantial
good which animated the heroes of Greece, and
which was anticipated by her people and her
friends, we have a government which requires
from two to three millions of dollars for its support, but which, at the same time, is swayed to
and fro by some one of the three potent and
irresponsible Plenipotentiaries of England, France,
and Russia! Is there anything more humiliating
or more degrading than this?

But this state of things could not go on much
longer. The Greeks resolutely took the matter
into their own hands, and by one master-stroke
they saved their country from its perilous and
degraded condition. This they accomplished by
that memorable revolution of September 3, 1843.
It accomplished a great deal of good, without
giving rise to evil consequences. That great
popular movement of a single day ended, in the
words of a Greek historian, in the acquisition of a
social compact, which is destined to protect, for
ages to come, the prerogatives of the throne and
the rights of the nation.

The Greeks, having established a form of
government such as they wished, showed themselves capable of governing themselves. They
commenced to rebuild their fallen city and to

preserve the renowned monuments of antiquity, which suffered not so much from the conqueror as they did from the ruthless hand of the antiquarian.

It was the antiquarian, and not the conqueror, who ruined the temples of antiquity and despoiled the city of Athens of its treasures. We can only feel, says the indignant Byron, or imagine, the regret with which ruins of cities, once the capitals of empires, are beheld ; the reflections suggested by such objects are too trite to require recapitulation. But never did the littleness of man, and the vanity of his very best virtues, of patriotism to watch and valor to .defend his country, appear more conspicuous than in the record of what Athens was and the certainty of what she now is. This theatre of contentions between mighty factions, of the struggles of orators, the exaltation and deposition of tyrants, and triumphs and punishment of generals, is now become a scene of petty intrigues and perpetual disturbance between the bickering agents of certain British nobility and gentry; the wild foxes, the owls. and serpents, in the ruins of Babylon were scarcely less degrading than such inhabitants. The Turks have the plea of conquest for their tyranny, and the Greeks have only suffered the fortunes of war incident to the bravest. But how are the mighty fallen, when two painters contest the privilege of plundering the Parthenon, and triumph in turn according to the tenor of each succeeding firman! Sylla could but punish, Philip subdue, and Xerxes burn Athens, but it remained for the petty antiquarian and his despicable agents to render her as contemptible as himself and his pursuits.

However, let us not forget that neither the conqueror, nor the antiquarian, nor time, the destroyer of all things, has succeeded in effacing the wonders of art; the principal monuments of the city, and the Acropolis with many of its monuments, were spared, and Athens, " even when under the government of a worthless slave, continued to be the favorite of all those who had an eye for art or for nature."

> " But lo! from high Hymettus to the plain
> The Queen of Night asserts her silent reign.
> No murky vapor, herald of the storm,
> Hides her fair face or gilds her glowing form.
> With cornice glimmering in the moonbeam's play,
> When the white column greets her grateful ray,
> And bright around with quivering beams beset,
> Her emblem sparkles o'er the minaret;
> The groves of olive scattered dark and wide,
> Where meek Cephisus sheds his scanty tide,
> The cypress saddening by the sacred mosque,
> The glimmering turret of the gay kiosk,
> And sad and sombre mid the holy calm,
> Near Theseus' fane, yon solitary palm,
> All tinged with varied hues, arrests the eye,
> And dull were his heart that passed them heedless by."

For the preservation of the "antiquities," a
society was formed under the name of the
"Archæological Society of Athens." The mem-
bers went to work with willing hearts and hands,
so that they succeeded in rendering the "National
Museum" the most interesting and perhaps the
richest museum of the world.

> Ever lovely, ever dear,
> How may I salute thine ear!
> O what size of words may tell
> Half the charms that in thee dwell!
> In thy sight are joy and pleasure
> Without stint and without measure.
> In thy breath is all that flings
> Sense and thought of choicest things.

Now, the progress Greece has made since her
independence is evident from what follows : —
Greece in 1834 had a population of 650,000
inhabitants. In 1870 she had 1,238,000 inhabitants, — that is to say, her population was doubled
in thirty-six years, — increasing more rapidly
than in Great Britain, and much faster than in
any other country of Europe. Greece, together
with the Ionian islands, has to-day a population
of one million and a half.

In 1830 there were in Greece 110 schools, and
the number of scholars amounted to 9,249. In
1860, there were in Greece 752 schools, with
52,860 scholars. In 1837 there were in the

University of Athens 52 scholars; in 1866 there were 1182. In regard to the commercial and maritime interests of the country, suffice it to say, that in 1871 Greece had 35,000 sailors; three times as many as Great Britain in proportion to her population. Her commerce with England in 1861 amounted to 923,000 English pounds; in 1871 it reached the sum of 2,332,000 pounds. Education is free. From the village school to the " great University " of Athens, education is free. Edmond About, in his work, "Contemporary Greece," speaks in the following terms concerning the Greek students: " I have seen in Greece all kinds of students, but I never saw the student who would not study." Rev. Joseph Cook thus eloquently portrays the intellectual progress of the Greek nation: —

" What has happened in Greece since she was liberated from Turkey ?

" Forty years ago not a book could be bought at Athens. To-day one in eighteen of the whole population of Greece is in school. Fifty years of independence and the Hellenic spirit have doubled the population of Greece, increased her revenues five hundred per cent, extended telegraphic communication over the kingdom, enlarged the fleet from 440 to 5,000 vessels, opened eight ports, founded eleven new cities, restored forty ruined towns, changed Athens from a hamlet of hovels to a city of 60,000 inhabitants, and planted there a royal palace, a legislative chamber, six type-foundries, forty printing establishments, twenty newspapers, an astronomical observatory, and a university with fifty professors and twelve

hundred students.   King Otho's German court, when he
came from Nauplia to Athens in 1835, lived at first in a shed
that kept out neither the rain nor the north wind.   On Constitution Peace in Athens, in 1843, the Hellenic spirit, without violence, and by the display of force for but a few hours,
substituted for personal power in Greece a constitutional
government as free as that of England.   George Finlay, the
historian of the Greek Revolution, and who fought in it,
affirms that, even before that event, degraded as the people
were politically, a larger proportion could read and write
than among any other Christian race in Europe.   Undoubt-
edly long bondage, acting on the native adroitness of the
race, taught the Greeks disingenuousness.   The old blood
produced an Alcibiades as well as a Socrates, a Cleon as
well as a Phocion; there was in it, as in American veins
to-day, a tendency to social, commercial, and political sharp-
dealing.   But after fifty years of independence the Hellenic
spirit devotes a larger percentage of public revenue to pur-
poses of instruction than France, Italy, England, Germany,
or even the United States.   Modern Greece, fifty years ago
a slave and beggar, to-day, by the confession of the most
merciless statisticians, its enemies, stands at the head of the
list of self-educated nations."

"'The Deity has changed in nothing these cities; but I
am not surprised thereby; for I know the Destiny is ever
striving to produce something new, and changes the weak as
well as the strong, by the power of Necessity.'" (PAUSANIAS.)

CHAPTER VII.

MODERN GREEK LITERATURE.

THE Septuagint, Polybius, and the New Testament were written in what is called Hellenistic Greek, or "ἡ κοινὴ διάλεκτος." I may in fact remark that Hellenistic Greek, or "ἡ κοινὴ διάλεκτος," first made its appearance in the Septuagint. For example, "ἔξελθε ἐκ τῆς γῆς σου, καὶ ἐκ τῆς συγγενείας σου ... πάντες ἐξέκλιναν, ἅμα ἠχρειώσθησαν τάφος ἀνεωγμένος ὁ λάρυγξ αὐτῶν," sounds just like modern Greek.

Of Polybius it may be said that the general run of his sentences is not so modern as the Septuagint, yet many of his peculiarities, or novelties, are decidedly modern. The New Testament is written in the language in which the newspapers are to-day printed in Greece. Everything about it is decidedly modern. The language of the New Testament needs no translation with us; it is as natural for a Greek, of fair education, to understand the New Testament "in the original Greek" as it is for an American to understand the language of an English paper.

To-day there are many books published in Athens, written by modern Greeks, in a style far above that of the New Testament; take, for instance : καὶ ἠρώτησαν αὐτοὺς λέγοντες· οὗτός ἐστιν ὁ υἱὸς ὑμῶν, ὃν ὑμεῖς λέγετε ὅτι τυφλὸς ἐγεννήθη ; πῶς οὖν ἄρτι βλέπει ; Ἀπεκρίθησαν αὐτοῖς οἱ γονεῖς αὐτοῦ, καὶ εἶπον οἴδαμεν ὅτι οὗτός ἐστιν ὁ υἱὸς ἡμῶν, καὶ ὅτι τυφλὸς ἐγεννήθη.   Now, in all this, with the exception of the word οἴδαμεν, for which the modern Greek will supply ἠξεύρομεν, everything else sounds decidedly modern.

We now pass into the "Roman period." Lebeck's edition of Phrynichus, "Eclogæ and Epitome," will perhaps give an idea as to the state of the spoken language about 180 years after Christ.

.   .   .   .   .

We come next to the Diocletian age. The following Nubian inscription by a King Silco, Corpus Insc. iii. p. 486, may serve as a type of the Greek spoken at that time in Æthiopia : —

Ἐγὼ Σιλκὼ βασιλίσκος Νουβαδῶν καὶ ὅλων τῶν Αἰθιόπων ἦλθον εἰς Τέλμιν καὶ Τάφιν, ἅπαξ δύο ἐπολέμησα μετὰ τῶν Βλεμμύων, καὶ ὁ θεὸς ἔδωκέν μοι τὸ νίκημα μετὰ τῶν ἐχθρῶν ἅπαξ, ἐνίκησα πάλιν καὶ ἐκράτησα τὰς πόλεις αὐτῶν, ἐκαθέσθην μετὰ τῶν ὄχλων μου· τὸ μὲν πρῶτον ἅπαξ ἐνίκησα αὐτῶν καὶ αὐτοὶ ἠξίωσάν με· ἐποίησα εἰρήνην μετ᾽ αὐτῶν καὶ ὤμοσάν μοι τὰ εἴδωλα αὐτῶν, καὶ

ἐπίστευσα τὸν ὅρκον αὐτῶν ὡς καλοὶ εἰσὶν ἄνθρωποι·
ἀναχωρήθην εἰς τὰ ἄνω μέρη μου· ὅτε ἐγεγονόμην βασιλίσκος οὐκ ἀπῆλθον ὅλως ὀπίσω τῶν ἄλλων βασιλέων
ἀλλὰ ἀκμὴν ἔμπροσθεν αὐτῶν. οἱ γὰρ φιλονεικοῦσιν μετ'
ἐμοῦ οὐκ ἀφῶ (cf. ἀφέωνται in New Testament) αὐτοὺς εἰς
χώραν αὐτῶν εἰ μὴ κατηξίωσάν με καὶ παρακαλοῦσιν
καθεσθῆναι. Ἐγὼ γὰρ εἰς κάτω μέρη λέων εἰμὶ καὶ εἰς
ἄνω μέρη αἴξ εἰμί· ἐπολέμησα μετὰ τῶν Βλεμμύων καὶ
Πρίμεως ἕως Τέλ[μ]εως ἐν ἅπαξ καὶ οἱ ἄλλοι Νουβαδῶν
ἀνωτέρω ἐπόρθησα χώρας αὐτῶν, ἐπειδὴ ἐφιλονείκησαν
μετ' ἐμοῦ· οὐκ ἀφῶ αὐτοὺς καθεσθῆναι εἰς τὴν σκιὰν εἰ μὴ
ὑποκλίνουσί μοι καὶ οὐκ ἔπωκαν νηρὸν ἔσω εἰς τὴν οἰκίαν
αὐτῶν. Οἱ γὰρ φιλονεικοῦσί μοι ἁρπάζω τῶν γυναικῶν
καὶ τὰ παιδία αὐτῶν.

．　　．　　．　　．　　．

From the age of Diocletian to the Byzantine
Period is but a step. Now, until the time of
Ptochoprodromus, in the eleventh century after
Christ, " artificial Attic " was still the language
of literature; but the popular dialect, often re-
ferred to by authors, keeps coming to the surface.
The following is a short specimen of the
popular style adopted in this period, from the
"Apophthegmata Patrum" :—

Ἦλθόν ποτε πατέρες εἰς Ἀλεξάνδρειαν κληθέντες ὑπὸ
Θεοφίλου τοῦ ἀρχιεπισκόπου ἵνα ποιήσῃ εὐχὴν καὶ καθέλῃ
τὰ ἱερά. Καὶ ἐσθιόντων αὐτῶν παρ' αὐτοῦ παρετέθη
κρέας μόσχιον. Καὶ ἤσθιον μηδὲν δακρινόμενοι καὶ λαβὼν

ὁ ἐπίσκοπος ἕν κοπάδιν ἔδωκε τῷ πλησίον αὐτοῦ γέροντι
λέγων, ἰδοῦ τοῦτο καλὸν κοπάδιν ἐστίν, φάγε ἀββᾶ. Οἱ
δὲ ἀποκριθέντες εἶπον. Ἡμεῖς ἕως ἄρτι λάχανα ἠσθίομεν
εἰ δὲ κρέας ἐστι οὐ τρώγομεν. Καὶ οὐκέτι προσέθετο οὐδὲ
εἰς ἐξαυτῶν γεύσασθαι αὐτοῦ.

The next period of "Greek literature" may be
reckoned from 622, the date of the Hegira, to
1099. We have here before our eyes "the tran-
sition in literature from the language of the grammarians to the language of the people."

Theophanes (758 – 816). Besides a host of
new words, and ancient words with new meanings, he has the following grammatical innovations : —

The endings -άδες, -άδων, -άδας, in nouns in -ᾶς ;
οἱ ἀμηράδες, emirs, τοὺς ἀμηράδας. The endings
-ις, -ιν for -ιος, -ιον ; ὁ κύρις τὸν κύριν. Ἄς λαλήσωμεν for λαλήσωμεν, and ἅς εἰσέλθωσι for εἰσελ-
θόντων. The perfect participle without reduplication, as σιδηρωμένος, καστελλωμένος πυρπολημέ-
νος. Ἥμισυν, half, indeclinable. The ending -ος
for ων ; ἀσχήμῳ for ἀσχήμονι ; ἀπὸ with the accusative. Ἀπὸ Ἀλεξάνδρειαν ; εἰς for ἐν. Ἐδίδα-
σκεν ἐν Κωνσταντινουπόλει, εἰς τὸ εὐκτήριον τῆς
ἁγίας Ἀναστασίας ; σὺν with the genitive as well
as ἅμα with the genitive, etc., etc.

The age of Malalas cannot be determined with
certainty. Professor Sophocles supposes that, as,

however, most of the grammatical innovations contained in the work that bears his name belong to the language of the eighth and ninth centuries, it may be assumed that he was contemporary with Theophanes. It would seem, further, that Greek was not his mother tongue.

I. The endings -ες for αι, as Πέρσες for Πέρσαι. Metaplastic dative plural ταῖς πλάκαις, from ἡ πλάκα, classical πλάξ πλακός. Participle active in οντα for -ον, and ἔντα for -εν; πεσόντα, οἰκοῦντα, ὄντα, μέλλοντα, παρέχοντα.

The accusative for the dative. The article before interrogative words. Ἄμα, with the genitive. Ἀπό, by, for ὑπό after passive forms. Μετά, with, followed by the accusative.

The anonymous biographer of Leo Armenius uses the following grammatical innovations: —

The ending -ουν for -ουσι; κυριεύουν for κυριεύουσι; ἐκ with the accusative καὶ εὐγενὸς for εὐγενής. The auxiliary ἃς for ἄφες.

Leo the Philosopher (A. D. 886 – 911), in his "Tactica," employs a considerable number of new words and the endings: -ος for -ης.

II. ἰδικός = proprium, as in Romaic. The ending -έσαι for -ει (second person sing. passive), οὐ for μή in the protasis, etc.

. . . . . .

Constantine Porphyrogenitus, who wrote all his works purposely "in the common and spoken

language," with the exception of the Life of St.
Basil, which was written in the artificial "Attic
Greek" of that period, gives us: The ending -αις
for αι; ἀλλάξιμον, gen. ἀλλαξίματος; σᾶς for ὑμῶν;
ἕνα for ἕν; μονογενῆ for the vocative of μονογενῆς;
τῶν for αὐτῶν; εἶσε for εἶ; σοῦ for σοι, as καλή-
σου ἡμέρα, "Good morning to you"; νὰ for ἵνα,
and ἕως with the accus. Ἅμα, with the subj. Μετά,
with, followed with the accus., etc.

An anonymous writer, known as "Theophanes
Continuatus," makes use of the expression, "the
common and impure language," which evidently
means the language of the illiterate. In his collection entitled "Theophanes Continuatus," we
find: Ἅλυ, gen. of Ἅλυς, χρυσὸς for χρυσοῦς.
The ending ας, κρασᾶς, *vitner*, and periphrastic
future subjunctive.

Cedrenus (A. D. 1057) wrote in ancient Greek,
but with "indifferent success." His work contains
but few grammatical innovations: Gen. in η from
ῆς; the numeral adverb ἑπτάϊ for ἑπτάκις.

.   .   .   .   .

Scylitzes gives us the following specimen of the
common dialect: ἐῶ σε ἔκτισα, φοῦρνε· ἐῶ ἵνα σε
χαλάσω = in modern Greek, ᾿εγώ σε ἔκτισα φοῦρνε,
ἐγώ νὰ σὲ χαλάσω, *I built thee, O oven, I will de-
molish thee!*

.   .   .   .   .

Anna Commena, who wrote a history of the

Byzantine War about the year 1100, alludes to
the common dialect. She has preserved the following popular tetrastitch : —

> Τό σάββατον τῆς τυρινῆς
> Χαρῆς ’Αλίξιε, ἐνόησές το,
> Καὶ τὴν δευτέραν τὸ πρωΐ·
> Εἶπα, καλῶς γεράκιν μου.

. . . . .

This closes the mediæval period of Greek literature.

Theodorus Prodromus (A. D. 1143–1180) may
be regarded as the earliest "modern Greek author."
He is said to have used the "popular dialect," or
"Romaic Greek," in its *entirety*. Before pro-
ceeding any farther, it may be well to give the
origin of the term "Romaic Greek."

ORIGIN OF THE NAME "ROMAIC."

In Professor Sophocles' "Romaic Grammar"
we find that when Constantine the Great trans-
ferred the seat of empire to Byzantium, he called
it Νέα ‘Ρώμη, *New Rome*. The popular name, however, was, and still continues to be, Κωνσταντινού-
πολις, *Constantinople*, that is Κωνσταντίνου πόλις,
the city of Constantine. The appellation *New Rome*
is now obsolete, except in connection with the
titles of its bishop. Thus, Γρηγόριος ἐλέῳ Θεοῦ
ἀρχιεπίσκοπος Κωνσταντινουπόλεως Νέας ‘Ρώμης καὶ

οἰκουμενικός πατριάρχης, *Gregory, by the mercy of
God Archbishop of Constantinople, which is New
Rome, and Universal Patriarch.* After that mem-
orable event the name of Ῥωμαῖοι, *Romans*, was
applied to the Greeks as well as to the genuine
Romans. The subjects of the Byzantine emperor
were sometimes distinguished from the Ἑσπέριοι
Ῥωμαῖοι, *Western Romans*, by the adjective Ἑῷοι,
Eastern. The Emperor's domain was known as
Ῥωμανία, *Romania*, the country of the Romans, a
derivative of Ῥωμᾶνος, Romanus, *Roman.*

The Greeks being thus changed into Romans,
it was natural that the name of the language
should undergo a corresponding transformation.
The adjective Ῥωμαίικος (trisyllabic), less correctly Ῥωμαῖκος, is derived from Ῥωμαῖος, after
the analogy of the classical Ἀχαιικός, from Ἀχαιός.
Hence ἡ Ῥωμαϊκή γλῶσσα, or simply τὰ Ῥωμαίικα,
Romaic, the language of the Romans.

The term ἡ Ἑλληνικὴ Γλῶσσα, or simply τὰ
Ἑλληνικά, is regularly applied now to the ancient
and present language of Greece.

Now, we have said that the first modern Greek
writer who can be said to have used the "Romaic
dialect" in its entirety was Theodorus Prodromus
(A. D. 1143 – 1180), nicknamed "Ptochoprodromus." He lived in the reign of the Emperor
Manuel Comnenus, was a monk, and addressed
to him a series of popular verses, στίχοι πολιτικοί,

preserved to us by Coray in the first volume of
his "Atacta," Paris, 1828. The burden of these
verses appears to be the poverty of learned men.
They are written with great spirit, and in a style
which may be termed "barbarous ancient Greek."
Since the emancipation of Greece the style commenced to show its native power, so that "Romaic
Greek" or "barbarous ancient Greek" is a thing
altogether of the past. The following is a specimen of his style:—

Τὴν κεφαλήν σου, Βασιλεῦ, εἰς τοῦτο τί μὲ λέγεις ;
Ἂν ἔχω γείτονάν τιναν κέχῃ παιδὶν ἀγόριν,
Νὰ τὸν εἰπῶ 'τι, Μάθε το γραμματικὸν νὰ ζήσῃ ;
Παρὰ κρανιαροκέφαλον πάντες νὰ μ' ὀνομάσουν.
Νὰ τὸν εἰπῶ 'τι, Μάθε το τζαγγάρην τὸ παιδίν σου.
Γείτοναν ἔχω πετζωτήν, τάχα ψευδοτζαγγάρην·
Πλὴν ἔνε καλοψουνιστής, ἔνε καὶ χαροκόπος.
Ὅταν γὰρ ἴδη τὴν αὐγὴν περιχαρασσομένην,
Λέγει ἅς βράσῃ τὸ κρασὶν καὶ βάλε τὸ πιπέριν·
Εὐθὺς τὸ βράσειν τὸ θερμόν λέγει πρὸς τὸ παιδίν του
Νά τό παιδίν μου, ἀγόρασε χορδόκοιλα σταμένου,
Φέρε καὶ Βλάχικον τυρίν ἄλλην σταμεναρέαν,
Καὶ δός με νὰ προγεύσωμαι, καὶ τότε νὰ πετζόνω.
Ἀφ' οὗ δὲ φθάσῃ τὸ τυρὶν καὶ τὰ χορδοκοιλίτζα.

.   .   .   .   .

Κἄν τέσσερα τὸν δίδουσιν εἰς τὸ τρανόν μουχρούτιν·
Καὶ παρευθὺς ὑπόδημαν ἐπαίρει καὶ πετζόνει·
Ὅταν δὲ πάλιν, βασιλεῦ, γεύματος ὥρα φθάσῃ,

'Ρίπτει τὸ καλαπόδιν του, ρίπτει καὶ τὸ σανίδιν,
Καὶ λέγει τὴν γυναῖκάτου, Κυρὰ καὶ θές τραπέζιν·
Καὶ πρῶτον μίσσον ἐκζεστόν, δεύτερον τὸ σφουγγάτον,
Καὶ τρῖτον τὸ ἀκριόπαστον ὀφθόν ἀπό μερίου.
Καὶ τέταρτον μονόκυθρον, πλὴν βλέπε νὰ μὴ βράζῃ.
'Αφ' οὗ δὲ παραθέσουσιν καὶ νίψεται καὶ κάτσῃ,
'Ανάθεμά με Βασιλεῦ καὶ τρισανάθεμά με,
Ὄνταν στραφῶ καὶ ἴδω τὸν λοιπὸν τὸ πῶς καθίζει,
Τὸ πῶς ἀνακομπόνεται νὰ πιάσῃ τὸ κουτάλιν,
Καὶ οὐδέν τρέχουν τὰ σάλια μου, ὡς τρέχει τὸ ποτάμιν.
Καὶ ἐγὼ ὑπάγω κ' ἔρχομαι πόδας μετρῶν τῶν στίχων.
Εὐθὺς ζητῶ τὸν ἴαμβον, γυρεύω τὸν σπονδεῖον·
Γυρεύω τὸν πυῤῥίχιον καὶ τὰ λοιπὰ τὰ μέτρα.
'Αλλὰ τὰ μέτρα ποῦ 'φελοῦν σ' τὴν ἄμετρόν μου πεῖναν;
Πότε γὰρ ἐκ τὸν ἴαμβον νὰ φάγω κοσμοκράτορ;
Ἢ πῶς ἐκ τὸν πυῤῥίχιον ποτέ μου νὰ χορτάσω;
Ἔδε τεχνίτης σοφιστὴς ἐκεῖνος ὁ τζαγγάρης.
Εἶπε τὸ Κύριε' λέησον, ἤρξατο ρουκανίζειν.

We give here some of his grammatical innovations as collected by Professor Sophocles. They will be found of importance to any one who may read his writings, and, in fact, a key to the Romaic dialect: —

I. N, annexed to words ending in a vowel: φόρειν, ἐκτενίσθην, γείτοναν, τινάν, ὑπόδημαν, Βραδύν, ἐκαῖέζουν, ἐσέν. II. The ending ες or αις for αι: τὲς τέσσαρες γωνίαις. III. The accent of proparoxytone nouns and adjectives retains its place:

ὁ κἄποιας γειτόνισσας, δεύτερην, σκουμπροπαλαμυδόπαστου. IV. Augmentative endings, -a: οὔρα, κομμάτια, κομματούρα. V. The adjective ending -έα for -εια: τὰς μακρέας μύτας. VI. The article οἱ for αἱ: οἱ ἀρχόντισσες, οἱ σάρκες. VII. Ἀτός, self; thus, Ἀτός του γίνεται Ἰατρός. VIII. Ἑαυτόν, self; thus, τρέφε τὸν ἑαυτόν σου. IX. Ποῦ or ὁποῦ for ὅς, who. X. The verbal ending -όνω or ώνω from the classical όω: πετσόνω, σηκώνω. XI. Ἐν, ἔνε, ἔνι εἶνε for ἐστί or εἰσί. XII. Periphrastic future by means of θέλω and the infinitive; thus, θέλεις σύρειν, the first example of the kind. XIII. Future subjunctive by means of νά and the imperfect or aorist indicative: νὰ 'ζουν, νὰ μὲ δίδαν, νά 'μαθα. XIV. Imperfect passive proparoxytone: ἠρχόμην and ἤρχουμουν, νά 'ργάζουμουν, γένουμουν. XV. The ending -ντασι for -ντο: thus, ἐπουλούντασι for ἐπωλοῦντο. XVI. The accusative for the dative, passim. XVII. The accusative for the genitive after numeral adverbs: ἅπαξ τόν χρόνον, once a year. XVIII. Νά and διά νά as in the Greek of the present day. XIX. Εὐθύς τό, followed by the aorist infinitive, is equivalent to the modern. Εὐθὺς ποῦ, as soon as. XX. All the prepositions take the accusative: σὺν τὴν ζήτησιν. XXI. Οὐδείς for ου, not.

Almost contemporary with Ptochoprodromus was Simon Sethos, who is the first prose writer in modern Greek.

The "Book of the Conquest of Romania and the Morea," Βιβλίον τῆς κουγκέστας τῆς Ῥωμανίας καί τοῦ Μωραῖος, by the Franks (French, Italians), now ascertained to be a translation from the French, belongs to the fourteenth century and represents the Romaic of that period. It is published by Buchon in the second volume of his "Recherches Historiques," Paris, 1845. Professor Sophocles states, that from the abuse it heaps upon the Greeks, because they, on more than one occasion, deceived the truth-loving Franks, but chiefly because the Latins were unable to induce that stiff-necked, perfidious, lying people to recognize the apostolic claim of the Holy Father, it is not difficult to perceive that the translator, as well as the original author, was a member of the Western church. The "Book of the Conquest" may be best described "as a rhyming chronicle, which might deserve the name of poor verse were it not so prosaic, or of bad prose were it not written in metre."

To the same period belongs the epic poem entitled "Belthandros and Chrysantza." This poem is without question a far more imaginative poem than the "Niebungelied." The writer possessed what is called "real genius." If our reason were disposed to deny this, our sensations on perusing his work will fully prove it. It is an infallible

proof of real genius when a writer possesses the
power to stir the feelings, or to affect the mind,
in the most lively manner, by a few words, and
with the most perfect simplicity of language.
Such a genius conspicuously marks both Shakespeare and the writer of " Belthandros and Chrysantza."

The poem, as Geldart remarks, is a romance
of knight-errantry, in which we can plainly trace
the effects of the crusades in Greece. The plot
of " Belthandros and Chrysantza" is simple but
imaginative. The hero is Belthandros (a Grae-
cism for Bertran), the son of Rhodophilus, King
of Romania, who has two sons, Bertran and
Philarmus, one of whom he loves, and the other
of whom of course he hates. Belthandros, the
unfortunate object of his ' father's displeasure,
accordingly takes a journey eastward, and after
heroic exploits performed at the expense of his
father's men-at-arms, who are despatched to bring
him back, he reaches Armenia, and the fortress of
Tarsus. Riding by the side of a small stream, he
espies a gleam of light in the running waters, and
follows up the course of the rivulet a ten days'
journey. It leads him to a magic building called
the Castle of Love, built of precious stones, and
surrounded and filled with every imaginable form
of wonder, in the way of automaton, birds and
beasts of gold, reminding us of Vulcan's work-

manship. Then follows an introduction to the
King of the Loves, the owner of the enchanted
palace, who gives him the task of choosing the
most beautiful out of forty women. He first
selects three, and having thus equalized the prob-
lem to that which Paris of old had solved, he
proceeds to award the palm to Chrysantza, who
turns out to be the daughter of the King of
Antiochia, and whose subsequent appearance at
the court of Rhodophilus reconciles the father,
and terminates the story with the slaying of the
fatted calf.

"Did the modern Greek language possess but
this single epic, to say that it is destitute of literature were a calumny indeed."

Emmanuel Gorgilas ('Εμμανουὴλ Γεωργιλλᾶς),
a native of Rhodes, belongs to the latter part of
the fifteenth century. He wrote several poems in
Romaic verse. About the same time the story of
Apollonius of Tyre ('Απολλωνίου τοῦ ἐν Τύρῳ) was
translated into Romaic from the Latin romance
Apollonius Tyrius, the supposed prototype of
Shakespeare's Pericles, Prince of Tyre.

The following works are attributed to Emmanuel Gorgilas.

1. Διήγησις εἰς τὰς πράξεις τοῦ περιβοήτου στρα-
τηγοῦ τῶν 'Ρωμαίων μεγάλου Βελισαρίου (ἐξεδόθη ἐν
Βενετίᾳ τῷ 1554 ὑπὸ Φραγκίσκου 'Ραμπατσέτου εἰς
4 τόμους. The work is metrical.

2. Τὸ Θανατικόν τῆς 'Ρόδου (ἀνέκδοτον ἐν τῇ Παρισιανῇ Βιβλιοθήκῃ).

3. Θρῆνος τῆς Κωνσταντινουπόλεως.

Demetrius Zenos (Δημήτριος ὁ Ζῆνος), who translated the Batrachomyomachia into the "Romaic dialect," represents the spoken language of the sixteenth century. This translation Martin Crusius, A. D. 1526–1607, translated into Latin. But almost the only examples of Modern Greek in the sixteenth century consist of letters and fragments of speeches, chiefly the utterances of ecclesiastics.

The "great work" of the seventeenth century, as Professor Geldart calls it, is one entitled "Erophile," written in the Cretan dialect, by one Chortakes, a Cretan. It is a tragedy, and opens with a monologue of Charon, the impersonation of Death, who speaks as follows: —

'Η ἄγρια[1] κ' ἡ ἀνελύπητη[2] κ' ἡ σκοτεινὴ Θωριά[3] μου,
Καὶ τὸ δρεπάν'[4] ὅπου βαστῶ,[5] καὶ ταῦτα τὰ γυμνά μου
Κόκκαλα, κ' ἡ πολλαῖς Βρονταῖς, κ' ἡ ἀστραπαῖς ὁμάδι.

[1] 'Η ἄγρια = ἡ ἀγρία (ὁ ἄγριος, -ία, -ιον).
[2] ἡ ἀνελύπητη for ἀνέλπιστος, ον, with sense of desperate.
[3] Θωριά = Θεωρία.
[4] δρεπάν = δρέπανον, ου, τό = Δρεπάνη.
[5] Βαστῶ = Βαστάζω.

"Οπου τὴν γῆν ἀνοίξασι, κ' ἐβγῆκ' ἀπού⁶ τὸν Ἄδη,
Ποιὸς εἶμαι μοναχά⁷ τωνε δίχως μιλιὰ⁸ μποροῦσι⁹
Νὰ φανερώσουν σήμερον σ' ὅσους μὲ συντηροῦσι.

. . . .

Ἐγῶμαι¹⁰ κεῖνος τὸ λοιπὸν¹¹ ἀπ' ὅλοι¹² μὲ μισοῦσι,
Καὶ σκυλοκάρδη¹³ καὶ τυφλὸ κ' ἄπονον μέ λαλοῦσι.
Ἐγῶμ' ἀπού τζὴ Βασιλεὺς¹⁴ τζὴ 'μπορουμένους οὔλους,
Τζὴ πλούσιους κ' ἀνήμπορους¹⁵ τζ' ἀφένταις καὶ τζὴ δούλους
Τζὴ νέους καὶ τζὴ γέροντας, μικροὺς καὶ τζὴ μεγάλους
Τζὴ φρόνιμους καὶ τζὴ λωλοὺς,¹⁶ κ' ὅλους ἀνθρώπους τζ'
          ἄλλους
Γιαμὰ,¹⁷ γιαμά ὄντε μοῦ φανῇ ρίχνω¹⁸ καὶ Θανατόνω.
Κ' εἰς τὸν ἀθὸ¹⁹ τζὴ νιότης τους τζὴ χρόνους τους τελειόνω
Λυόνω τζὴ δόξαις καὶ τιμαῖς τὰ 'νόματα μαυρίζω
Τζὴ δικαιοσύνας διασκορπῶ, καὶ τζὴ φιλιαῖς χωρίζω,
Τζ' ἄγριαις καρδιαῖς καταπονῶ, τζὴ λογισμοὺς ἀλλάσσω
τζ' ἐλπίδες ρίχνω s' μιὰ μεριὰ, καὶ τζ' ἔγνοιαις κατατάσσω
Κ' ἐκεῖ που μὲ πολὺ θυμὸ τὰ 'μάτια μου στραφοῦσι,

---

⁶ ἀπού = ἀπό.
⁷ μοναχάτωνε = by themselves ; so ποτέ μου (never) in my life.
⁸ μιλιὰ = ὁμιλία, -ας.
⁹ μποροῦσι = δύνανται.
¹⁰ Ἐγῶμαι = (Ἐγώ) εἶμαι.
¹¹ τὸ λοιπὸν = in truth, finally (common in modern Greek).
¹² ἀπ' ὅλοι μὲ μισοῦσι = all men hate (me).
¹³ σκυλοκάρδη = hound-hearted.
¹⁴ τζὴ Βασιλεὺς, i. e. τοὺς Βασιλέϝς, contracted for τοὺς Βασιλέϝας.
¹⁵ ἀνήμπορους = μικρούς, ἀδυνάτους (weak).
¹⁶ λωλοὺς = μανιώδης.
¹⁷ Γιαμὰ γιαμὰ ὄντε, as soon as ; etymology δίαμα ὄντε χρόνον.
¹⁸ ρίχνω = ρίπτω.
¹⁹ ἀθὸ = ἄνθος, flower.

Χώραις χαλοῦν, ἀλάκαιραις,[20] κόσμοι, πολλοί βουλοῦσι.
Ποῦ τῶν Ἑλλήνω ἡ Βασιλειαίς; ποῦ τῶ Ῥωμιῶν ἡ τόσαις
Πλούσιαις καὶ μπορεζόμεναις χώραις; ποῦ τόσαις γνώσαις;

Φτωχοί[21] στὸ λάκκο κατοικοῦν, βουβοὶ μὲ δίχως[22] στόμα
Ψυχαῖς γδυμναῖς[23] δὲν ξεύρω ποῦ στὴ γῆ λιγάκι[24] χῶμα.
Ὦ πλήσια[25] κακορρίζικοι[26] καὶ γιάντα δὲ θεωροῦσι
Τζὴ μέραις πῶς λιγαίνουσι, τζὴ χρόνους πῶς περνοῦσι;
Τὸ ψὲς[27] ἐδιάβη, τὸ προχθὲς πληὸ δὲν ἀνιστυρᾶται,
Σπίθα[28] μικρὴ τὸ σήμερο στὰ σκοτεινὰ λογᾶται.
Σέναν ἀνοιγοσφάλισμα[29] τῶν ἄμματι ἀποσώνω
Καὶ δίχως λύπησι καμιὰ πᾶσ᾽[30] ἄνθρωπο σκοτώνω
Τὰ κάλλη σβύνω, κ᾽ ὄμορφο πρόσωπο δὲ λυποῦμαι,
Τοὺς ταπεινοὺς δὲ λεημονῶ, τοὺς ἄγριους δὲ[31] φοβοῦμαι
Τοὺς φεύγουν φτάν᾽ ὀγλήγορα, τοὺς μὲ ζητοῦν μακραίνω
Καὶ δίχως νὰ μὲ κράζουσι συχνὰ τζὴ γάμους ᾽μπαίνω.
Φτωχοὶ τ᾽ ἀρπᾶτε φεύγουσι, τὰ σφίγγετε πετοῦσι,
Τὰ περμαζόνετε σκορποῦν, τὰ κτίζετε χαλοῦσι.

---

[20] ἀλάκαιραις, Cretan, for ὁλόκληραι.
[21] Φτωχοί = πένητες (ἄνθρωποι).
[22] μὲ δίχως = without. The μὲ is pleonastic.
[23] γδυμναῖς = for γυμναῖς.
[24] λιγάκι = ὀλίγον.
[25] πλήσια = μάλα,
[26] κοκορρίζικοι = ill-fated. Τὸ ριζικὸ is modern Greek for fate. The idea is the same as in πεπρωμένον (common in modern Greek) εἱμαρμένη, that which is deep fixed like a root in the ground. ρίζα.
[27] τὸ ψὲς, yesterday evening.
[28] Σπίθα = Σπιθαμή.
[29] ἀνοιγοσφάλισμα, from ἀνοίγω and σφαλίζω, i. e. ἀσφαλίζω, to make fast, hence, to shut.
[30] πᾶσα for πάντα.
[31] δὲ for δὲν = οὐ.

Σὰ σπίθα³² σβύν' ἡ δόξα σας, τὰ πλούτησας σὰ σκόνη³³

Σκορπούσηνε καὶ χάνονται, καὶ τ' ὄνομά σας λυόνει

Σὰ νᾶτον³⁴ μὲ τὸ χέρι σας γραμμένο εἰς περιγιάλι

Στὴ διάκρισι τζή θάλασσας, γὴ χάμαι³⁵ στὴν πασπάλη

. . . . .

Σ' ἐδιάλεξα εὐγενέστατε Μουρμούρ' ὑψηλότατε

'Ρήτορα 'π' ὅλαις τζ ἀρεταῖς³⁶ καὶ τζὴ τιμαῖς γεμάτε,

Μὲ τ' ὄνομά σου τοῦτο μου τὸν κόπον νὰ στολίσω,

Καὶ χάρι ἀπὸ τζὴ χάραις σου πλήσα νὰ σου χαρίσω.

Γιατί³⁷ ὅσω σὲ θεωρῶ ψηλὸ,³⁸ σὲ βλέπω κάλλο τόσο

Μὲ σπλάγχνος ἀνεξίκακο, κ' ἄμετρη καλοσύνη —

Κ' εἶσαι 'π τὴν 'περηφάνησι μακρὰν τοῦ κόσμου κείνη

Τὴ σκοτεινὴ, ποῦ δὲ γεννᾷ λάβρα, οὐδὲ φῶς χαρίζει

Μὰ τζίκνα³⁹ μόνο καὶ καπνὸ τὰ τρίγυρα γεμίζει.

The next writer we shall notice is Franciscus Scuphos, who flourished about the year 1669. He was born in Crete and was educated in Italy, and was also professor at the Greek school in Venice. He wrote a work on Rhetoric, which may be regarded, in the words of an English scholar, a living example of the fact that the oratory of the ancients continues to live in the oratory of modern Greece.

---

[32] Σὰ σπίθα = ὡς σπινθήρ. Lat. scintilla.

[23] σὰ σκόνη = ὡς κονιορτός (dust).

[34] Σὰ νᾶτον = ὡσὰν.

[35] χάμαι, Cretan, for the modern χάμου, the ancient χαμαί.

[36] τζ ἀρεταῖς = τὰς ἀρετάς.

[37] Γιατί = ἐπειδήπερ (γάρ).

[38] ψηλὸ = ὑψηλὸν = μέγαν.

[39] τζίκνα, a curious corruption and metathesis for κνῖςα.

In the eighteenth century we are met by the
names of Kosmas the Aetolian and Rhegas of
Pherae, both scholarly men, and the great fore-
runners of Greek independence. The following
oath administered by Rhega to all his confeder-
ates, is an example of his deadly intolerance to
tyranny : —

'Ω Βασιλεῦ τοῦ κόσμου ὁρκίζομαι εἰς σέ,
Στὴν γνώμην τῶν τυρράνων νὰ μὴν ἐλθῶ ποτέ.
Μήτε νὰ τοὺς δουλεύσω, μήτε νὰ πλανεθῶ,
Εἰς τὰ ταξίματά των νὰ μὴ παραδοθῶ.
Ἐνόσῳ ζῶ σ' τὸν κόσμον, ὁ μόνος μου σκοπός
Τοῦ νὰ τοὺς ἀφανίσω νὰ ἦναι στραθερός.
Πιστὸς εἰς τὴν πατρίδα συντρίβω τὸν ζυγόν
Κἰ ἀχώριστος νὰ ζήσω ἀπὸ τὸν στρατηγόν.
Κ' ἄν παραβῶ τὸν ὅρκον, ν' ἀστράψῃ ὁ οὐρανός
Καὶ νὰ μὲ κατακαύσῃ νὰ γέν' ὡσὰν καπνός.

Here is another war-song, which contributed
in no small degree to fire the Greeks with that
enthusiasm for liberty which soon resulted in the
insurrection : —

Παιδιὰ τοῦ Ἡρακλέους ὁρμᾶτε, μὲ σπαθιὰ
Κρατεῖτε μ' ἕνα χέρι, μὲ τ' ἄλλο τὴν φωτιά,
Ὁρμήσατε γενναίως, δράμμετε ὅλοι μαζή
Καὶ δείξατε τῶν Ἑλλήνων τὸ γένος ὅτι ζῆ.
Σπετσιῶται, καὶ Ὑδριῶται, κὶ ἀδέλφια Ψαρριανοί,
Ἐις τ' Ἀρχιπέλαγόν μας Τοῦρκος ἂς μὴ φανῇ.
Ἄν τις ὅμως τολμήσῃ νά παρρουσιασθῇ

Στὰ Βάθη τῆς θαλάσσης ἀς καταποντισθῇ —
Ὡς πότε παλληκάρια νὰ ζῶμεν σ' τά στενά
Σπηλιάς νὰ κατοικῶμεν σ' τὰ ὄρη καὶ βουνά;

Rhegas was betrayed to the Turks by the *Christian* government of Austria, and was by them put to death on the spot, at Belgrade.

The following inscription was engraved on the tombstone of Rhegas and Kosmas: —

Οὗτοι ἐλευθερίαν θηρώμενοι ἀγλαόμορφον
Εὗρον ἐνὶ ξυλόχοις Ὀκρυόεντα μόρον·
Χαίρετε Θηρευταὶ κοιμώμενοι, ἐσόκεν ἠὼς
Ἔλθῃ ἀπ' Ὀλύμπου λαμπάδ' ἀνισχομένη·
καὶ τότ' ἐγειρόμενοι πολίῳ βρόμῳ ὀρνυμενάων
δαίμονες εἰς ἄγραν σπεύδετ' ἀλεξίκακον.

In 1777, was born at Larissa, in Thessaly, Constantinus Cumas, author of a great number of geographical, mathematical, and philosophical works. He was known under the name " ὁ φιλόσοφος " (the philosopher). Most of the learned Greeks of those times were from Rumelia, which province was in higher repute on this account than any other in Greece. Numbers of the " Kleptes " were men of scholastic attainments. Having been abroad, and seen a better state of things, as well as having acquired refinement from books, they could not submit to the degradation that awaited them among the Turks, and therefore retired to the mountains and lived in independence. In some of the wildest and most dreary mountains were many of the most intelligent of our people, and in the dress of shepherds were to be found men such as Constantinus Cumas.

Constantinus Cumas was one of those lettered Greeks who began to propose the cultivation of the spoken language. Their plan was as follows: —

I. The ancient inflections are to be preferred to the corresponding modern and mediæval inflections.

II. All barbarous or foreign words and idioms are to be banished.

III. All new words are to be formed by derivation and composition after the analogy of the ancient language.

IV. The ancient orthography of words of Greek origin is to be preferred.

The following is a specimen of Cumas' style: —

Ἀλλ' εἶναι, πρὸς Διὸς, φρόνιμος τέκτων ὅστις ἀγοράζει σκεπάρνιον καὶ πριόνιον τὰ ὁποῖα ἐμποδίζονται ἀπὸ τὴν χρύσωσιν καὶ τοὺς ἄλλους στολισμοὺς νὰ ἐκπληρώσωσι τὰ ἴδια αὐτῶν ἔργα, ἤγουν τὸ ἕν νὰ πελεκᾷ τὸ δὲ ἕτερον νὰ πριονίζῃ; ἀπαράλλακτα πάσχει, νομίζω ὅστις διὰ νὰ στολίσῃ τὴν γλῶσσαν μὲ γενικὰς ἀπολύτους καὶ δοτικὰς καὶ χωρὶς ἀνάγκην λέξεις ἀσυνειθίστους, κινδυνεύει νὰ τὴν καταστήσῃ ἀκατάληπτον εἰς τοὺς ἀκούοντας ἢ ἀναγινώσκοντας.

The following is a catalogue of Constantinus
Cumas' published works:—

<table>
<tr><td></td><td align="right">Vols.</td></tr>
<tr><td>Κωνικῶν τομῶν ἀναλυτικὴ πραγματεία τοῦ 'Αββᾶ Καΐλλου. 1803</td><td align="right">1</td></tr>
<tr><td>Σειρὰ μαθηματικῶν καὶ φυσικῶν πραγματειῶν. 1807</td><td align="right">8</td></tr>
<tr><td>'Αδήτου χημείας ἐπιτομὴ. 1808</td><td align="right">2</td></tr>
<tr><td>Σύνοψις πειραματικῆς φυσικῆς. 1812</td><td align="right">1</td></tr>
<tr><td>Βειλάνδου 'Αγάθων. 1814</td><td align="right">3</td></tr>
<tr><td>Σύνταγμα φιλοσοφίας. 1818–1819</td><td align="right">4</td></tr>
<tr><td>Τεννεμάλου ἱστορία τῆς φιλοσοφίας. 1818</td><td align="right">1</td></tr>
<tr><td>Σύνοψις ἱστορικῆς χρονολογίας. 1818</td><td align="right">1</td></tr>
<tr><td>Σύνοψις παλαιᾶς γεωγραφίας μὲ 3 πίνακας. 1818</td><td align="right">1</td></tr>
<tr><td>Σύνοψις ἐπιστημῶν (ἀριθμητικῆς, γεωμετρίας, νεωτέρας γεωγραφίας, ἀστρονομίας, λογικῆς καὶ ἠθικῆς). 1818</td><td align="right">1</td></tr>
<tr><td>Λεξικὸν τῆς Ἑλληνικῆς γλώσσης. 1826</td><td align="right">2</td></tr>
<tr><td>Βειλάνδου 'Αβδηρῖται. 1827</td><td align="right">2</td></tr>
<tr><td>Ἱστορία τῶν ἀνθρωπίνων πράξεων. 1830–32</td><td align="right">12</td></tr>
<tr><td>Γραμματικὴ. 1833</td><td align="right">1</td></tr>
<tr><td>'Αδριανοῦ Βάλβη γεωγραφία. 1838–1840</td><td align="right">5</td></tr>
<tr><td></td><td align="right">45</td></tr>
</table>

The great name that appears at the end of the
eighteenth century is that of Adamantius Coraes,
the great patriot and linguistic reformer, and one
of the most celebrated literati of Europe, as
Professor Geldart and others justly assert. Born
at Smyrna, on April 27, 1748, the two sentiments
which formed his main-springs of action through-

out life, were early developed, namely, patriotism, synonymous in his case with hatred of the
Turk, and a passion for learning. His historian
informs us that in his native town he was greatly
assisted in his lingual and other studies by the
Dutch consular chaplain, Bernhard Keum, of
whom he makes frequent and affectionate mention in his "Autobiography and Correspond-
ence." At the age of twenty-four he became his
father's mercantile agent at Amsterdam, where he
spent six years, but the ledger was the least
interesting of his books, and in 1778 he was
recalled. He returned with the greatest reluc-
tance, because his darling project was to study
medicine in France, in order that, should he be
obliged to live among the Turks, he might
exercise among them the only profession which
procured respectful treatment for the Greeks.
After four melancholy years at Smyrna, his
wishes were at length complied with, and in 1782
he arrived at Montpellier. He distinguished himself in this famous medical school, and, having
obtained his diploma, removed to Paris in 1788,
where, instead of practising his profession, he
engaged in literary labors, most of them having
a patriotic aim. Here he wrote letters to his
countrymen, encouraging them in the struggle
for freedom to which Rhegas was already insti-
gating them; and here he pursued those studies

which have established his fame as a European
scholar. Napoleon selected him to prepare a
translation of Strabo's Geography, the first volume of which was presented to the Emperor in
1805. In a letter dated Leyden, July 22d, of
that same year, Wyttembach, writing to Larcher,
calls Coraes "not only a Grecian but a veritable
Greek." In 1807 his edition of Isocrates procured for him the title of "Patriarch of Greek
Philology," and in 1814 he received an official
letter inquiring if he would accept a Greek chair
in the Collége Royal. . . . . About the first week
of April, 1833, Coraes, having extended his hand
to reach a cup of coffee, fell to the ground and
received injuries from which he died the 10th
of April, 1833. He was buried at "Mont Par-
nasse," and the following inscription was engraved
on his tombstone : —

· *ΑΔΑΜΑΝΤΙΟΣ ΚΟΡΑΗΣ*

ΧΙΟΣ

῾Υπὸ ξένην μέν ἴσα δὲ τῇ ῾Ελλάδι πεφιλημένην γῆν
τῶν Παρισίων

ΚΕΙΜΑΙ.

His published works are as follows : —

La Médecine Clinique. 1787. Montpellier.
Μετάφρασις ἐκ τοῦ γερμανικοῦ τοῦ Selle.
Introduction à l'étude de la Nature et de la Médecine.
Ibid.

Catéchisme Orthodoxe Russe. (From the German of Plato, Archbishop of Moscow.)

Vade-mecum du Médecin. Montpellier. (From the English.)

Esquisse d'une Histoire de la Médecine. Paris. 1767. (From the English.)

Pyretologiae Synopsis. Montpellier. 1786.

Ἀδελφικὴ διδασκαλία, an Answer to Πατρικὴ διδασκαλία, a Forgery of the Turkish Government, published under the name of Anthimus, Patriarch of Jerusalem, for the purpose of allaying the tumultuary tendencies of the Greek subjects of the Porte.

Les Caractères de Théophraste. 1799.

Traité d'Hippocrate, des airs, des eaux et des lieux. Paris. 1806.

Ibid., second edition with Greek title. 1816.

Βεκκαρίου περὶ ἀδικημάτων καὶ ποινῶν. Paris. 1802, 1823.

Σάλπισμα πολεμιστήριον. Paris. 1803. (On the death of Rhegas.)

Ἡλιοδώρου Αἰθιοπικὰ Βιβλία δέκα. Paris. 1804. In two Volumes.

Lettre du Docteur Coray sur le testament secret des Athéniens, dont parle Dimarque dans la harangue contre Demosthènes.

Διάλογος δύο Γραικῶν κατοίκων τῆς Βενετίας. 1805. καὶ ἐν Ὕδρᾳ. 1825.

Πρόδρομος Ἑλληνικῆς Βιβλιοθήκης. 1809 – 1827. Ἑλληνικὴ Βιβλιοθήκη. Paris. 1807 – 1835. 15 volumes. (Consisting of editions of classical authors, with notes.)

Πάρεργα Ἑλλ. Βιβλιοθήκης. 1809 – 1827. 9 volumes.

Ἰλλιάδος ῥαψωδίαι Δ. 1811 – 1820.

Διατριβὴ αὐτοσχέδιος περὶ τοῦ περιβοήτου δόγματος τῶν σκεπτικῶν φιλοσόφων Νόμῳ καλόν, Νόμῳ κακόν.

Ἄτακτα. Paris. 1818 – 1825. 2 volumes.

Συνέκδημος ἱερατικός. 1831.

Σύνοψις ἱερᾶς Κατηχήσεως.

Αὐτοβιογραφία. 1833.

Besides a great many articles in the "Logios Hermes," a Greek periodical published in Vienna, on philological and political subjects.

On his death he left his library and manuscripts to the gymnasium at Chios, the birthplace of his ancestors. His unpublished works are more numerous, if not more voluminous, than those which have been given to the world. Besides this, the margins of many of his books are crowded with notes in his handwriting.

The following is a catalogue of the works which were bestowed by him to the library of Chios, and which remain as yet unpublished.

Adnotationes in Athæneum.
Notes sur Eschyles.
Ἰλιάδος Ῥαψωδία Ε, ἕως τὸν 250 στίχον.
Σημειώσεις εἰς τοὺ Ἀθήναιον καὶ Ἡρόδοτον.
Ὕλη Λεξικοῦ Γαλλογραικικοῦ.
Γραμματικαὶ Σημειώσεις.
Ἴσον τῶν σταλθεισῶν σημειώσεων εἰς E. Barcker, διὰ τὴν νέαν ἔκδοσιν Λεξικοῦ Hederius.
Ἐξηγήσεις εἰς τὸν Ἀπολλώνιον περὶ συντάξεως.

Γαληνοῦ εἰς τὸ περὶ χυμῶν Ἱπποκράτους, σελ. 1 - 401, κείμενον σελ. 4 - 75 σημ. 1 - 170 ἀντίγραφον.

Ἀρεταίου μετάφρασις Γαλλικὴ, ἀδιόρθωτος καὶ ἀτελὴς, σελ. 1 - 407. -

Σημειώσεις εἰς τὸ προσωρινὸν Πολίτευμα τῆς Ἑλλάδος. Observationes miscelaneae, pag. 1 - 905.
Idem sine paginatione.
Idem in Athæneum, pag. 1 - 139.

Λεξικολογία.

Μετάφρασις Ἡροδότου εἰς τὸ Γραικικὸν, σελ. 1 - 1250 ἕως τὸν παράγρ. 56 τοῦ 7 Βιβλίου.

Ἀφορισμῶν Ἱπποκράτους, μετάφρασις Γαλλικὴ ἀδιόρθωτος καὶ ἀτελὴς, σ. 1 - 241.

Plus l'art de la médecine, pag. 1 - 10 et une table le tout incoplet.

Κείμενον καὶ σημειώσεις εἰς τὸ περὶ διαίτης ὀξέων, καὶ εἰς τὸ περὶ ἀρχαίας Ἰατρικῆς τοῦ Ἱπποκράτους, σελ. 116 τὸ Κείμενον, αἱ σημ. σ. 117 - 408.

Σημειώσεις κατὰ Γαληνοῦ ἐκ τῶν αὐτοῦ συγγραμμάτων σελ. 1 - 1067. Ἔτι τινὲς σημειώσεις εἰς τὰ συγγράμματα τοῦ Ἱπποκράτους σελ. 1 - 21.

Γραμματικὴ τῆς Γραικικῆς γλώσσης ἀτελείωτος. Collationes des manouscris Grecs, pag. 1 - 84.

Στίχοι Ἰωάννου Τζέτζου. 1 - 141.

Περὶ μέτρων, σελ. 1 - 48. .

Σχόλια εἰς τὸ Ἀπολλωνίου περὶ συντάξεως, σελ. 1 - 24.

Λεξικολογία ἀπό τὸ Ἑλληνικὸν εἰς τὸ Γραικικόν.

Λεξικὸν διαφόρων συγγραφέων εἰς τὸν Ἱπποκράτην. Adnotationes in varios Auctores Græcos.

Ἄλλη Λεξικολογία ἀπὸ τὸ Ἑλληνικὸν εἰς τὸ Γραικικόν.

Few countries, Geldart says, none certainly save Germany, can show such a literary Hercules as Adamanties Coraes, the second Leo Allatius of Greece.

The next writer we shall notice is Constantinus Oekonomos, who was contemporary with Coraes. He was a native of Thessaly, and had received a superior education. He soon became remarkable for his opposition to some of the doctrines and practices which had before prevailed amongst the Greeks, or, at least, had not been openly opposed. A Greek historian informs us that the bishop soon viewed him with dislike, being a man inferior in education, talents, and soundness of opinion, and at length interdicted his public preaching. Oekonomos had a sincere desire to establish better principles amongst his countrymen, and intended to introduce all possible improvements in the system of education, and was disposed to forward everything that might prove beneficial to them. He did not, therefore, allow himself to be discouraged by the bishop's opposition, but made a journey to Constantinople to obtain permission of Gregorius, the patriarch, to preach where he pleased. In this he succeeded; and, after his return to Smyrna, preached with more zeal and boldness than before. The character of Oekonomos was of the most sincere, frank, and friendly description, with the most

kind and willing disposition. He combined an
extraordinary decision and independence. His
historian informs us that he regarded the ob-
servance of ceremonies, by many so much insisted
on, as a matter of small importance compared
with the feelings they were designed to cultivate
or to express. Oekonomos devoted his attention
and time much to the establishment of schools.
He acted in this co-operation with various enlightened Greeks, who were anxious for the
greater extension of knowledge among the Greeks,
and had taken pains to introduce the Prussian
system of instruction in the schools he was
endeavoring to establish.

Jacob Rhizos Nerulos, known under the appellation of "the modern Aristophanes of Greece,"
was contemporary with Oekonomos. He was
the unsparing satirist of the "Logios Hermes,"
and his style was and is still known under the
appellation of the "Nerulian style."

To illustrate the above I give three short extracts, taken respectively from the "Αὐτοβιογραφία" of Coraes, the treatise "Περὶ Προφορᾶς" of
Oekonomos, and the "Κορακίστικα," a satirical
comedy of Nerulos, in which I need hardly say
the Κόρακες are the followers of Coraes.

*Αἱ ἐκδόσεις μου δὲν ἔλειψαν ὅμως νὰ μοῦ γεννήσωσι
καὶ ἐχθροὺς, ὀλίγους τινὰς σχολαστικοὺς, ἐνωμένους μὲ
ὄχι πολλοὺς τοῦ ἱερατικοῦ τάγματος, οἱ ὁποῖοι μὲ κατεπο-*

λέμησαν ἀγρίως ὡς καινοτόμον ὄχι μόνον εἰς τὰ περὶ παιδείας, ἀλλὰ καὶ εἰς αὐτήν μου τὴν θρησκείαν. Μετανοῶ τώρα, ὅτι τοὺς ἀντεπολέμησα κ᾽ ἐγώ· φρονιμώτερα ἤθελα πράξειν, ἂν ἀκολουθοῦσα τὸ σοφὸν παράγγελμα τοῦ Ἐπικτήτου, "Ἔδοξεν αὐτῷ." — CORAES, Αὐτοβιογραφία.

Τὸ περὶ γνησίας τῶν Ἑλληνικῶν γραμμάτων προφορᾶς πολύκροτον πρόβλημα, πρὸ τριῶν ἤδη αἰώνων εἰς τὴν Εὐρώπην ἀναφυὲν, ὑπῆρξε πολλάκις εἰς πολλοὺς πολλῶν καὶ μεγάλων συζητήσεων ὑπόθεσις. Πρῶτος ὁ σοφὸς Ἔρασμος περὶ τῷ 1520 ἀπολακτίσας τὴν ἕως τότε συνήθη καὶ νενομισμένην, ἐπενόησεν ἄλλην παντάπασι νέαν καὶ ἀνήκουστον τῆς Ἑλληνικῆς γλώσσης ἐκφώνησιν, τὴν ὁποίαν καὶ παρέδωκεν εἰς τοὺς ὀπαδούς του ὡς μόνην ἀληθινὴν καὶ γνησίαν, καθ᾽ ἣν τάχα καὶ οἱ παλαιοὶ Ἕλληνες ἐπρόφερον τὴν γλῶσσάν των. — OECONOMOS Περί προφορᾶς.

Εἶναι δύο χρόνια τώρα ὁποῦ ὁ πατέρας μου ἀρρωστεῖ ἀπ᾽ ἕν ἀλλόκοτο πάθος τὸ νὰ ὁμιλῇ κορακίστικα, καὶ ἄλλο δὲν κάμνει παρά νά σκαλίζῃ λεξικά, νὰ πλάττῃ λέξεις ἀνήκουσταις καὶ παράξεναις, νὰ διαβάζῃ κἄτι διαβολόχαρτα τυπωμένα, ὁποῦ τὰ ὀνομάζουν λόγιον Ἑρμῆ καὶ νὰ γράφῃ καὶ νὰ λαλῇ μιὰ γλῶσσα, ὁποῦ τὴν δημιουργεῖ ὁ ἴδιος. Τὶ νὰ κάμω; γιά νὰ τὸν ὑποχρεώσω, βιάζω τὸν ἑαυτόν μου νὰ μάθω αὐταῖς ταῖς ἀηδεστάταις φλυαρίαις, καὶ μ᾽ ὅλον ὁποῦ δὲν γυρνᾷ ἡ γλῶσσα μου, σ᾽ αὐτὰ τὰ καταραμένα κορακίστικα, μ᾽ ὅλον τοῦτο, ἐπειδὴ καὶ τὰ λατρεύει, βιάζομαι κ᾽ ἐγώ νὰ τὸν ὁμιλῶ τῇ γλῶσσα του, καὶ εἰς κάθε λέξι δική του ὁποῦ ἤθελα προφέρει μὲ δίδει τὴν εὐχή του. — NERULOS, Κορακίστικα.

Modern Greece has not produced many author-esses. But among these, Angelica Pala, chiefly known by the following ode "On the Death of Lord Byron," is certainly the most distinguished. She belongs to the beginning of the nineteenth century.

1.

Τοὺς λαμπροὺς ὑμνους τῆς νίκης ἀφίνων
Κλανθμῶν ἠχεῖ ἡρώων ὁ στρατός·
Πικρῶς λυποῦντ᾽ αἰ ψυχαὶ τῶν Ἑλλήνων,
Τ᾽ ἀκούει μακρόθεν καὶ χαίρει ὁ ἐχθρός.

2.

Ὁ φίλος ἦλθε· πλὴν μόλις τὸν εἶδον
Σκάπτουν κλαίοντες τὸν τάφον αὐτοῦ,
Ἰδοῦ τὸ τέλος ἐνδόξων ἐλπίδων,
Καὶ τὸ τρόπαιον θανάτου σκληροῦ.

3.

Ἦλθε νὰ ἐμπνεύσῃ ὡς ἄλλος Τυρταῖος
Εἰς κάθε στῆθος πολέμων ὁρμήν.
Πλὴν, φεῦ, ὁ Βάρδος ἐλπίσας ματαίως
Ἰδοῦ μένει εἰς αἰώνιον σιωπήν.

4.

Ὡς δένδρον κεῖτ᾽ ὁπ᾽ ἐκόσμει μεγάλως
Τὴν κορυφὴν μουσικοῦ Παρνασσοῦ.
Νῦν πρὸ ποδῶν φθείρουσά του τὸ κάλλος
Πνοὴ τὸ ἔρριψ᾽ ἀνέμου σφοδροῦ.

5.

Ἑλλὰς! ἐὰν τὸ σῶμα του ἡ Ἀγγλία
Νὰ φέρῃ εἰς μνῆμα ζητᾷ πατρικόν.
Εἰπέ, Μουσῶν ὦ μητέρα γλυκεῖα,
Εἶναι τέκνον μου ὁ υἱός τῶν Μουσῶν.

6.

Καταφρονῶν τῶν ἐρώτων τοὺς θρήνους,
Ἡδονῆς μὴν ἀκούων τὴν φωνήν
Ἐξήτει ἐδὼ ἡρώων τοὺς κινδύνους
Τάφον ἂς ἔχῃ ἡρώων 'στὴν γῆν.

The great lyrical poet of Greece is, however, Athanasios Christopulos, the so-called modern Anacreon. He was born at Kastoria, in Macedonia, in 1772, and died in Moldavia, where he held the office of judge, in 1847. Professor Geldart states that his undoubted genius was consecrated chiefly to the glory of the wine-bottle, yet he wrote some love-songs of exquisite tenderness and beauty, which have been copied without acknowledgment by various modern poets. Consciously or unconsciously, the "Nightingale" of Christopulos is certainly at the foundation of the "Swallow" of Tennyson. Inasmuch as the nightingale sings, and the swallow only twitters, my readers will agree with Professor Geldart in preferring the Greek to the English poet in this particular case.

Christopulos and two other very popular poets of Modern Greece, Vallariotes and Solomos, wrote for the common people in vernacular Romaic. The following extracts, taken respectively from the works of these three great poets, may serve as examples:—

OLD AGE.

Νὰ ἡ τρίχες σου ἀρχίζουν
'Αθανάσιε ν' ἀσπρίζουν!
  Νὰ δακρύων ἐποχή!
Νὰ σέ λέγει καὶ ὁ Ἔρως,
Φίλε πλέον εἶσαι γέρος,
  'Στὸ ἐξῆς καλὴ ψυχή.
Τὴ νεότητα χαιρέτα,
Τὰ φιλήματ' ἄφησέ τα,
Ξέχασέ τα παρευθύς,
Καὶ ἀρχίνα μέ ὑγεία
Τὰ πικρὰ τὰ γερατεῖα
  Σ' τὸ ἐξῆς νὰ τὰ γευθῆς.
Δὲν σὲ πιάνουν τὰ λουλούδια,
Δὲν σὲ πρέπουν τὰ τραγούδια,
Πῆγ' ἐκεῖνος ὁ καιρός·
Τώρα τάφος πλησιάζει,
Τώρα θάνατος φωνάζει,
  Τώρα χάρος λυπηρός!
Ὅθεν πλέον ἑτοιμάσου,
'Ρῆξε ὅλα τὰ καλάσου
  Πὲ τὸν κόσμον Ἔχε Γειά!

Καὶ τὰ δάκρυα βάστα μόνον
Εἰς τὴν λύπην κ' εἰς τὸν πόνον
Μιὰ μικρὴ παρηγοριά !

ANSWER TO THE PRECEDING.

Πᾶ ! ἡ τρίχες μ' ἂν ἀσπρίζουν
Μήπως τάχατε πικρίζουν ;
Τὶ ἔχ ἡ ἄσπρη τους βαφή ;
Τοιγὰρ τ' ἄσπρο θανατόνει ;
Ἤ φιλῶντας ἀγκυλόνει
Τὰ χειλάκια σ' τὴν ἀφή ;
Το τριαντάφυλλό μας πρῶτον
Τὸ λουλούδι τῶν Ἐρώτων
Εἶναι ἄσπρο καθαρό.
Καὶ τὸ κόκκινο ἡ φύσις
Τὸ συγκέρασεν ἐπίσης
Μ' ἔνα χρῶμ' ἀσπρουδερό.
Ἡ μυρτιὰ τῆς Ἀφροδίτης
Εἰς τὸ πράσινο κλαδί της,
Μέσ' σ' τὰ φύλλα τὰ χλωρά
Ὅλα κάτασπρα, σὰν χιόνι,
Τὰ λουλούδιά της φυτρόνει
Τ' ἀνθηρά, καὶ τρυφερά.
Καὶ ὁ Δίας ὁ μεγάλος
Γιὰ τῆς Λήδας του τὸ κάλλος
Κύκνος γίνηκε μιὰ φορά.
Ν' ἀπόδειξ' εἰς κάθε μέρος
Ἄσπραις τρίχαις θέλ' ὁ Ἔρως
Σὰν τοῦ κύκνου τὰ φτερά !

Τὸ λοιπὸν κέγ' ὅσο θέλει,
Ἃς ἀσπρίζω δὲν μὲ μέλει,
Παντελῶς δὲν μὲ λυπᾷ·
Ὅτι ὅσο πάντ' ἀσπρίζω,
Τόσο πλέον νοστιμίζω,
Τοσ' ὁ Ἔρως μ' ἀγαπᾷ.

THE NIGHTINGALE.

Κίν' ἀηδονάκι μου καλό,
Κίνα καὶ πάγε 'στὸ γιαλό.
Τὴν ἀκριβὴ ποῦ ξεύρεις,
Νὰ πᾷς νὰ μὲ τὴν εὕρῃς·
Καὶ σὰν τὴν βρῇς νὰ τὴν ἰδῇς
Ἀρχίνα κεῖ νὰ κελαδῇς
Γλυκὰ γλυκὰ μὲ χάρι
Νὰ σκύψῃ νὰ σὲ πάρῃ
Ἂν σ' ἐρωτήσῃ τί σ' ἐσύ;
Καὶ ποιός σὲ στέλνει ἀπ' τὸ νησί;
Εἰπὲ, πῶς εἶμαι δῶρο
Πουλὶ στεναγμοφόρο!
Πῶς ὁ ἀφέντης μου ἐδῶ
Μὲ στέλνει νὰ σὲ τραγουδῶ·
Τὰ πάθη μου νὰ κλαίγω
Μὲ μέλος νὰ σ' τὰ λέγω.
Ὕστερα σκύψε ταπεινά
Καὶ λάλησέ την σιγανά,
Καὶ ὅρκισ' την σ' τὰ κάλλη
Στὸν κόρφο νὰ σὲ βάλῃ·
Ἄχ ἀηδονάκι μ' δὲν βαστῶ

Θὰ σὲ τὸ πῶ, Εἶσαι πιστό;
Ἐπίβουλο μὴ γένης
Στὸν κῆπον ποῦ ἐμπαίνεις.

BACCHI LAUDES.

Ὅταν πίνω τὸ κρασάκι
Στὸ χρυσό μου ποτηράκι
Καὶ ὁ νοῦς μου ζαλισθῇ. ·
Τότ ἀρχίζω καὶ χορεύω,
Καὶ γελῶ καὶ χωρατεύω,
Κ’ ἡ ζωή μ’ εὐχαριστεῖ.
Τότε παύουν ἠ φροντίδες
Τότε σβύνουν ἠ ἐλπίδες
Τότε φεύγουν οἱ καπνοί.
Κ’ ἡ καρδιά μου γαληνίζει,
Καὶ τὸ στῆθός μου ἀρχίζει
Ν’ ἀνασαίνῃ ν’ ἀναπνῇ.
Γιὰ τὸν κόσμον δὲν μὲ μέλει,
Ἄς γυρίζῃ ὅπως θέλει,
Τὸ κρασάκι μου νὰ ζῇ.
Ἡ κανάτα νὰ μὴ στύψῃ
Ἀπ’ τὸ πλάγι νὰ μὴ λείψῃ
Ν’ ἀποθάνωμε μαζί!

.   .   .   .   .

Dionysius Solomos was born in the island of Zacynthos in 1798 (April 8), and died the 21st of November, 1857. The following Ode to Liberty, written by him in the "month of May," 1823, is justly admired for its simplicity and imagination, and it has with justice become "The National Song of Greece." It is played on all great national holidays:—

1.

Σὲ γνωρίζω ἀπὸ τὴν κόψι
Τοῦ σπαθιοῦ τὴν τρομερή,
Σὲ γνωρίζω ἀπὸ τὴν ὄψι,
'Ποῦ μὲ βία μετρᾴει τὴν γῆ.

2.

'Απ' τὰ κόκκαλα βγαλμένη
Τῶν 'Ελλήνων τὰ ἱερά,
Καὶ 'σὰν πρῶτα ἀνδρειωμένη,
Χαῖρε, ὦ χαῖρε, 'Ελευθεριά!

3.

'Εκεῖ μέσα ἐκατοικοῦσες,
Πικραμμένη, ἐντροπαλὴ,
Κ' ἕνα στόμα ἀκαρτεροῦσες
῎Ελα πάλι νὰ σοῦ 'πῇ.

4.

῎Αργειε ν' ἄλθη ἐκείνη ἡ 'μέρα,
Καὶ ἦταν ὅλα σιωπηλὰ,
Γιατὶ τὰ 'σκιαζε ἡ φοβέρα
Καὶ τὰ 'πλάκονε ἡ σκλαβιά.

5.

Δυστυχής! Παρηγορία
Μόνη σοῦ ἔμενε νὰ λὲς
Περασμένα μεγαλεῖα
Καὶ διηγῶντας τα νὰ κλαῖς.

6.

Καὶ ἀκαρτέρει καὶ ἀκαρτέρει
Φιλελεύθερην λαλιὰ,
"Ενα ἐκτύπαε τ' ἄλλο χέρι
'Απὸ τὴν ἀπελπισιὰ.

7.

Κ' ἔλεες· πότε, ἄ! πότε βγάνω
Τὸ κεφάλι ἀπὸ τσ' ἐρμιαῖς;
Καὶ ἀποκρίνοντο ἀπὸ 'πάνω
Κλάψαις, ἄλυσες, φωναῖς.

8.

Τότε ἐσήκονες τὸ βλέμμα
Μὲς τὰ κλάϋματα θολό,
Καὶ εἰς τὸ ροῦχο σου ἔσταζ' αἷμα
Πλῆθος αἷμα Ἑλληνικό.

9.

Μὲ τὰ ροῦχα αἱματωμένα,
Ξέρω ὅτι ἔβγαινες κρυφὰ,
Νὰ γυρεύῃς εἰς τὰ ξένα
"Αλλα χέρια δυνατά!

10.

Μοναχὴ τὸν δρόμο επῆρες
'Εξανάλθες μοναχή·
Δὲν εἶν' εὔκολαις ἡ θύραις,
'Εὰν ἡ χρεία ταῖς κουρταλῇ.

11.

Ἄλλος σοῦ ἔκλαψε εἰς τὰ στήθια,
Ἀλλ' ἀνάστασιν κἀμμιά.
Ἄλλος σοῦ ἔταξε βοήθεια,
Καὶ σὲ 'γέλασε φρικτά.

12.

Ἄλλοι, ὠϊμέ! σ' τὴν συμφορά σου
Ὁποῦ ἐχαίροντο πολύ,
Σύρε ν' αὔρης τὰ παιδιά σου,
Σύρε, ἐλέγαν οἱ σκληροί!

13.

Φεύγει ὀπίσω τὸ ποδάρι,
Καὶ ὁλογλήγορο πατεῖ
Ἤ τὴν πέτρα, ἤ τὸ χορτάρι,
Ποῦ τὴν δόξα σοῦ ἐνθυμεῖ.

14.

Ταπεινότατη σοῦ γέρνει
Ἡ τρισάθλια κεφαλὴ
Σὰν πτωχοῦ 'ποῦ θυροδέρνει,
Κ' εἶναι βάρος του ἡ ζωή.

15.

Ναί! ἀλλὰ τώρα ἀντιπαλεύει
Κάθε τέκνο σου μὲ ὁρμή,
Ποῦ ἀκατάπαυστα γυρεύει
Ἤ τὴν νίκη ἤ τὴν θανή.

16.

Ἀπ᾽ τὰ κόκκαλα βγαλμένη
Τῶν Ἑλλήνων τὰ ἱερὰ,
Καὶ ᾽σὰν πρῶτα ἀνδρειωμένη,
Χαῖρε, ὦ χαῖρε, Ἐλευθεριά!

17.

Μόλις εἶδε τὴν ὁρμὴν σου
Ὁ Οὐρανὸς, ποῦ γιὰ τσ᾽ ἐχθροὺς
Εἰς τὴν γῆν τὴν μητρικὴν σου
Ἔτρεφ᾽ ἄνθια καὶ καρποὺς.

18.

Ἐγαλήνευσε· καὶ ἐχύθη
Καταχθόνια μιὰ βοή,
Καὶ τοῦ Ῥήγα σου ἀπεκρίθη
Πολεμόκραχτη ἡ φωνή.

19.

Ὅλοι οἱ τόποι σου σ᾽ ἐκράξαν,
Χαιρετῶντας σε θερμὰ,
Καὶ τὰ στόματα ἐφωνάξαν
Ὅσα αἰσθάνετο ἡ καρδιά!

20.

Ἐφωνάξανε ὡς τ᾽ ἀστέρια
Τοῦ Ἰονίου καὶ τὰ νησιὰ,
Καὶ ἐσηκώσανε τὰ χέρια
Γιὰ νὰ δείξουνε χαρά.

21.

‘ Μ’ ὅλον ’που ’ναι ἀλυσωμένο
Τὸ καθένα τεχνικὰ,
Καὶ εἰς τὸ μέτωπο γραμμένο
Ἔχει· ψεύτρα Ἐλευθεριά.

22.

’Γκαρδιακὰ, χαροποιήθη
Καὶ τοῦ Βάσιγκτον ἡ γῆ (the land of Washington)
Καὶ τὰ σίδερα ἐνθυμήθη
’Ποῦ τὴν ἔδεναν καὶ αὐτή.

23.

Ἀπ’ τὸν πύργον του φωνάζει,
’Σὰ νὰ λέῃ σὲ χαιρετῶ,
Καὶ τὴν χῆτην του τινάζει
Τὸ Λεοντάρι τὸ Ἰσπανό.

24.

Ἐλαφιάσθη τῆς Ἀγγλίας
Τὸ θηρίο, καὶ σέρνει εὐθὺς
Κατὰ τ’ ἄκρα τῆς Ῥουσσίας
Τὰ μουγκρίσματα τσ’ ὀργῆς.

25.

Εἰς τὸ κίνημά του δείχνει,
Πῶς τὰ μέλη εἶν’ δυνατά.
Καὶ εἰς τοῦ Αἰγαίου τὸ κῦμα ῥίχνει
Μιὰ σπιθόβαλη ματιά.

These twenty-five stanzas will suffice to give
to the reader an idea of this unequalled poem.
The poem is composed of one hundred and fifty-
eight stanzas.

Besides his "Ode to Liberty," Solomos wrote
a lyric poem on the death of Lord Byron, of one
hundred and sixty-six stanzas, commencing as
follows: —

1.

Ἐλευθεριὰ, γιὰ 'λίγο πᾶψε
Νὰ χτυπᾶς μὲ τὸ σπαθί.
Τώρα σίμωσε καὶ κλᾶψε
Εἰς τοῦ Μπάιρον (Byron) τὸ κορμί.

2.

Καὶ κατόπι ἂς ἀκλουθοῦνε
Ὅσοι ἐπράξανε λαμπρά !
Ἀποπάνου του ἂς χτυποῦνε
Μόνον στήθια ἡρωϊκά.

3.

Πρῶτοι ἂς ἔλθουνε οἱ Σουλιῶτες
Καὶ ἀπ' τὸ Λείψανον αὐτό
Ἂς μακραίνουνε οἱ προδότες
Καὶ ἀπ' τὰ λόγια ὁποῦ θὰ 'πῶ.

4.

φλάμπουρα, ὅπλα τιμημένα,
Ἂς γυρθοῦν κατὰ τὴ γῆ,
Καθὼς ἤτανε γυρμένα
Εἰς τοῦ Μάρκου τὴ θανή.

Ποῦ εἶν θὰ λένε σαστισμένοι
Τὸ Λεοντάρι τὸ Ἀγγλικό;
Εἶναι ἡ χῆτη του πεσμένη,
Καὶ τὸ μούγκρισμα βουβό.....

Solomos wrote, besides these two poems we
have noticed, many other songs and sonnets, all
evincing the creative power and masterly genius
of the poet. The following sonnet, entitled "Ἡ
Ξανθούλα" (The Golden-haired Girl), is sung by
young and old in Greece: —

1.

Τὴν εἶδα τήν Ξανθούλα
Τὴν εἶδα 'ψὲς ἀργά,
Ποῦ ἐμπῆκε σ' τὴ βαρκούλα
Νὰ πάῃ σ' τὴν ξενητειά.

2.

Ἐφούσκονε τ' ἀέρι
Λευκότατα πανιά,
Ὡσὰν τὸ περιστέρι,
Ποῦ ἁπλόνει τὰ φτερά.

3.

Ἐστέκονταν οἱ φίλοι
Μὲ λύπη, μὲ χαρά,
Καὶ αὐτὴ μὲ τὸ μαντίλι (handkerchief)
Τοὺς ἀποχαιρετᾷ.

4.

Καὶ τὸ χαιρετισμό της
'Εστάθηκα νὰ ἰδῶ,
῞Ως 'ποῦ ἡ πολλὴ μακρότης
Μοῦ τό 'κρυψε καὶ αὐτό.

5.

Σ' ὀλίγο, σ' ὀλιγάκι
Δὲν ἤξερα νὰ 'πῶ,
῍Αν ἔβλεπα πανάκι,
῍Η τοῦ πελάγου ἀφρό.

6.

Καὶ ἀφοῦ πανί, μαντίλι
'Εχάθη σ' τὸ νερό,
'Εδάκρυσαν οἱ φίλοι
'Εδάκρυσα κ' ἐγώ.

7.

Δὲν κλαίγω τὴ βαρκοῦλα
Δὲν κλαίγω τὰ πανιὰ,
Μόν', κλαίγω τὴν Ξανθοῦλα,
Ποῦ πάει σ' τὴν ξενητιά.

8.

Δὲν κλαίγω τὴ βαρκοῦλα
Μὲ τὰ λευκὰ πανιὰ,
Μόν' κλαίγω τὴν Ξανθοῦλα
Μὲ τὰ ξανθὰ μαλλιά.

Aristoteles Valaorites, who died twelve or fifteen years ago, was "a voluminous poet," full of power and imagination. The following "Νεκρική ᾠδή" may serve as an example:—

Τὴν αὐγὴ μὲ τὴ δροσούλα ἐξεφύτρωσ' ἕνα ῥόδο
Τὴν αὐγὴ μὲ τὴ δροσούλα ἐμαράθηκε τὸ ῥόδο!
Γιὰ μιὰν ἄνοιξι μονάχα στὰ περίφανα κλαριά του
Ἐτραγούδησε τ' ἀηδόνι ἔκαμε καὶ τὴ φωλιά του....
Σὰν ἡ ἄνοιξι γυρίσῃ καὶ τ' ἀηδόνι σὰ γυρίσῃ
Τὴ φωλιά του ποῦ θὰ στήσῃ;....

Ὅταν ἔβγαινε ἡ σελήνη, ὅταν ἔβγαιναν τ' ἀστέρια
Μὲ ἀγάπη τὸ ἐθεωροῦσαν, τοῦ ἀπλώνανε τὰ χέρια.
Σὰν νὰ ἠθέλαν ἐκεῖ ἐπάνω νὰ τὸ πάρουν τὸ καϋμένο,
Ἔλεγαν πῶς εἶν' ἀδέρφι, ἔλεγαν πῶς πλανημένο
Τ' οὐρανοῦ τὸ μονοπάτι τ' ὀρφανὸ θὰ εἶχε χάσῃ
Ὢχ! ἀστέρια! ὤχ! ἀστέρια! γρήγορα ποῦ θὰ σᾶς
        φθάσῃ!
Κ' ἄποιοι ποῦ ἤκουσαν τ' ἀηδόνι στὸ κλαρί του νὰ λαλῇ.
Εἶπαν δὲν εἶναι τραγοῦδι, μυρολόγι εἶν' ἐκεῖ....
Κί ὅσοι εἶδαν τὰς ἀκτίνας τῶν ἀστέρων τοῦ οὐρανοῦ
Νὰ γελοῦν νὰ παιγνιδίζουν μὲ τὰ φύλλα τοῦ οὐρανοῦ
Εἶπανε τὰ φῶτα ἐκεῖνα ἄχ! δὲν εἶναι τῆς χαρᾶς
Εἶπαν ὅτι εἶναι τὰ φῶτα νεκρικῆς κεροδοσᾶς.

.   .   .   .   .   .

Τὴν αὐγὴ μὲ τὴ δροσούλα ἐξεφύτρωσε ἕνα ῥόδο
Τὴν αὐγὴ μὲ τὴ δροσούλα ἐμαράθηκε τὸ ῥόδο

Μὴν ἐπέρασεν ἐκεῖθεν ὁ Βοριὰς ὁ παγωμένος
Καὶ σὰν εἶδε τέτοιο ῥόδο ὁ σκληρὸς ἐρωτεμένος
    ῎Αρπαξε τὴ μυρωδιά του
    Καὶ τὴν πῆρε στὰ φτερά του ; . . . .

   •   •   •   •   •

Δὲν τὸ ξεύρω! Κάποιος εἶπε ὅτι ἐψές τὸ βράδυ βράδυ
Εἶδε κάποιονε νὰ φεύγῃ σὰν καπνὸς μὲ τὸν ἀγέρα.
Τ' ἄλογό του ἦτο μαῦρο σὰν τῆς νύχτας τὸ σκοτάδι
    Κ' ἐλαφρό σὰν τὸν αἰθέρα,
Εἰς τὸ χέρι του ἐβαστοῦσε, ἀχαμνό ξεγυμνωμένο
    ῎Ενα ῥόδο μαραμμένο.
῞Οταν ἔφευγε ἀκλουθῶντας τοῦ πελάου τὴν ἄκρη ἄκρη
    ῎Αχ δὲν ἔχυν' ἕνα δάκρυ,
Μόνον ἔλεγε στὸ κῦμα, ποῦ τὸν βλέπει καὶ τραβιέται,
    " Κύματά μου εἰπέτε, εἰπέτε
Δὲν εἶν' ὤμορφο τὸ ῥόδο ; " Μόνον λέγει στὸ χορτάρι
    Ποῦ ὑποκάτω ἀπ τὸ ποδάρι
Τοῦ ἀλόγου του πεθαίνει. " Δὲν εἶμ ἄξιος κ' ἐγὼ
    Τέτοιο ῥόδο νὰ φορῶ ; "
Τέτοια ῥόδα καὶ τοῦ Χάρου κάνουν ὤμορφα τὰ στήθια
    Εἶναι ἀλήθεια, εἶν' ἀλήθεια !

A very popular poet of Greece is Zalocostas, who has been dead some fifteen years or more, — a voluminous translator from Italian poets, as Professor Geldart states, and, as an original writer, full of power and imagination. The following may serve as an example : —

Ὦ πλήρης,σεπτῶν ἀναμνήσεων χώρα,
Ὦ γῆ κλεινῶν ἄθλων, ὦ γῆ ποθητὴ,
Τὸ αἷμα ποιοῦσα ἡμῶν ! διὰ τί
Μ' ὀργὴν καὶ μὲ ἄλγος σὲ βλέπομεν τώρα ;
Ἀλλοίως, φεῦ, ἄλλην σ' ἐβλέπομεν ὅτε
Ἀγῶνες καὶ μόχθοι ὑπῆρχον κοινοί,
Κ' ἐπίθετον ἄλλο δὲν εἴχομεν ἢ
Ἑλλήνων βλαστοὶ καὶ Χριστοῦ στρατιῶται.

.   .   .   .   .

Ὦ αἶσχος, ὦ νόμοι σκληροῦ πεπρωμένου !
Ὦ μάρτυρες, ποία ἐπῆλθ' ἐποχή !
Τὰ τέκνα ὑμῶν ὀρφανὰ, δυστυχῆ,
Ὡς στίγμα τὸ ὄνομα φέρουν τοῦ ξένου.

.   .   .   .   .

Εἰς ζόφεον χάος τὰ ρεύματα χύνων.
Τῶν δούλων καὶ μαύρων τοῦ ἔθνους στιγμῶν,
Παρήρχετ' ὁ χρόνος βαρὺς στεναγμῶν,
Καὶ τ' ὄνομ' αὐτὸ τῶν προγόνων μας σβύνων.

.   .   .   .   .

Ἐν,πρώτοις τὸ πῦρ ἐξερράγ' εἰς τὸ Σοῦλι
Ἐκεῖ οἱ γενναῖοι πατέρες ἡμῶν
Ἐκραύγασαν πάντες μὲ μέγαν θυμόν·
Ἀλήπασα, τρέμε· δὲν εἴμεθα δοῦλοι.

.   .   .   .   .

Κτυπᾶτε ἀνδρεῖοι ! Φωναὶ ἀμαζόνων
Ἀντήχουν ἐν μάχαις πυρὸς μεταξὺ,
Κτυπᾶτε ! κ' ἡ Χάϊδω μὲ ξίφος ὀξύ
Ἡραίου τὰς τάξεις μαχίμων γειτόνων.

.   .   .   .   .

Τὶς ἦν ὁ κακοῦργος ἐξ οὗ ὀλεθρία
Ἐξῆλθεν ἡ πρώτη ἐρίδων σπορά;
Ὦ, εἴθε μελλόντων αἰώνων ἀρὰ
Εἰς τὴν κεφαλήν του νὰ πέσῃ βαρεῖα!

Ἃς ἦναι παντοῦ βδελυκτόν τ᾽ ὄνομά του
Ἀτάραχον ὕπνον νὰ μὴ κοιμηθῇ
Πλησίον του δέ τις νὰ μὴν εὑρεθῇ
Παρήγορος ἄλγους ἐν ὥρα θανάτου!

Εἰς τοῦ τύμβον ἐκεῖνον πλησίον
Ἠνεῴχθη μὲ πάταγον χάσμα·
Καὶ τῆς γῆς ἐκ τῶν σπλάγχνων τῶν κρύων
Ἐτινάχθη δεκάπηχυ φάσμα.
Ἆ! δὲν ἦτο τοῦ νοῦ μου ἀπάτη,
Μήτε φροῦδον τοῦ φόβου μου πλάσμα.
Βλοσυρὸν περιέστρεφε ᾽μάτι,
Καὶ λαμπάδα φλογῶν διαπύρων
Μὲ τὴν ἄσαρκον χεῖρα ἐκράτει.
Ἐθερμάνθη ἐπ᾽ ἄμετρον γύρον
Ὁ αἰθήρ, καὶ ἡ γῆ, καὶ οἱ λίθοι,
Καὶ ἡ κόνις αὐτὴ τῶν μαρτύρων.

Τοὺς γενναίους μας μάρτυρας εἶδα,
Ὅσοι ἔπεσον πίστεως φίλοι
Διὰ μίαν θανόντες πατρίδα.
Κατηφεῖς, σκυθρωποὶ καὶ ὀργίλοι,
Κατεδείκνυον μέλη θλασμένα
Καὶ πληγῶν διαχαίνοντα χείλη.

Of the so-called "Kleptic Ballads," the pride of modern Greece, the following may serve as a specimen:—

THE BURIAL OF DEMOS.

Ὁ ἥλιος ἐβασίλευε, κ' ὁ Δῆμος διατάζει·
Σύρτε, παιδιά μου, σ' τὸ νερόν, ψωμὶ νὰ φᾶτ' ἀπόψε.
Καὶ σὺ, Λαμπράκη μ' ἀνεψιέ, κάθου ἐδώ κοντά μου·
Νά! τ' ἄρματά μου φόρεσε, νὰ ἦσαι καπιτάνος·
Καὶ σεῖς, παιδιά μου, πάρετε τὸ ἔρημο σπαθί μου,
Πράσινα κόψετε κλαδιά, στρῶστέ μου νὰ καθίσω,
Καὶ φέρτε τὸν πνευματικὸ νὰ μ' ἐξομολογήσῃ·
Νὰ τὸν εἰπῶ τὰ κρίματα ποῦ ἔχω καμωμένα,
Τριάντα χρόνι' ἁμαρτωλός, κ' εἴκοσι πέντε κλέφτης·
Καὶ τώρα μ' ἦρθε θάνατος, καὶ θέλω ν' ἀποθάνω.
Κάμετε τὸ κιβούρι μου πλατύ, ψηλὸ νὰ γένῃ,
Νὰ στέκ' ὀρθὸς νὰ πολεμῶ, καὶ δίπλα νὰ γεμίζω.
Κ' ἀπὸ τὸ μέρος τὸ δεξὶ ἀφῆστε παραθύρι,
Τὰ χελιδόνια νὰ ρχωνται, τὴν ἄνοιξιν νὰ φέρουν
Καὶ τ' ἀηδόνια τὸν καλὸν Μάϊ νὰ μὲ μαθαίνουν!

Among the numberless and nameless poems of the modern Greeks I agree with Professor Geldart in saying, that I know nothing in any language more beautiful of its kind than the following:—

Εἰς τὸ ρεῦμα τῆς ζωῆς μου
Διὰ τί νὰ σ' ἀπαντήσω;
Δι' ἐμὲ ἀφ' οὗ δὲν ἦσο
Διατί νὰ σὲ ἰδῶ; ....

Καὶ μὲ ἔκαμες ἀπαύστως
Στεναγμοὺς νὰ ὑποφέρω,
Καὶ γελᾶς διότι κλαίω,
Διὰ σὲ καὶ θρηνωδῶ.

Στέρξε, κάμε ἢ νὰ ζήσω
Ἢ νὰ παύσῃ ἡ πνοή μου·
Ἴσως, ἴσως στὴν θανήν μου
Πλέον μεταμεληθῆς.

Δὲν ζητῶ, οἱ στεναγμοί μου
Τὴν καρδίαν σου ν' ἑλκύσουν·
Θέλω μόνον, ὅταν σβύσουν
Τῆς ζωῆς μου αἱ στιγμαί,
Ἕνα στεναγμὸν θρηνώδη
Ὡς χαιρετισμὸν ν' ἀφήσῃς,
Καὶ εἰς τὸν τάφον μου νὰ χύσῃς
Ἕν σου δάκρυ δι' ἐμέ.

A modern Greek, Mr. Apostolos Arsakios, who, I believe, is still living at Athens, when but eighteen years old wrote an "Idyl" which closely resembles the style of Theocritus. Mr. Arsakios wrote this "Idyl" to congratulate Napoleon the First for a son which was born to the emperor, but we really believe that the main object of the author was to induce the conqueror of Austerlitz to help the Greeks, who were then striving for independence. The following lines may give an idea of his style:—

ΕΙΔΥΛΛΙΟΝ.

Θύρσις καὶ Δάφνις.

Θύρσις.

Πᾷ σε, γέρων, ἀδρανεῖς φορέοντι πόδες τὸν ἀκιδνόν;
Πᾷ δ' ἄρ' κεκμακὼς, μέγα τ' ἀσθμαίνων ἀλάλασαι,
Καὶ τοσσοῦτος ἱδρὼς περιδίδρομε σῶμα γεραιόν;

Δάφνις.

Πάντοσ' ἐμὸν, ποιμὰν, πῶῦ σκίδνατ' ἔνθα καὶ ἔνθα
'Εκπάγλῳ θορύβῳ, νεμέθω τε πόας τε λελαθός·
Κἠγὼν δὲ βραδύπουν μόλις ὥρμασ' ἤλυσιν ἄρθρων,
Σκίμπωνι σκολιῷ σκηρίπτων γῆρας ἀφαυρὸν,
Ἔνθα καὶ ἔνθ' ὁ γέρων μεθέπων φυξήλιδα ποίμναν,
Καὶ ταραχᾶς παγάν· κίκυς μὰν οὐκ ἔτι πρόσσω
Ἔμπεδα βαινέμεναι, τρομέοντί τε γυῖα γεραιῶ
'Εμμόχθῳ γε δρόμῳ· Τὰ δὲ μοι πάντ' ἔννεπε, τέκνον
Θύρσι, πόθεν βόμβος με, πόθεν δ' ἁ ἔκπαγλος ἀχὼ,
Χάλκειον προλιποῦσα δαφοινᾶς βρόχθον 'Εννεῦς,
'Εμβρέμετ' ἀέριος; σμαράγῳ μὰν πάντα ταράττει;

Θύρσις.

'Αλλὰ σὲ γὰρ δὴ ταῦτα, πάτερ φίλε, μὴ θορυβούντων,
Γάλλων χάρματος ἐργ', ἰδ ὅσους Γάλλοισιν ἀδελφοὺς
'Ελλάνων ξυνέδεσσε μέγας φὼς χειρὶ βαρείᾳ.

Δάφνις.

Τόσσων μὰν λέγε, Θύρσι, τί τούτιον εὐφροσυνάων;
Οὐ μάν τοι νίκησιν ἀγαλλόμενοι κροτέοντι·
Νίκαι μὲν γὰρ τοῖς δ' ἐθάδες νῦν ἠδὲ βέβαιοι,
Οὐδέ τις οἰσεῖ τόσσον ἀγάκροτον ἄσπετον ἦδος.

Θύρσις.

Οὐδέ τι τοιοῦτον.   Τάδε νῦν, φίλος, ἄρρεν ἐγείρει
Ναπολέοντι τέκος δαμάρατον γ᾽ ἀναθῆλαν·

Δάφνις.

Ἀλλὰ τὺ γὰρ δὴ τοῦτο, πόθεν, πῶς, ὦ ᾽γαθὲ, ἔγνως ;

Θύρσις.

Λείμακα μὲν κἠγὼν, καθ᾽ ὑδρηλὸν μάλα νόμευον
Αἰφνίδιος ὄχ᾽ ὁ δοῦπος ἀφίκετο· φαίνετο δ᾽ ἦμες
Πρᾶτα μάχας τέκμωρ, διά τε κρότον οὐρανομήκη
Καὶ βλοσυρὸν πλατάγημα· τὸ μὰν βομβεῦον ἐκεῖνο
Καὶ πολύφλοισβον ἔλειφ᾽ ὑσμάνας, χάρμα δὲ μᾶλλον
Φράσδεν· ὄϊς γῶν μοι Κωρύδων εὐ᾽ τῷδε νομεύειν
Μίμνεν, ἐγὼν εὐθὺς δὲ περάσσας λαῖτμα θαλάσσας
Κραιπνὰ μάλ᾽ ὥστε νέος (τόδε γὰρ νεότητος ὄνειαρ)
Ἤλυθον ἐσ νᾶσον τὰν γείτονα, ἔνθα θριάσδεν
Δᾶμος ἅπας ἕλλην Κερκύρας φαίνετο χαίρων.
Οὐδὲ μεταλλάαν οἷος τ᾽ ἦν χάρματος αὐτῷ
Τούτιον ἀρρήτω· τὸ γὰρ οὐκ οἷον τ᾽ ἀβακέμμεν
Τοὐπιφανὲς ᾤοντο· βοὰς δὲ κατ᾽ ἠδ᾽ ἀλαλατὼς
Καὶ κότον ἀλλάλοισιν ἐόντα τίν᾽ ὤλεσε χάρμα,
Παντᾷ δ᾽ ἦν φίλτρον, παντᾷ γάνος ἠδ᾽ ἴα γῆρυς.
"Ζώη ΝΑΠΟΛΕΩΝ ! Ζώη βασιλεὺς δὲ ὁ ῾Ρώμας !"
Κράσδεκον μεγάλως, πίλως· δ᾽ εἰς ἠέρα πέμπον·
Κ᾽ ἔγνων, Δάφνι, μόγις, ὅτι δὴ ταῦτ᾽ ἄρρεν ἐγείρει
Ναπολέοντι τέκος, ῾Ρώμας βασιλεὺς, ἀναθῆλαν·
Παντᾷ δ᾽ εὐρυτάταν τριπλᾶ μάλ᾽ ἠδὲ τετραπλᾶ
Τόσσα τι χάρματος ἔργα κατ᾽ ἀρχὰν γίνετ᾽ Ἄνακτος.

Another modern Greek, Mr. Demetrius Schoinas, composed a "Pindaric Ode," in April, 1811, for the purpose of congratulating Napoleon the First for the son that was born to him: —

Στροφὴ γ!

Λίπεν δ' ἄψ Θῶκον ἔνθα θάασ-
σε νύγμασι χαρᾶς·
'Ιριν ἔκ τε ποδά-
νεμον δ', ὠνόμαξεν 'Αθανάτως
ἐπ' ἀγοράνδε καλέσαι,
ἀπὸ δ' ὦρτο τάχ' ἀγγελέοισα· ἐπεὶ
δὲ Διὸς μεθ' ὁμάγυριν ἆλθον ἱε-
ρὰν, τοῖσιν ῥα ἔνεπε παγ-
χρυσέῳ ἐν δαπέδῳ
Ζεύς· παρὰ δ' ἄγγελος ἔ-
στα δεξιὸς "Αρτεμις οἱ
'Ιστε νῦν Θεοὶ, ἰδὲ τέρ-
πεσθε· ἁμὸς γὰρ μεγακλεής.

Writing in "classical Greek" has of late years been generally the habit of all educated Greeks. The following extract from an essay, "Περὶ τοῦ εἰ ἐξῆν καὶ ταῖς γυναιξὶ ταῖς δραματικαῖς ἐπιδείξεσι παρεῖναι," written by a well-known doctor of Athens, may serve as an example: —

Τῶν ἀρχαίων οὐδὲν περὶ τούτου βέβαιον καταλελοιπό-
των, οἱ νεώτεροι διττὴν ἡμῖν ἰδέαν παρέδωκαν, ἐκ διαμέ-
τρου διάφορον· οἱ μὲν γὰρ αὐτῶν μάλιστα εἰσήγαγον εἰς
τὰ θέατρα τὰς γυναῖκας, οἱ δὲ ἀπέκλεισαν εἰς τὸ παντελές.

.... Ἐν δὲ τῇ Σπάρτῃ, ὅπου καὶ τὸ τῶν γυναικῶν φῦλον μέρος τῆς πολιτείας ἐκ τοῦ νόμου συνίστα, ἐξεῖναι, φασὶ, καὶ αὐτὰς τὰς εὐγενεστέρας, οὐ μόνον εἰς τὸ θέατρον εἰσιέναι, ἀλλ' (ὅπερ καὶ τοῦθ' ὁμολογουμένως ἐκείναις ἀπηγόρευται) καὶ χορεύειν ἐπὶ σκηνῆς, καὶ ὑποκρίνεσθαι, καὶ μισθὸν ἐπὶ τούτῳ λαμβάνειν παρὰ τοῦ χορηγοῦ. Ταῦτα μὲν ἐκεῖνος. Οἱ δὲ ἄλλοι οὐκ ἄξια λόγου ταῦτα κρίναντες, καὶ θεατρίαις ἁπλῶς ἀνοίγουσι τὸ θέατρον, καὶ τόπον αὐταῖς ἀποδιδόασιν ὡρισμένον.

Before closing this chapter, a few words are due to our contemporaries. The writings of many modern Greek prose authors, as, for instance, the "Ἱστορία τῆς Ἑλληνικῆς ἐπαναστάσεως," by Spyridon Tricupes, and "Δοκίμιον ἱστορίας τῆς Ἑλληνικῆς γλώσσης," by D. Mavrophredes, are well known, and have been reviewed in some of the leading English journals. Professor Asopios is well known by his "Εἰσαγωγὴ εἰς Πίνδαρον," and Professor Damalas by his "Περὶ ἀρχῶν." Papparegopulos' History of Greece is remarkable, as Professor Geldart states, for its clear and simple style and the unstudied purity of its language. I close this chapter with the following extract from Plutarch's "Life of Cæsar," as translated by Mr. A. R. Rangabes, "Εἰς τὴν καθομιλουμένην" (in the spoken language), late Greek Ambassador in Paris, and well known not only as a scholar and archæologist, but also as a poet: —

Ἡ γνώμη λοιπὸν αὕτη ἐφάνη φιλάνθρωπος, καὶ ἰσχυρὸς ὁ λόγος, ὅστις ἐρρέθη περὶ αὐτῆς. Δι᾽ ὅ, οὐ μόνον οἱ μετ᾽ αὐτὸν ἐγερθέντες παρεδέχοντο τὴν πρότασιν αὐτοῦ, ἀλλὰ καὶ πολλοί τῶν προομιλησάντων, ἀρνούμενοι τὰς ἰδίας των γνώμας, παρεδέχοντο τὴν ἐδικήν του, ἕως ὅτου ἦλθεν ἡ σειρά τοῦ Κάτωνος καὶ τοῦ Κάτλου. Οὗτοι δ᾽ ἠναντιώθησαν μεθ᾽ ὁρμῆς, καὶ ὡς ὁ Κάτων μετὰ λόγου ἔρριψε καὶ ὑπόνοιαν κατ᾽ αὐτοῦ, καὶ ἐξανέστη κατ᾽ αὐτοῦ βιαίως, οἱ μὲν ἄνδρες παρεδόθησαν ὅπως θανατωθῶσι· κατὰ δὲ τοῦ Καίσαρος, ἐν ᾧ ἐξήρχετο τῆς βουλῆς, πολλοὶ τῶν νέων τῶν φρουρούντων τὸν Κικέρωνα τότε ὁρμήσαντες, ἔστρεψαν γυμνά τὰ ξίφη κατ᾽ αὐτοῦ. Ἀλλὰ λέγεται ὅτι ὁ Κουρίων, περικαλύψας τότε αὐτὸν διὰ τῆς τηβέννου του, τὸν ἐξήγαγε. Καὶ ὁ Κικέρων, ὅταν οἱ νέοι προσέβλεψαν εἰς αὐτόν, ὅτι ἔνευσεν ἀποφατικῶς, φοβηθεὶς τὸν δῆμον, ἢ τὸν φόνον ὅλως ἄδικον καὶ παράνομον θεωρῶν. Τοῦτο ὅμως δὲν ἠξεύρω πῶς ὁ Κικέρων ἂν εἶναι ἀληθὲς, δὲν τὸ ἔγραψεν εἰς τὸν περὶ τῆς ὑπατείας λόγον του· κατηγορεῖτο δ᾽ ὕστερον ὅτι δὲν ὠφελήθη τότε ἐκ τῆς εὐκαιρίας ἥτις ἀρίστη παρουσιάζετο εἰς αὐτόν κατὰ τοῦ Καίσαρος, ἀλλ᾽ ἐδειλίασεν ἐνώπιον τοῦ δήμου, ὅστις ὑπερτάτως ηὐνόει τὸν Καίσαρα.

CHAPTER VIII.

DIFFERENCE BETWEEN THE OLD ATTIC AND THE MODERN GREEK.

THE only difference that exists between the old pure Attic and the modern Greek or *common dialect*, is as follows : —

The common dialect is a loose Attic with a mixture of Macedonian and Alexandrian words. It adopts various new forms, as ψεῦσμα, νῖκος, νουθεσία, ἐκχύνειν, στήκω, ὀμνύω for ψεῦδος, νίκη, νουθέτησις, ἐκχέειν, ἵστημι, ὄμνυμι; it admits various poetical words, as αὐθεντεῖν, *to lord it;* ἀλέκτωρ for ἀλεκτρυών; ἔσθω for ἐσθίω; βρέχω, *to rain,* etc.; it uses old words in new senses, as συνίστημι, *I prove;* ὀψώνιον, *wages;* ἐρεύγεσθαι, *eloqui;* γεννήματα, *fruit;* λαλιά, *language;* and it frames new words and new compounds, as γρηγορῶ, παιδιόθεν, αἱματοχυσία. It ceases to employ the dual; entirely abandons the use of the optative in *oratio obliqua;* uses the infinitive instead of the future participle after verbs of *going, sending,* etc.; admits ει with the subjunctive, ὅταν, καὶ, ἵνα, with the present indicative; and, finally, shows a tendency to *analysis*, by using prepositions where the case-terminations would have been originally sufficient to express the meaning, and by employing the active with ἑαυτὸν instead of the middle. (ἐτάραξεν ἑαυτὸν = ἐταράξατο. See Farrar's "Greek Syntax.")

The dual number, which does not exist in modern Greek, is not found in the Æolic dialect, and, in fact, being altogether unnecessary, early begins to vanish and to be treated as quite subordinate to the plural. The dual number may be termed "a superfluous exuberance," adding but little force to the language.

Such being the changes which have passed over the Greek language, we still hold that it has lost neither the elasticity nor the life of the ancient Greek. Her words are not, so to speak, "congealed," and "void of life," as are the words of the French and — with the exception of the German — the words of other languages, which retain the meaning once given them. It may be said that this produces indefiniteness and want of clearness; but for all that, this is one of the strongest proofs of the life of the language. This is the reason why the "New Hellenistic," though somewhat under-a new garment, is the traditional language of the old Greeks, which for the last thirty centuries runs through the Grecian heaven, at times shining with all its usual light, at times scarcely visible and clouded by mist, but never extinguished. It is not and cannot be termed the daughter of the old Greek, just as the term is applied to modern languages derived from the Latin, because these languages are shoots from the root of the withered, dried, and grafted trunk of the Latin, whilst the modern Greek is the same old trunk, variously tried, withered as to some of its branches, but for the most part producing new branches in the place of the ones withered, never losing its vitality, and promising, under a careful cultivation, to become the same old shady and far-spreading tree which it was formerly.

Modern languages, such as the French and the Italian, are founded, as a modern Greek scholar asserts, upon the "popular Latin"; but this Latin is, so to speak, in ruins, and it is from its ruins that these languages arose invested with new forms, new idioms, and a new life. Notice how the following Latin words, *caballus, annulus, bovis, pater, mater, fratris, soror, pellis, oculus, ovum, testa, niger, instrumentum, corpus* (*corporis*), become, so to speak, mutilated in the Italian *cavallo, annello, bove* or *bue, padre, madre, fratello* (especially from *fratellus*), *sorella, pelle, occhio, nove, testa, nero, strumento, corpo,* and in the still worse French, *cheval, anneau, bœuf, père, mère, frère, sœur, peau, œil, œuf, tête, noire, instrument, corps.* The three genders in Latin are compressed into two. From the demonstrative pronoun *ille, illa,* the definite article *le, la* results; and from the numeral *unus, una, unum,* the indefinite article *uno, una, un,´une;* similar changes have occurred in the Greek language, but when? In the Homeric and Attic times *only.*

The forms of the verbs were likewise so much changed that it was necessary to add separate personal pronouns, to distinguish the persons, which has never occurred in the Greek language. *J'aime, tu aimes, il aime, nous aimons, vous aimez,* instead of *āmō, ămās, ămăt, ămūmus;* instead of the one perfectum, three were formed, *defini, indefini, anterieur.* Besides this, another *new* tense was added, the "conditional," which does not *really* exist in the Latin. Thus, in the Italian we have the forms *venderei, venderesti, venderebbe;* and in the French, *je vendrais, tu vendrais, il vendrait,* etc. Words of either foreign, German, Greek, or Celtic origin have crept into the language and are so thoroughly woven with the whole fabric of the language that they can never be eradicated: on the other hand, the foreign idioms which have been introduced into the Greek language are, for the most part, superficial; they are spots which can easily be rubbed out, and are by no means deep and indelible colors.

These languages, accordingly, are justly termed

"her daughters," but the "New Hellenistic" is one and the same old Greek; or, as a modern Greek scholar calls it, "the newest phase of the old Greek,"—to which state it has come slowly through many centuries, not violently, or accidentally, but unassisted, and by means of those very laws lying in her own nature.

It may not be out of place here to remark, if we look to the matter of pronunciation in a practical point of view, what has already been stated by a recent scholar who travelled in Greece, viz.: A knowledge of Greek, with the modern Greek pronunciation, will obviate the necessity of engaging an interpreter when travelling in Greece, Turkey, Egypt, and Asia Minor. Greek, as the language of the most thriving mercantile race, is the medium of communication between many of the various nations of the East. Again, by discarding the pronunciation now prevalent, and adopting instead the modern Greek, and by studying the Greek "as a living language," I will mention what scholars like Ross and Tassow have already noticed, "that great light may be thrown upon the meaning of classical authors." Besides, it is a fact that the knowledge of Greek as a living language is of chief significance in the verbal criticism of the New Testament and the Septuagint.

CHAPTER IX

THE word "prosody" retains among the modern Greeks the signification of the old grammarians, — "the doctrine of accentuation." In this sense it differs entirely from "prosody" as the word is to-day understood by those who study the Greek as a foreign language. We do not believe in the statements of J. Vossius and many others, that prosody meant simply "metrical quantity" or "musical rhythm," and that the genuine prosody of the Greek words was always in "unison of sound with the poetical rhythm" or "the quantity of the syllables," etc.

Now, that "prosody," as a modern Greek scholar asserts, meant among the ancient Greeks "καὶ τὰς ἐν τῷ διαλέγεσθαι τάσεις τῆς ἐγγραμμάτου φωνῆς," viz. the "grammatical accents," is evident from what follows.

Aristotle (350 B. C.) calls definitely the "accent of a word prosody." "Παρά δὲ τὴν προσῳδίαν ἐν μὲν τοῖς ἄνευ γραφῆς διαλεκτικοῖς οὐ ῥάδιον ποιῆσαι λόγον" . . . . "But from accent, in discussions which are not committed to writing, it is not easy to frame an argument." (Σοφιστ. ἐλέγχ. α, βλ. καὶ ἐφεξῆς). Again, treating of "the parts of Rhetoric," Aristotle recommends "πῶς τοῖς τόνοις χρῆσθαι, οἷον ὀξείᾳ καὶ βαρείᾳ καὶ μέσῃ, ... and on the manner in which we should employ its tones, viz., the *acute*, the *grave*, and the *intermediate*," .... from which he says "harmony results."

Accordingly, if musical intonation really was characteristic of ancient Greek accentuation, this feature has been most faithfully preserved. Professor Geldart remarks that the Greeks, especially when excited in preaching or public speaking, intone so melodiously that something very like a tune is heard of which the higher tones are always the more emphatic syllables. .... Aristoxenus, a pupil of Aristotle (330 B. C.), teaches that "πρῶτον ἁπάντων, τὴν τῆς φωνῆς κίνησιν διοριστέον τῷ μέλλοντι πραγματεύεσθαι περὶ μέλους, αὐτὴν τὴν κατὰ τόπον· οὐ γὰρ εἷς τρόπος αὐτῆς ὢν τυγχάνει· κινεῖται μὲν γὰρ καὶ διαλεγομένων ἡμῶν, καὶ μελῳδούντων, τὴν εἰρημένην κίνησιν· ὀξὺ γὰρ καὶ βαρὺ δῆλον ὡς ἐν ἀμφοτέροις τούτοις ἐστὶ (Αριστοξ. ἁρμονικ. στοιχ. Βιβλ. γ, ἐν τόμῳ α, σελ. 3, τῆς ἐκδόσ. Μεϊβομ). Again, "Δύο δέ τινες εἰσιν ἰδέαι κινήσεως (of the voice), ἥ τε συνεχὴς καὶ ἡ διαστηματική. Τὴν μὲν οὖν συνεχῆ λογικὴν εἶναι φαμέν· διαλεγουμένων γὰρ ἡμῶν οὕτως ἡ φωνὴ κινεῖται κατὰ τρόπον, ὥστε μηδαμοῦ δοκεῖν ἵστασθαι·

κατὰ δὲ τὴν ἑτέραν, ἣν ὀνομάζομεν διαστηματικὴν, ἐναντίως πέφυκε γίνεσθαι· καὶ γὰρ ἵστασθαί τε δοκεῖ, καὶ πάντες τὸν τοῦτο φαινόμενον ποιεῖν οὐκέτι λέγειν φασὶν, ἀλλ᾽ ᾄδειν· διόπερ ἐν τῷ διαλέγεσθαι φεύγομεν τὸ ἱστάναι τὴν φωνὴν, ἂν μὴ διὰ πάθος ποτὲ εἰς τοιαύτην κίνησιν ἀναγκασθῶμεν ἐλθεῖν· ἐν δὲ τῷ μελωδεῖν τοὐναντίον ποιοῦμεν· τὸ μὲν γὰρ συνεχὲς φεύγομεν, τὸ δ᾽ ἱστάναι τὴν φωνὴν ὡς μάλιστα διώκομεν. . . .

Dionysius the Thracian (66 B. C.) defines the accent "φωνῆς ἀπήχησιν ἐναρμονίου ἢ κατὰ ἀνάτασιν ἐν τῇ ὀξείᾳ ἢ κατὰ ὁμαλισμὸν ἐν τῇ βαρείᾳ, ἢ κατὰ περίκλασιν ἐν τῇ περισπωμένῃ." Cicero (60 B. C.), speaking of the acute (acutum), grave (gravum), and the circumflex (circumflexum), says, that from these, results. . . . "quidam cantus" (Cicer. Orator. 17), so that, as Oekonomos asserts, grammatical prosody in Latin was translated accentus (ac-cino = ad cano, viz. ad cantum). Dionysius of Halicarnassus (30 B. C.) mentions as of like name or meaning "prosody" and "accent": τάσεις φωνῆς αἱ καλούμεναι προσῳδίαι. The same one, treating "περὶ μαθήσεως γραμμάτων," says "πρῶτον τὰ ὀνόματα τῶν γραμμάτων ἐκμανθάνομεν· ἔπειτα τοὺς τύπους καὶ τὰς δυνάμεις· εἶθ᾽ οὕτω τὰς συλλαβὰς καὶ τὰ ἐν αὐταῖς πάθη· καὶ μετὰ τοῦτο ἤδη τὰς λέξεις καὶ τὰ συμβεβηκότα αὐταῖς, ἐκτάσεις τε λέγω καὶ συστολὰς καὶ προσῳδίας." . . . . Sextus (190 B.C.) enumerates and distinctly calls "τὰς τῶν Γραμμα-

τικῶν προσῳδίας, ὀξεῖαν καὶ βαρεῖαν καὶ περισπω-
μένην." Hence it results from the testimony
of the different authors mentioned, and of many
others omitted for the sake of brevity, that prosody
meant by no means 'what Vossius and Henninius
and others have asserted, "a singing and melody
in unison of sound with the poetical rhythm,"
but simply the "accent accompanying the pronunciation of a word," or "τὸ λογῶδες μέλος τὸ ἐν
τοῖς ὀνόμασιν," as Aristoxenus justly remarks.

Erasmus himself never recommended the disuse
of the Greek accent in pronunciation, and very
well draws out the distinction between accent and
quantity as follows.

He puts his lesson into the mouth of a bear,
who is made to say, "There are some men so
obtuse as to confound stress with length of sound,
while the two things are as different as possible."
A sharp sound is one thing, a long sound is another. Intensiveness is not the same thing as
extensiveness. And yet I know learned men,
who, in sounding the words ἀνέχου καὶ ἀπέχου,
lengthened the middle syllable with all their
might and main, just because it has the acute
accent, though it is short by nature; in fact, as
short as a syllable could be. Why, the very don-
keys might teach us the difference between accent
and quantity, for they, when they bray, make the
sharp sound short and the deep one long.

The "followers of Erasmus" in Germany, however vicious their pronunciation in other respects, invariably read Greek so that the accent is heard, and never dream that they are sacrificing quantity.

Professor Geldart asserts, "that our prejudice against accents is for the most part insular, and deepened moreover by the insular peculiarities of our pronunciation. This is especially the case with respect to long and short υ, which we ordinarily pronounce in exactly the same manner, namely as *you*. The result of this is, that when we want to show the difference between long and short υ, we have no other means open to us than that of laying a stress on the long υ and leaving the short unaccented. In ηὐτύχει and ὑπεύθυνος we pronounce the υ as *you*, i. e., really long, and we only distinguish between the long υ in the one case and the short υ in the other by flying in the face of the Greek accent, and reading the words respectively ηὖτυχει and ὑπευθύνος. In this case, so far from preserving the true quantity by the use of the Latin accent, we are only covering a false one."

Now, there is no human language without its accents of prosody — whether written or not — fixed or represented by analogy or custom. Because, as Oekonomos remarks, the accent tends to the unity of the word, concentrating its syllables

into one whole, and rendering the meaning of the
word clear. Thus, the accentual, or, so to speak,
"belonging to speaking," prosody of the common
dialect differed from the poetical prosody. Hence
it results, that Vossius and his followers are
wrong in affirming that the accents of the words
were always in unison with the metre of the
verses and the quantity of the syllables. This is
evident, as a modern Greek says, because, first,
the whole nation were not poets; and again, because the accents as a consequence would have
been unsteady or indefinite, being changed to suit
the quantity of syllables, which at times vary,
becoming either long or short, for the completion
or perfection of the metre, — that is to say, the
accents could not then have had a definite and
fixed location in the common dialect or in conversation; the laws and meaning of the language
would no longer have been unvarying, and it
could not have been a satisfactory medium of
communication for the people (who certainly did
not converse with each other in verse), or for
philosophers themselves. This reminds us how
Lucianus, the famous writer, a native of Samo-
sata, in a witty way says that Venus, once en-
raged against the inhabitants of Abdera, caused
them all to be seized with a poetical frenzy,
so that the one could not understand the
other!

We conclude, therefore, that there exists in the Greek language the definite accentuation of words as old as the language itself. Oekonomos says that the Greek language expressed from the earlier times the stress of its sounds, ·that is to say, the accentual prosody of the words, definitely according to the custom of each dialect. The Dorians, for instance, have the peculiarity of using the circumflex accent in barytone futures, as in ᾀσῶ δωσῶ λεξοῦντι (λέξουσι). The Æolians again, by putting the acute accent on the penultimate, say φρόνην, κάλην, νόην instead of φρονεῖν, etc. They likewise, in words of two syllables, place the acute accent on the penultimate, whilst others accent the same words on the last syllables; for instance, σύφος or σόφος κάλος, τράχυς, ὄξυς, πήλευς, θῦμος αὖως instead of αὐὼς (ἀὼς, ἠὼς) θυμός, etc., and the adverbs κάλως, σόφως instead of ὧς. Thus, the Bœotians were wont to say ὑγίεις instead of ὑγιὴς (ει = η). In like manner were formed χαρίεις, αἰγλήεις, τελήεις. In like manner, although Plato wrote ταχυτῆτα, he also wrote θεότητα, ἀνθρωπότητα, τρατηζότητα, κυαθότητα, etc.

The Attics used to say, τουτὶ, ταυτὶ, ἐκεινωνί instead of ταῦτα, τοῦτο, ἐκείνων. They likewise said, πόνηρε καὶ ἄληθες καὶ ἄντικρυς and ἐλθέ, εἰπέ, εὑρέ. They also said, διέτης, τριέτης and δίετες, τρίετες, etc., while others accent the same words on the last syllable. The Ionians and the Attics said, ἀληθείη,

ἀναιδείη, εὐκλείη, κατηφείη, whilst, on the other
hand, the Attic tragedians in these very words
accent the antepenult.

Now, these variations of accent are simply dialectic. They by no means change the fact, that
there is a definite law of accentuation in the Greek
language.

This definite law of accentuation existed even
before the Greek language was divided into dialects. So long as the Greeks remained a tribe
of small numbers, inhabiting one and the same
country, they spoke one and the same language,
and the greatest harmony prevailed as respects
the accent and pronunciation of the words. But
when the Greeks commenced to scatter and to
migrate into different countries, then, in time,
their language also began to differ by certain
variations and distinctions, and hence the dialects
arose.

Similar dialectic variations exist to this day in
the Greek language, but the people understand
each other without any difficulty whatever. These
dialectic variations do not alter the language, consequently the rules of accentuation are uniform,
although the people adapt them to suit their
idiomatic peculiarities. Poetic prosody likewise
teaches the uniform accentuation of words. This
is evident because many short syllables become
long in both the arsis and the thesis, by means

of the accent, which, as Oekonomos asserts, lengthens somewhat the quantity in pronunciation. For instance, the Homeric ὑποδεξίη (Ἰλ.), ἀκομιστίη (Ὀδ. φ), κακοεργίη (Ὀδ. χ), ἀεργίη (Ὀδ. ω), ἱστίη (Ὀδ. ξ), ἰλίου (Ἰλ. ο), ἀγρίου (Ἰλ. χ), ὁμοιίου (Ἰλ. ε), ὑπεροπλίῃσι (Ἰλ. α) lengthen ι by means of the accent, naturally short in these words. Oekonomos also says, that ο and ε become long in Αἰόλου (Ὀδ. κ), ἀπὸ ἔθεν (Ἰλ. ζ), ἱππότην (᾽Επιγραμμ. Παυσαν. θ, 10), Θεαγένην (Αὐτ. στ. 11, 2), etc. Likewise in the ἀγυιὰ καὶ ὀργυιὰ (Herod. and Xenop.). Now, it is only by the placing of the accent on the antepenultimate that final α becomes short, as, for instance, ἄγυιαν (Ἰλ. υ, 254), ὄργυι᾽ ὑπὲρ (Ὀδ. 1, 328). It is on this account that the Attic tragedians, by shortening the last syllable, used the Æolic forms ἥμιν, ὕμιν instead of ἡμῖν, ὑμῖν, etc.

Now, we believe that the accents always existed in the Greek language. There is no language without its accents. Aristophanes of Byzantium (200 B. C.) might have introduced written accents, in order to preserve the true pronunciation of Greek at the time when it was becoming the vernacular of many Oriental races, but accents existed long before Aristophanes, and, in fact, long before the Homeric era. Accents, we say, always existed, but the ancient Greeks did not generally write them. The fact that

many of the inscriptions that have been discovered are without accents does by no means
prove that accents did not exist among the ancient Greeks. Now, the modern Greeks seldom,
if ever, put any accents on capital letters, that
is to say, on words composed of capitals, and it
would not be strange if the ancient Greeks likewise were accustomed to leave off the accents
from inscriptions, which were generally written
with capitals. It is, however, worthy of remark
that a verse of Euripides, with accentual marks,
has been discovered written on the walls of Her-
culaneum. It was natural for the ancient Greeks
to pronounce their language correctly, even without marking the syllables on which the stress
ought to fall by means of the accent. To this
day, many women of Greece, in writing to their
husbands away from home, usually write without
the accents. But do they not know how to pronounce their language just as well as those who
make constant use of written accents? To pronounce correctly, to lay the stress on the syllable
on which the accent falls, is natural to every
Greek, although he may do it unconsciously. He
is taught to pronounce according to accent from
early childhood; he pronounces correctly, although he may not know the laws of prosody.

We said that accents have always existed in
the Greek language. Homer (1000 B. C.) says

Τρῶας and Τρωάς (Ἰλ. χ, 57). Ἀλλ᾽ εἰσέρχεο τεῖχος, ἐμὸν τέκος, ὄφρα σαώσῃς Τρῶας καὶ Τρωάς, μηδὲ μέγα κῦδος ὀρέξῃς. Now, how could Homer otherwise than by means of the accent distinguish between the male and female inhabitants? Oekonomos also brings the example of δμώων καὶ δμῶας (ὁ δμὼς· Ὀδ. ξ, 59 and 399) from δμωῶν καὶ δμωὰς (ἡ δμωή, Ὀδ. 121 and 25, 45, 154). How could he distinguish finally λάων and λαῶν (Ἰλ. φ, 314) unless by means of the accent? It is by means of the accent, Oekonomos says, that Homer lengthened in the arsis or thesis the short syllable of the penult and the antepenult, as ἴμεναι, ἀρόμεναι, ὄϊες, κακοεργίη, ἀγρίου, ὁμοίου, etc.; he also shortened the long syllable, or the one before it, by means of the accent, as ἐγείρομεν, βούλεται, ἀποθείομεν instead of ἐγείρωμεν, βούληται, ἀποθείωμεν. Compare also the ἐπειὴ μεμαὼς Ἀχιλεύς, Ἀχιλῆος, Ὀδυσεὺς, Ὀδυσῆος, because it is on account of the force of the following accent that the one of the consonants was omitted. The ancient grammarians spoke in detail concerning these facts, as did also the great scholar Hernnanus in his " Elementa doctrinæ metricæ," page 56, etc.

Again, Aristophanes (430 B. C.), by means of the accent, shows the difference in the meaning of the words: Βόειος δημὸς (oxytone) from δῆμος (Βατρ. 40, Ἱππ. 95) and διαπεινῶμεν from διαπίνομεν (Bœotian, διαπεινᾶμες καὶ διαπίνομες). His con-

temporary, Isocrates, played upon the words καὶ
νοῦ with καινοῦ (γραφιδίου καινοῦ, καὶ βιβλίου καινοῦ, and so on). Plato (390 B. C.) distinctly says,
"Πολλάκις ἐπεμβάλλομεν γράμματα, τὰ δ᾽ ἐξαιροῦ-
μεν, παρ᾽ ὃ βουλόμεθα ὀνομάζοντες, καὶ τὰς ὀξύτητας
μεταβάλλομεν, οἷον Διῒ φίλος· τοῦτο ἵνα ἀντὶ ῥήματος ὄνομα ἡμῖν γένηται, τό, τε ἕτερον αὐτόθεν ἰῶτα
ἐξείλομεν, καὶ ἀντὶ ὀξείας τῆς μέσης συλλαβῆς βαρεῖαν ἐφθεγξάμεθα· ἄλλων δὲ τοὐναντίον ἐμβάλλο-
μεν γράμματα, τὰ δὲ βαρύτερα φθεγγόμεθα. Τούτων
τοίνυν ἕν καὶ τὸ τῶν ἀνθρώπων ὄνομα πέπονθεν, ὡς
ἐμοὶ δοκεῖ· ἐκ γὰρ ῥήματος ὄνομα γέγονεν, ἑνὸς γράμ-
ματος, τοῦ α, ἐξαιρεθέντος, καὶ βαρυτέρας τῆς τελευ-
τῆς γενομένης, ἐντεῦθεν ὁ ἄνθρωπος (ἐστὶν) ἀναθρῶν
ἃ ὄπωπε. . . . . "We often put in and leave out letters in words, and give names as we please, and
change the accents. Take, for example, the words
Διῒ φίλος. In order to convert these into a noun
we omit one of the iotas, and sound the middle
syllable grave instead of acute; as, in other words
also, letters are inserted, and the grave is changed
into an acute. . . . . The name ἄνθρωπος, which
was once a phrase and is now a noun, appears
to be a case just of this sort; for one letter,
which is the α, has been omitted, and the acute
of the last syllable has been changed to a
grave. . . . . Hence man, of all animals, is rightly
called ἄνθρωπος, meaning ὁ ἀναθρῶν ἃ ὄπωπεν.
Again, Aristotle (350 B. C.) says: Παρὰ δὲ τὴν

προσῳδίαν ἐν μὲν τοῖς ἄνευ γραφῆς διαλεκτικοῖς οὐ ῥάδιον ποιῆσαι λόγον, ἐν δὲ τοῖς γεγραμμένοις καὶ ποιήμασι λόγον μᾶλλον· οἷον καὶ τὸν Ὅμηρον ἔνιοι διορθοῦνται πρὸς τοὺς ἐλέγχοντας ὡς ἀτόπως εἰρηκότα..... "Τὸ μὲν οὐ καταπύθεται ὄμβρῳ," λύουσι γὰρ αὐτὸ τῇ προσῳδίᾳ λέγοντες τὸ οὐ ὀξύτερον. Καὶ τὸ περὶ τὸ ἐνύπνιον τοῦ Ἀγαμέμνονος, ὅτι οὐκ αὐτὸς ὁ Ζεὺς εἶπε..... "δίδομεν δέ οἱ εὖχος ἀρέσθαι," ἀλλὰ τῷ ἐνυπνίῳ διδόναι.

" But from accent, in discussions which are not committed to writing, it is not easy to frame an argument, but rather in writings and poems; as, for instance, some defend Homer against those who accuse him as having spoken absurdly, —

Τὸ μὲν οὐ καταπύθεται ὄμβρῳ, —

for they solve this by accent, saying that οὐ is to be marked with an acute accent. Also about the dream of Agamemnon, because Jupiter himself does not say,

δίδομεν δέ οἱ εὖχος ἀρέσθαι,

but says to the dream διδόναι. Such things, therefore, are assumed (explained) from accent."

Although the Greek language from its earlier times had " accents," their use became more prevalent in both writing and speaking after the time of Aristophanes (200 B.C.), who is also considered as their inventor.

*Οἱ χρόνοι καὶ οἱ τόνοι καὶ τὰ πνεύματα, ᾿Αριστοφάνους
ἐκτυπώσαντος γέγονε πρός τε διάκρισιν τῆς ἀμφιβόλου
λέξεως, καὶ πρὸς τὸ μέλος τῆς φωνῆς συμπάσης, καὶ τὴν
ἁρμονίαν, ὡς ἂν ἐπᾴδοιμεν φθεγγόμενοι. Σκέψαι δ᾿ ὡς
ἕκαστον αὐτῶν φυσικῶς ἅμα καὶ οἰκείως, καθάπερ τὰ ὄργανα, ἐσχημάτισται καὶ ὠνόμασται· ἐπειδὴ καὶ ταῦτα
ἔμελλε τῷ λόγῳ ὥσπερ ὄργανα ἔσεσθαι· ἑώρακε γὰρ καὶ
τὴν μουσικὴν οὕτω τὸ μέλος καὶ τοὺς ἀριθμοὺς σημαινομέ-
νην· καὶ πῆ μὲν ἀνιεῖσαν, πῆ δ᾿ ἐπιτείνουσαν, καὶ τὸ μὲν
ὀξὺ τὸ δὲ βαρὺ ὀνομάζουσαν, κ. τ. λ. (᾿Αρκαδ. Παρὰ Βι-
λοϊσῶν· Προλεγόμ. εἰς ῞Ομηρον. σελ. ια.)*

Now, it results from what has been said, and
from the direct testimony of the different authors
mentioned, and of many whose testimony might
have been cited, that grammatical accent or prosody is essentially different from "poetical prosody." The modern Greeks in pronouncing according to accent agree in every respect with the
direct testimony of the ancient grammarians, the
divine Plato, Aristotle, Cicero, Plutarch, Aristoxenus, Sextus, Nicanor (120 B. C.), Aristophanes,
Dionysius of Halicarnassus, and of many others.
The statement of Professor Sophocles that all
vowel sounds in modern Greek are isochronous
is incorrect, because in many instances we pronounce more or less the grave as well as the
acute accent. We distinguish the acute accent,
as Oekonomos justly remarks, by pronouncing

the word more emphatically, or by raising the
voice, and especially so in questions, as τίς τὸν
ἔκαμε κριτήν ; we pronounce likewise the circumflex, though rarely, by prolonging the voice. This
is especially to be noticed in Thessaly and Epirus,
in which countries the people pronounce εἶδα =
ἴδα; and δῶμα as if it were δόόμα, etc.

Now, to attempt to pronounce the Greek according to the principles of Latin accentuation is
simply absurd. It is a fact that Latin prosody in
some instances agrees with Greek accentuation,
but in many respects there is a wide difference
between the two. To begin with, the Latin accentuation of many words renders doubly sure
the accuracy and correctness of the accentuation
of the modern Greeks. For instance, the proparoxytone words, Ἀπόλλωνος, Ὠρίωνος, εἴδωλον,
ἔρημος, ἐνέργημα, παράκλητος, the ancient Latin
poets used likewise to pronounce by marking
the antepenultima with the acute accent, as Apŏl-
linis, Oriŏnis (sæ | vūmque O | rīonis | ensem, Hor),
īdolum (Auson). Now, those who pronounce
simply according to the quantity of syllables,
pronounce as if the words were written, εἰδῶλον,
Ἀπολλῶνος, and so forth, and thus, as Oekonomos
puts it, act in violation of the principles of both
the Grecian and Latin Muse. The Latins never
accent the last syllable of a word. On the other
hand, the Greek language possesses many such

nouns, and hence this difference alone suffices to put an insurmountable barrier between the Latin and Greek prosody. The Latin tongue, being fashioned after the Æolic dialect, keeps, generally speaking, its accentuation, especially so in words of two syllables, which the Æolians pronounced by placing the accent on the penultima, as αὖως ἔμμι (ἀὼς, εἰμὶ). Many words of three syllables they pronounced by placing the acute accent on the penultima, as Ἀχίλλευς ἤ Ἀχίλλης, Ὑδύσσευς. Latin: Achilles, Ulysses. Oxytone or paroxytone trisyllabic words the Æolians used to pronounce by placing the acute accent on the antepenultima, for instance, δύνατος instead of δυνατὸς, and so on. But even in the accentuation of words of two and three syllables, generally speaking, the Æolians differed materially from the Latins. Thus, the Æolians pronounced κατὰ, σιῶ, ἰὼν, and, again, ἱέρης, Μνασίας, etc. Again, Oekonomos justly remarks, that Latin prosody materially differed from the Greek, inasmuch as the Latins accent the antepenultimate even when the last syllable is, according to the Greeks, long. On the other hand, the Greek prosody always strictly observes the last syllable of every word and its change in respect to the cases, and places the accent according to the quantity of the last syllable. For instance, the Latins say Philosóphia, Histȯria, Theológia, Ecclésia, and the genitives Córporum, ángeli, and so on, placing the accent on the antepenultimate, which fact is in direct violation of the principles of Greek prosody, which is always directed in the accentuation of a word by the quantity of the last syllable. Again, the change of the accent by contraction is a thing unknown among the Latins, as *cáreo* = χαρέω, χηρέω, χηρεύω, χηρόω, -ῶ, and δέκω, δείκω, κνύω, δόκω, *dúceo* = δοκέω, hence δοκῶ. There are, besides, numberless other peculiarities of the Greek language, both dialectic and perpetual, which divide and separate its prosody from the Latin. But however well Latin prosody has been fashioned and formed by her glorious poets and writers, yet it never could attain, imitate, or approach, either the euphony, the elasticity, or the manifold and very rich variety of the Grecian prosody. Finally, it is a fact that modern Philology, owing to the great changes which have passed over the Latin language, ever since the second century after Christ, has been unable to ascertain the original sound of her letters. Thus we claim that it is inconsistent with well-established principles and facts to attempt to pronounce Greek according to Latin accentuation. There is certainly much similarity between the Greek and Latin, but this similarity or resemblance is not, as a Greek says, that of one egg to another, neither that of one drop of water to another. The Latin language resembles the Greek language just as a daughter resembles her mother, or just as a sister might resemble her sister; or, as Oekonomos says, however strong a resemblance there may be between the two languages, the warbling of a Procne (swallow) differs from that of a nightingale.

Now, that the accent plays a most important part in the meaning of a word, is manifest from the following collection of words, which are written alike, but distinguished from each other in meaning by the accents. The distinguished scholar, Gottlob Hoffman, said in reference to this point, "Why! anybody can easily distinguish the word δία from διὰ and μόνη from μονὴ (μένω) and some other similar words simply by the meaning!" However, there are many words and many nouns in the Greek language distinguished from each other *simply* by means of the accent, but without which all the soothsayers of the world could never tell the meaning.

A.

'Αγελαῖος, *belonging to a herd.*

'Αγέλαιος, *of the herd* or *multitude;* ἀγ. ἄνθρωποι, opp. to ἄρχοντες.

"Αγη, in good sense, *wonder, reverence, awe;* in bad sense, *envy, hatred.*

'Αγή, -ῆς, *breakage, piece, splin-*
ter; κωπῶν ἀγ. Æsch. Pers. 425.

"Αγητος, *Agetus,* a Spartan.

'Αγητός, *admired, famous.*

'Αγκῦρα, *Ancyra,* a city of Galatia.

"Αγκυρα, *an anchor.*

'Αγόραιος, *to be bought in the market;* as in most Edd. of the N. T. ἄρτος.

Ἀγοραῖος, belonging to the ἀγορά, Ζεὺς ἀγοραῖος.

Ἄγων, ἄγοντος, leading.

Ἀγών, -ῶνος, a contest.

Ἀδολέσχης, chatterer; ἀδολεσχής, subtle. Joh. Philoponus.

Ἀθρόος, -α, -ον, very rarely -ος, -ον, assembled in crowds. Eustath. p. 1387.

Ἄθροος, -ον (a. priv. θρόος), noiseless, only in gramm.

Ἀθῷος, -ον, unpunished, scot-free.

Ἄθωος, -η, -ον, of Mount Athos. Æsch. Ag. 285.

Αἶθος, -εος, a burning heat, fire.

Αἰθός, -ή, -όν, burnt, fire-colored, fiery. Pind. p. 8, 65. Bachyl. 12.

Αἶνός, -ου, ὁ, 1, a tale, story, hence, a fable; 2, praise.

Αἰνός, -ή, -όν, Ep. word = δεινός, dread, dire, fearful.

Αἰόλος, -η, -ον, easily turning, quietly moving.

Αἴολος, -ον, the god of the winds.

Αἰπεῖα, fem. of Αἰπύς, high and steep; lofty.

Αἴπεια, -ας, -η, 1, Æpēa, a city of Messenia; 2, a city in the island of Cyprus, later, Soli.

Αἶπος, -εος, τό, a height, a steep, a hill. Æsch. Ag. 285, etc.; πρὸς αἶπος ἰέναι, ὁδοιπορεῖν.

Αἰπός, -η, -όν, Ep. for αἰπύς, high, lofty, usu. of cities.

Ἀκή, ἡ, 1, a point, edge; 2, silence, etc.

Ἄκη, -ης, ἡ, Ace, the earlier name of the city Ptolemaïs in Phœnicia.

Ἀκήλητος, inexorable.

Ἀκηλητός, spotless. Joh. Philop.

Ἀκίς, -ίδος, ἡ, a point-barb, a splinter.

Ἆκις, -ιδος, ὁ, Acis, a river of Sicily. Theoc. 1, 69.

Ἄκρις, -ιος, 1, the extremity; 2, Acris, a city of Libya. Diod.

Ἀκρίς, -ίδος, a locust.

Ἀκροβόλός, one that throws from afar, a skirmisher.

Ἀκρόβολος, -ον, struck from afar.

Ἁλία, -ας, an assembly, gathering.

Ἁλιά, -ας, a salt-cellar.

Ἅλις, adv., in heaps, in crowds, in swarms.

Ἁλίς, -ίδος, saltness.

Ἁλωά, a threshing-floor.

Ἁλῷα, a festival of Demeter.

Ἄμητος, -οῦ, ὁ, a reaping, harvesting.

Ἀμητός, *the harvest gathered in.*

Ἀμυγδαλῆ, -ῆς, oft in Theophr. *the almond-tree.*

Ἀμυγδάλη, -ης, *an almond.*

Ἄρα, Ep. ρα, *then, straightway,* etc.

Ἀρά, ᾶς, *a curse.*

Ἀραιός, -η, -ον, *thin, narrow, weak.*

Ἀραῖος, -αία, *prayed against, accursed.*

Ἄργης, -ου, ὁ, *Arges* or *Cyclops.* Hes. Th. 140.

Ἀργῆς, *a kind of serpent.*

Ἀργής, -ῆτος, *white, bright.*

Ἄργος, -ου, ὁ, *Argus,* son of Jupiter and Niobe, and King of Argos.

Ἀργός, -ή, -όν, *shining, bright.*

Ἄρνειος, -εία, -ειον, *of a lamb* or *sheep;* κρέα.

Ἀρνειός, -οῦ, ὁ, *a young ram just full-grown.*

Ἀρνός, *a sheep,* etc.

Ἄρνος, *Arnus,* a river of Etruria, now the *Arno.*

Ἁρπαγῆ, -ης, *seizure, rapine.*

Ἁρπάγη, -ης, *a hook,* esp. for drawing up a bucket.

Ἄρσις, -εως, ἡ, *raising up.*

Ἀρσίς, -ίδος, *arrow-point.* Pharor.

Ἀρτίτοκος, *new-born.*

Ἀρτιτόκος, *having just given birth;* μήτηρ.

Ἀρτίτομος, *just cut.*

Ἀρτιτόμος, *having just cut.*

Ἀσφόδελος, ὁ, *asphodel.*

Ἀσφοδελός, *producing asphodel.*

Αὐλητής, *a flute-player.*

Αὐλήτης, *a farm-servant.*

B.

Βαιός, -α, -ον, *little, insignificant.*

Βαῖος, *Bæus,* a man.

Βάκχειος, *belonging to Bacchus* or *his rites.*

Βακχεῖος, sub. -πούς, *a metrical foot of three syllables,* ⏑ — — or — — ⏑.

Βασίλεια, *a queen, princess.*

Βασιλεία, *a kingdom.*

Βηλός, -οῦ, ὁ, *the threshold.*

Βῆλος, -ου, *Belus,* a Babylonian deity.

Βίος, -ου, *life.*

Βιός, *a bow.*

Βληχρός, -ά, -όν, *weak, nerveless.*

Βλῆχρος, *a woody plant,* flowering late.

Βροτός, -οῦ, ὁ, *mortal, man.*

Βρότος, *blood* that has flowed from a wounded man, *gore.*

Βυσσός, -οῦ, *the depths of the sea;* water-deeps.

Βύσσος, a fine yellowish *flax*, and the *linen* made from it (cotton).

Γ.

Γαῦλος, a *round-built Phœnician merchant-vessel.*

Γαυλός, -οῦ, *a milk-pail, a water-bucket.*

Γέλοιος, *laughable, absurd.*

Γελοῖος, *exciting laughter, merry.*

Γλαυκός, -η, -ον, *bright, gleaming*, etc.

Γλαῦκος, an edible fish of gray color.

Γόνος, -ου, *that which is begotten, a child.*

Γονός, *corn-land, a sown field* (Hom.), usu. in phrase, Γονὸν ἀλωῆς.

Γυρός, -ά, -ον, *round*, Lat. *curvus.*

Γῦρος, -ου, *a round ring, circle.*

Δ.

Δειρή, -ῆς, *the neck, throat.*

Δείρη, a city and promontory.

Δῆμος, -ου, *a country district.*

Δημός, -οῦ, *fat, tallow.*

Δημοσία, adv. *publicly.*

Δημόσια, -τὰ, neut. *public things.*

Δία, acc. *of* Ζεύς.

Διά, prep. *by, through.*

Διογενής, *noble, born of Jove.*

Διόγένης, *Diogenes, a man's name.*

Διχοτόμος, *cutting in two.*

Διχότομος, -ον, pass., *cut in half, divided equally.*

Δόκος, ὁ, *opinion.*

Δοκός, *beam.*

Δόλιος, -α, -ον, *crafty, deceitful.*

Δολιός, -ον, ὁ, *Dolius*, a slave of Laertes in Ithaca.

Δρυμός, an *oak-coppice, thicket.*

Δρύμος, *Drymus*, a city of Phocis.

Ε.

Εἶπε, *he said.*

Εἰπέ, *say thou.*

Ἔλευσις, *coming, arrival.*

Ἐλευσίς, -ῖνος, *Eleusis*, a city.

Ἐξαίρετος, -ον, *taken out, picked.*

Ἐξαιρετός, -ή, -όν, *that can be taken out.*

Ἔπαινος, *approval, praise.*

Ἐπαινός, -η, -ον, *exceedingly awful.*

Ἐπαρχία, *a province.*

Ἐπάρχια, a woman's name.

Ἐρινεός, *the wild fig-tree.*

Ἐρίνεος, *of wool, woollen.*

Ἔτος, *a year.*

Ἐτός, *in vain.*

Εὐανθής, *flowery.*

Εὐάνθης, *Euanthes,* a name.

Εὐγενής, *well-born* (a civil, polite man), εὐγενὴς ἄνθρωπος.

Εὐγένης, *Eugenes,* a poet of the Anthology.

Εὐμενής, *well-disposed.*

Εὐμένης, *Eumenes,* a brave Athenian at Salamis.

Εὔκλεία, *renown, good fame.*

Εὔκλεια, *Euclia,* an appellation of Diana.

Εὐσθενής, *stout, lively.*

Εὐσθένης, *Eusthenes,* a name.

Z.

Ζωρός, -ον, *pure, sheer.*

Ζῶρος, *Zorus,* founder of Carthage.

Ζωή, *life.*

Ζώη, τὸ ἐπάνω τοῦ μέλιτος, καὶ γάλακτος. Eust. p. 906, 52.

H.

Ἤμων, *slinger.*

Ἡμῶν, gen. pl. of ἡμεῖς.

Ἡράκλειος, -α, -ον, *belonging to Hercules.*

Ἡρακλεῖος, *herculean.*

Ἥττων, compart.

Ἡττῶν, part. of ἡττάω.

Θ.

Θεά, fem. of Θεός.

Θέα, *a seeing.*

Θερμός, -ή, -ον, *warm, hot, boiling.*

Θέρμος, -ον, *the lupine,* esp. *lupinous,* used in Athens to counteract the effects of drink.

Θόλος, *a dome.*

Θολός, *mud, dirt.*

Θυμός, -οῦ, 1, *the soul;* 2, *wrath,* etc.

Θύμος, -ον, *thyme,* Lat. *thymus.*

I.

Ἰά, ἡ, *voice.*

Ἴα, old Ion. *one;* plural, *violet.*

Ἰδέ, *and.*

Ἴδε, *behold.*

Ἰδοῦ, imp. aor. mid.

Ἰδού, *lo! behold.*

Ἰδρύμενος, part. pres.

Ἰδρυμένος, part. perf.

Ἰός, *rust,* etc.

Ἴος, -ιος, *one of the Sporades,* etc.

Ἰπνός, -ὁ, *an oven.*

Ἴπνος, *Ipnus,* a place in Locris.

Ἱπποκόμος, *keeping* or *grooming horses,* etc.

Ἱππόκομος, *horse-haired,* etc.

Ἱπποκορυστής, -οῦ, *equipping, arming horses.*

Ἱπποκορύστης, *Hippocorystes,* masc. prop. noun.

K.

Καιρό;, -οῦ, 1, *strictly the right measure ; 2, the right measure of time.*

Καῖρος, also καίρως, *threads, slips, or thrums on the beam of the loom.*

Καλλισθενής, *adorned with strength.*

Καλλισθένης, *Callisthenes*, an orator.

Κᾶλον, *dry wood, fire-wood.*

Καλόν, neut. of καλό;.

Καλῶς, adv. from καλός.

Κάλως, *a rope.*

Καμπή, *a bending, winding,* as of a river.

Κάμπη, *a caterpillar.*

Κεῖνος for ἐκεῖνος.

Κεινός, *empty.*

Κηλητής, *a charmer.*

Κηλήτης, *charmed.*

Κεράστης from κέρας.

Κεραστής from κεράννυμι.

Κῆρος, *Cerus*, a river.

Κηρός, *wax.*

Κλειτό;, -ή, -όν, *renowned, famous.*

Κλεῖτος, *Clitus,* a proper name.

Κλείω, *to tell of, make famous.*

Κλειώ, *Clio,* one of the Muses.

Κνῆκος, *the thistle.*

Κνηκός, *yellow.*

Κνημό;, *woody.*

Κνῆμος, *Cnemus,* a name.

Κόμπος, *pride.*

Κομπός, *proud.*

Κριός, *a ram.*

Κρῖος, a proper name.

Κτᾶσθαι from κτάομαι.

Κτάσθαι from κτείνω.

Κυκέω, *Imix.*

Κυκεῶ, accus. of κυκεών.

Κύρτος, *a creel.*

Κυρτός, *crooked.* Eust. p. 907.

Κύρτος, *a fishing-basket.*

Κυρτός, *curved, bent, arched.*

Λ.

Λάβη, *pretext.*

Λαβή, *handle.*

Λαός, -ον, *the people.*

Λᾶος, the name of a city.

Λάρος, *a ravenous sea-bird ; the gull.*

Λαρό;, -ά, -ον, *pleasant, nice.*

Λέπας, *a bare rock.*

Λεπάς, *a limpet.*

Ληνός, *a wine-press.*

Λῆνος, *wool.*

Λιθοβόλο;, *throwing stones.*

Λιθόβολος, *struck with stones.*

Λίχανος, *fore-finger.*

Λιχανός, *string of a harp.*

M.

Μακρός, *long.*

Μάκρος, *length.*

Μαλακία, *softness.*

Μαλάκια, *water-animals* of soft substance.

Μονή, *a staying* (convent).

Μόνη, fem. of Μόνος.

Μόχθηρος, *laborious.*

Μοχθηρός, *wretched.*

Μυιῶν, gen. from μυία; μυιών, *muscle.*

Μυλλός, *awry, crooked.*

Μύλλος, an *edible fish.*

Μυλών, *a place for a mill,* etc.

Μύλων, a city.

Μυρίοι, *infinite in numbers.*

Μύριοι, *ten thousand.*

N.

Νέος, *young.*

Νεός, *fresh land, fallow.*

Νομός, *a pasture.*

Νόμος, *a law.*

Ξ.

Ξανθός, *golden, yellow.*

Ξάνθος, *a proper name.*

Ξενών, *a room for strangers.*

Ξένων, *a proper name.*

O.

Ὄκνος, *delay.*

Ὀκνός, -ή, όν, *idle, cowardly.*

Ὅμως, *nevertheless.*

Ὁμῶς, *equally,* etc.

Ὄρος, *a mountain.*

Ὀρός, *the watery* or *serous part of milk.*

Οὔκουν, *not therefore, so not.*

Οὐκοῦν, *therefore, accordingly.*

Οὖρος, *a mountain.*

Οὐρός, *a trench.*

Οὐρά, *tail.*

Οὖρα, *boundaries.*

Π.

Πατροκτόνος, *parricidal.*

Πατρόκτονος, *slain by a father.*

Πείθω, *to persuade.*

Πειθώ, *persuasion,* etc.

Πίων, *fat.*

Πιών, 1, aor.; 2, part. of πίνω.

Πλατάγη, *rattle.*

Πλαταγή, *rattling sound.*

Πλυνός, *washing-trough.*

Πλύνες, *washed.* Schol. Aristophanes' Plut. 1062.

Ποῖος, ποία, ποῖον, *of what nature?*

Ποιός, -ά, -όν, *of a certain nature, kind,* etc.

Πότος, *a drinking-bout; carousal.*

Ποτός, -ή, -όν, verb, adj. of πίνω, *drunk, for drinking.*

Πρωτόγονος, *first-born.*

Πρωτογόνος, *bringing forth first.*

Πρωτότοκος, *first-born.*

Πρωτοτόκος, *bearing her first-born.*

Πυρρός, *flame-colored.*
Πύρρος, *Pyrrhus,* a man's name.
Πῶρος, -ου, *tufa-stone.*
Πωρός, -ά, -όν, *blind; miserable.*

P.

Ῥινή, *file.*
Ῥίνη, *shark.* Joh. Phil.
Ῥίπη, *town-wall.*
Ῥιπή, *blast of wind.* Eust. p. 301.
Ῥοδών, *a rosebud.*
Ῥόδων, ἡ, *Rhodon,* masc. prop. name.
Ῥόδιος, adj., *Rhodian,* of Rhodes.
Ῥοδιός, subst., *Rhodius,* a river.

Σ.

Σάρων, -ωνος, *a lewd fellow.*
Σαρῶν, from σαίρω, *sweeping.*
Σῆς, gen. fem. of σός.
Σής, *a moth.*
Σκάφη, *a hole, trench.*
Σκαφή, *a digging.*
Σκύμνος, *lion's whelp.*
Σκυμνός, *young of* every other wild beast.
Σπαρτός, -ή -όν, *sown, scattered.*
Σπάρτος, *the shrub.*
Σταφυλή, *a bunch of grapes.*

Σταφύλη, *the level* or *the plummet* in a carpenter's bench.
Συνοικία, *a community.*
Συνοίκια, *a public feast in honor of Theseus.*
Συρμός, 1, *anything that draws, drags,* or *tears along with violence;* 2, *fashion, mode.*
Σύρμος, *Syrmus,* a proper name.

T.

Ταυροκτόνος, *slaying bulls.*
Ταυρόκτονος, *killed by a bull.*
Τηλεμάχος, *fighting from afar.*
Τηλέμαχος, a name (son of Ulysses).
Τηλεφανής, *appearing afar.*
Τηλεφάνης, *Telephanes,* a prop. name.
Τομός, *cutting.*
Τόμος, *a volume.*
Τορός, *piercing, thrilling.*
Τόρος, *a borer* used in trying for water.
Τροχός, *a wheel,* etc.
Τρόχος, *a running course.*

Υ.

Ὑβός, -η, -ον, *hump-backed.*
Ὕβος, *the bunch* or *hump of a camel.*
Ὕβρις, *insolence.*
Ὑβρίς, *a night-bird of prey.*

Φ.

Φαιδρός, -α, -ον, *beaming, bright.*
Φαῖδρος, *Phædrus*, a pr. name.
Φόρος, *a tribute, tax.*
Φορός, *bearing, carrying.*
Φυλακή, *a watching* or *guarding a watch.*
Φυλάκη, *Phylace*, a city.

X.

Χαλαζοβόλος, *showering hail;* νέφη.

Χαλαζόβολος, *stricken with hail.*
Χαροπό-, -η, -ον, *glad-eyed, bright-eyed.*
Χάροπος, a man's name.

Ω.

Ὦμος, *the shoulder.*
Ὠμός, *raw, rough,* etc.
Ὠχρός, *pale.*
Ὦχρος, *paleness.*

Again, many proper nouns are formed from substantives by transposition of the accent. For instance: —

Ἀκέστης, from ἀκεστής.
Ἄρητος and Ἀρήτη, from ἀρητὸς, ἀρητή.
Αὔγη, from αὐγή.
Βαῖος, from βαιὸς.
Γλαῦκος, from γλαυκὸς.
Γόργος and Γοργώ, from γοργὸς.
Διογένης, from διογενὴς.
Εὐπείθης, from εὐπειθὴς.

Κλεῖτος, from κλειτὸς.
Λεῦκος, from λευκὸς.
Λῶτος, from λωτὸς.
Μεγασθένης, from μεγασθενὴς.
Πύρρος and Πύρρα, from πυρρὸς, -ρὰ.
Σμεῖκρος or Σμῖκρος, from σμικρὸς.
Φαῖδρος and Φαίδρα, from φαιδρὸς, -δρὰ.

In like manner, to this day, many nouns become proper simply by a change of the accent, some of which are either local and idiomatic, so to speak, to certain places, whilst other nouns are common to all the Greeks. For instance: Χρῦσος, from χρυσὸς, like χρύσης (Ἰλ. a) and "Χρῦσος Εἰσιδό-

τοῦ Ἀθηναῖος" (Olyp. 236), found in an Attic inscription. Σταῦρος, from σταυρός. Λάμπρος, from
λαμπρός. Φόρος, from φορός. Ῥίζος, from ῥιζόεις,
whence the "ῥιζοῦς θεσσαλίας χώρα." Σῖμος, from
σιμὸς, whence Σίμων Σιμωνίδης, Σιμμίας Σίμμιχος (a
diminutive Bœotian appellation), and many others
which I might enumerate, as well as numberless
other forms or innovations of the accent both in
ancient and modern Greek, which show the care
we ought to exercise in pronouncing Greek.

Now, many believe that the ancient Greeks
pronounced the verses, such as "the hexameters"
and "the iambic" simply according to the "quantity of the syllables," and that they entirely overlooked or neglected the accent. But this does not
seem so certain, and there are many things that go
to show that the Greeks, in pronouncing the verses,
never neglected or overlooked the accent.

No language ever uses in poetry "an accentual
prosody" directly opposite and antagonistic to
the one in prose. In pronouncing Latin verse
we sometimes overlook or, so to speak, neglect
the natural accent of the words for the sake of
the rhythm.

But this fact by no means proves the necessity
of pronouncing Greek verse in like manner. In
the first place, who assures us that Virgil himself
pronounced his verses in the manner now prevalent? We can only form a meagre idea from

Quintilian concerning Latin versification, from the fact that he did not speak in detail about these things. Now, Geldart affirms that just because the Latin accent, however fallaciously applied to Greek, does in a remarkable manner tend to preserve to a great extent (though by no means completely) the quantity of syllables, the notion has arisen that it could not be otherwise preserved. That this notion is completely false is practically shown even in Latin, in which we have to recognize, and do recognize, the length of the many long syllables, which it is impossible even according to the Latin system to accent. It is, besides, a well-known fact that many distinguished European scholars asserted that we ought by no means to neglect accent in pronouncing Latin verse. Again, Homer lengthened by means of the accent not only the short syllable in the arsis, but also in the thesis, as Αἰόλου, and so on. He likewise shortened, as we have already remarked, the syllable before or after the accent simply by means of it. He at times used the syllable accented on the thesis as a short one, as ἵ | ππους ἄλε | ται (Ιλ. λ, 192) instead of ἄληται; sometimes even the accent causes one λ to be omitted, as in Αχιλεὺς, and so on. And, in short, the ancient poetry was by no means separated from the accents of prose. (See Herrmann, "Elementa doctrinæ metricæ.")

Aristotle says that the iambic metre is mostly used in common conversation. "Ὁ δ' ἴαμβος αὐτή ἐστιν ἡ λέξις ἡ τῶν πολλῶν · διὸ μάλιστα πάντων τῶν μέτρων ἰαμβεῖα φθέγγονται λέγοντες." "For the iambic measure is most of all adapted to conversation. And as an evidence of this we most frequently speak in iambic in familiar discourse with each other." Plutarch says concerning the "iambic measure" "τὰ μὲν λέγονται παρὰ κροῦσιν, τὰ δὲ ἄδονται · . . . . . τὸ δὲ παρὰ τὴν κροῦσιν λέγεσθαι · (εἶναι τὸ αὐτὸ καὶ ἡ παρακαταλογή.") Oekonomos says, "παρακαταλογή" is what the moderns call "recitativum," a sort of address, in which the poems are pronounced, as the Italians say, "quasi parlando," whilst the term "καταλογάδην" and "ἡ καταλογή" means "τὸ τὰ ἄσματα οὐκ ὑπὸ μέλει λέγειν."

Dionysius of Halicarnassus describes the movableness, transposing, or changing of the accents which takes place in the odes. Now, what difference there exists between hexameters and iambics on the one hand and lyric odes on the other is evident. Demosthenes himself distinguishes the "metrical" (as, for instance, the Homeric verses) from those that are sung, such as the odes of Pindar, the "dithyrambic," the "choruses," the strophes and others which are uttered, so to speak, by a varying melody of the voice: "Ὥστε καὶ τοὺς τῶν ἐμμέτρων καὶ τοὺς τῶν ᾀδομένων ποιητὰς καὶ πολλοὺς τῶν συγγραφέων ὑποθέσεις

τὰ ἐκείνων ἔργα τῆς αὐτῶν μουσικῆς πεποιῆσθαι"
(Λογ. ἐπιτάφ).   Dionysius of Halicarnassus, treating of the changes which are necessary for the
composition or formation of harmony, teaches
that they must be· "διάφοροι καὶ αἱ τάσεις τῆς
φωνῆς, αἱ καλούμεναι προσῳδίαι, κλέπτουσαι τῇ
ποικιλίᾳ τὸν κόρον."   So that, recommending the
same rules for the formation of harmony in both
metrical and prose writings, he distinctly asserts
the importance and the necessity of respecting
the accent both in metrical and prose writings.
In another passage he says, " Μουσική τις ἦν καὶ ἡ
τῶν πολιτικῶν λόγων ἐπιστήμη, τῷ ποσῷ διαφέρουσα
τῆς ἐν ᾠδαῖς καὶ ὀργάνοις, οὐχί τῷ ποιῷ· καὶ γὰρ ἐν
ταύτῃ καὶ μέλος ἔχουσιν αἱ λέξεις καὶ ῥυθμὸν καὶ
μεταβολὴν καὶ πρέπον."   Now, as a modern Greek
says, if the orators pronounced according to
rhythm and according to the accents, why not
the poets also?   And if the speeches of the orators
must be read according to the accents, why not
read the poems in like manner?   Dionysius also
compares many rhetorical passages of the same
rhythm with poetical verses of like rhythm, for
instance that of Demosthenes,

" Μήτ' ἰδίας ἔχθρας μηδεμιᾶς ἕνεκα,"

and says that it is exactly an elegiac pentameter,
just like

" Κοῦραι ἐλαφροπόδων ἴχνε' ἀειράμεναι."

He compares in like manner many other passages

of the same orator, saying merely that these prose
passages differ from the poems, inasmuch as the
former are "poetical, rhythmical, and melodious,"
whilst the poems are in rhythm — that is to say
"accordant in harmony" and "according to measure" and "musical" — "ἔῤῥυθμα καὶ ἔμμετρα καὶ
μελῳδικά," because the poems possess in succession
similar metres and rhythms arranged according
to verse, period, or strophe, whilst the rhetorical
phrases or the so-called "oratorical cadences" have
rhythm, but not the same in succession. On the
contrary, they are irregular and wandering, and
mixed obscurely with others, so that the rhetorical
phrase becomes, as Aristotle termed it, "μήτε ἔμ-
μετρος μήτε ἄῤῥυθμος," neither "metrical nor void
of rhythm."

We must remark that Dionysius, who is justly
called a·very critical scholar, by no means considered the poems as void of accent, as some have
supposed, because he would naturally have said so.

Oekonomos says that one can observes many
other hexameter passages in Demosthenes, such as,

Τὸν γὰρ ἐν ᾿Αμφίσσῃ πόλεμον, δι᾿ ὃν εἰς ᾿Ελάτειαν.
᾿Ηλθε Φίλιππος . . . .

Also

Τῶν ἄλλων ῾Ελλήνων πολλάκις ἐστεφανῶσθαι (περὶ Στεφ.),

as well as in many other writers, for instance St.
Chrysostom : —

Κἂν τῶν ἡλιακῶν ἀκτίνων λαμπροτέρα οὖσα τύχῃ, ...
Τοῦ καπνοῦ προσέφλεξε, καὶ ἡμαύρωσεν ἅπασαν (περὶ ῾Ιερωσ.), etc.

Aristiades, the Κοϊντιλιανὸς (Quintilian), recommends "τεττάρων στοχάζεσθαι ἐννοίας τε πρεπούσης, καὶ λέξεως, καὶ ἁρμονίας, καὶ ῥυθμοῦ· προκαθηγεῖται μὲν ἡ ἔννοια πάντως, ἧς ἄνευ οὔτε αἵρεσις οὔτε φυγή τινος ἐγγίνεται· ταύτης δὲ μίμημα λέξις, καὶ πρὸς τὴν τοῦ πέλας ἀκοήν τε καὶ πειθὼ πρώτως ἀναγκαία· αὕτη δὲ ὀξύτητητάς τε καὶ βαρύτητας προσλαβοῦσα μετὰ διαστημάτων, συγκεχυμένην (perhaps συγκεχυμένων) μὲν, ἐγέννησεν ἁρμονίαν· λόγοις δὲ τοῖς συμφώνοις τεταγμένων ῥυθμὸν." Now, if accent, which tends to mark the word clearly, were overlooked in the recitation of poems, it is evident that so much confusion and doubt would have resulted as to render the meaning of the verse extremely obscure. Aristotle (350 B. C.) likewise recommends as the first excellence of poetical recitation the *clearness of words.* Now, how can *words* possess *clearness* if we do not respect their accents? "Ἡ γὰρ λέξις, ἤτοι ἡ διὰ τῶν ὀνομάτων ἑρμηνεία, τὴν αὐτὴν ἔχει δύναμιν καὶ ἐπὶ τῶν ἐμμέτρων καὶ ἐπὶ τῶν λόγων." Quinctilian recommends "that poems should be read in such a manner that the reader may appear rather to be pronouncing a "prose passage" and "without metre," whilst the prose passages of the orators should be recited just like poems; that is to say, neither the rhythm of the poems ought to be sung, nor the harmony of the words (in prose) to be confounded with the stupid and rude or

unpolished conversation of the rabble. That is
what Cæsar meant, saying, "if you sing the poem
you sing it badly, if you read it you sing it well."

Finally, not one of the old grammarians recommends the reading of the poems simply according
to the quantity of syllables. On the contrary,
Tryphon (Τρύφων) censures the practice, calling
it "τὰ κατὰ πόδα, κακόμετρα." And Erasmus
also distinguished *accent* from *quantity*, and com-
plained because in his church neither the quantity of the syllables nor the accent of the words
was kept with accuracy, especially in "musical
odes." "*Accentus non indicat doctrinam quantitatis
syllabicæ*" .... and "*Chorus ecclesiasticus nec in
psalmis recitandis nec in canticis solemnibus ullum
habet brevium aut longarum delectum, ne tonorum
quidem admodum magnam rationem*," etc. (Dialog.
de rect. Linq. Græc. pronunt.)

It becomes evident, therefore, that the customary pronunciation of those who pronounce simply according to the quantity of syllables cannot
be the safe or correct way of pronunciation.
"For what purpose,"— a modern Greek exclaims,
—"for what purpose were the poets of Greece
compelled to compose metres (and especially the
heroic) in every respect and directly opposite to
the accentual prosody of the words, and, so to
speak, without any foundation in the very nature
of the language? Or, perchance, did they not

compose verses for their fellow-citizens, whom
they sought to teach and to please? What more
than the neglect or the absence of accents from
the poems could render them incomprehensible
to the many?"

Vossius and his followers blamed the so-called
"πολιτικοὺς στίχους" (popular verses) of the modern Greeks, which possess rhythm, simply by
means of the accent and the number of the syllables. But it becomes evident from these popular
verses that our fathers, in pronouncing the verses
of Homer and of the other poets, observed also
the accent together with the quantity, because
the "popular verses" are only imitations of many
Homeric and other old verses pronounced simply
according to accent without regard to quantity.
Attention to the quantity of syllables had disappeared from the common conversation of the
multitude at the time even when the language had
passed its prime. But even whilst the language
was at its acme, the unpolished multitude did not
distinguish between the long and short with as
much emphasis and precision as the poets and the
orators were accustomed to do. Oekonomos says,
that many syncopated words extant in both the
poets and the orators give evidence of the fact,
e. g. οἴομαι and οἴδασθα into οἶμαι and οἶσθα, κεβλὴ
from κεβαλὴ instead of κεφαλῆ, σαυκῶς from σα-
βακῶς, βλώσκω instead of μολίσκω (μλόσκω), με-

σημβρία from μεσημερία (μεσημρία), χέρνιβον (χερόνιβον), Λαπίθης (λαο-πίθης), Λαγέτης, Λάγος (λαὸν ἄγων), and numberless other forms, both dialectic and common to all, as well as those words resulting from syncope and synizesis, and these Attic words which, although terminating in a long vowel, accent the antepenult, e. g. εὔγεως, Μενέλεως, etc., show "that the multitude pronounced rather hurriedly and not so clearly and distinctly the long vowel sounds." The circumflex, pronounced somewhat hurriedly, was confounded easily with the acute, as in the Homeric, τὸ μὲν οὖ instead of οὔ or οὐ, as well as οὖτις, transformed into οὖτις (Od. I. 366).

But the comedians, imitating the common conversation of the people, made many innovations or changes in the rhythm, at times shortening the long syllables, then introducing trochaic and iambic together with anapestic measures, thus endeavoring to imitate the voluble manner of conversation extant among the common classes.

A modern Greek asserts that after the language had passed its prime the distinction between the long and short syllables was much neglected. Finally, the absence of great poets, the absence of the theatres, the confusion of dialects, and other like changes, caused the general neglect of quantity. About the year 170 (B. C.) Pausanias, a pupil of Herodes the Athenian, somewhat distin-

guished as a "stump-speaker," was often blamed
because he confounded long and short syllables,
just as his Cappadocean compatriots were wont
to do. But this did not at all interfere with
the genuine prosody of the spoken language.
"Poetical prosody" is one thing and "prosody
of accents" is another. The former deals with
the quantity of syllables, the latter considers the
location of special stress. The former changes
with the rhythm of the poem, the latter has a
fixed position in every word. After "poetical
prosody" became less prominent, the prosody
of accent remained an inseparable peculiarity.
Our contemporary poets used this as the foundation of verse-making, dividing the metres of the
verses no more according to quantity, which the
ignorant and unpolished multitude could no longer
appreciate, but only according to the accent and
the number of the syllables, from which arises the
so-called "popular rhythm," which has a very
close connection with the musical rhythm of the
ancients. Those who composed these verses bor-
rowed, so to speak, the peculiarity of this versi-
fication from the ancients, i. e. from the trochaic
metre of Æschylus' Pers. : —

Ὦ βαθυζώνων ἄνασσα Περσίδων ὑπερτάτη,
Μῆτερ ἡ Ξέρξου γηραιά, χαῖρε Δαρείου γύναι.

Having simply kept the accents, they formed verses
of fifteen syllables, e. g.

Τϊος Αἰνείου γνήσιος Ἀσκάνιος τὴν κλῆσιν
Ἀπὸ Κρεούσης γυναικὸς, τῆς θυγατρὸς Πριάμου,
Τὴν πόλιν Ἀλβαν ᾤκησε σὺν τοῖς περιληφθεῖσι.

For this reason Eustathius (1118 A. D.) termed
these verses of fifteen syllables "trochaic verses."
Again, Oekonomos says that from the iambic of
Aristophanes, which has two metres, e. g.

Δήμητερ, ἁγνῶν ὀργίων
Ἄνασσα, συμπαραστάτει.

Verses of eight syllables were formed, such as
those composed by Symeon Metaphrates about
1050 A. D.

Ἀπὸ ῥυπαρῶν χειλέων
Ἀπὸ βδελυρᾶς καρδίας
Ἀπὸ ἀκαθάρτου γλώσσης
Ἐκ ψυχῆς ἐῤῥυπωμένης
Δέξαι δέησιν Χριστέ μου

And again, from the same syllables, simply by
changing the accent, the harmony of the verses
was also changed by "συζυγίας."

Νῦν αἱ Δυνάμεις οὐρανῶν
Ἀνθρώποις συγχορεύσατε

According to the Anacreontic,

'Ερῶ τε δῆτα κ' οὐκ ἐρῶ
Καὶ μαίνομαι κ' οὐ μαίνομαι.

Alexander Apollinarius (350 A. D.) is generally
believed to have been the first who wrote in these
so-called "popular verses." He rendered, at any
rate, into hexameter verse the psalter, and, in fact,
many of the writings of the Church. Professor
Sophocles states that the "ἀκάθιστος ὕμνος" is the
office of the Virgin, partly read and partly sung,
all standing, on the Saturday of the fifth week in
Lent. And as Georgius Pisides (A. D. 617) was
the readiest versifier of that period, it has been
conjectured that he was the author of the principal part of it. The distinctive portions of this
office are its twenty-four οἶκοι, *houses, stations.*
Their rhythm is accentual, i. e.

῎Αγγελος πρωτοστάτης
Οὐρανόθεν ἐπέμφθη
Εἰπεῖν τῇ Θεοτόκῳ τὸ Χαῖρε·
Καὶ σὺν τῇ ἀσωμάτῳ φωνῇ
Σωματούμενόν σε θεωρῶν, Κύριε,
'Εξίστασο καὶ ἵστατο κραυγάζων πρὸς αὐτὴν τοιαῦτα.

However, many scholars suppose that it was
Apollinarius (350 A. D.) who composed this in-

stead of Pisides. Compare with the above the Anacreontic verses of similar "συζυγίας," such as

Πέμπετε τῶν δ' ἀπ' οἴκων, — Ἠπνοιᾶισι ζεφύρου,
Θοὰς ἀκάτους ἐπ' οἶδμα λίμνας (Εὐριπ.)
Δεῦρο καλεῖν νόμος ἐσ χορόν
Ἀσπίσι καὶ λόγχαις Ἀχαιῶν — ἄνακτας ·
Ἑλλάδος ἐνναέτησιν
Ἁλίου προσέβαλεν ἅρμα (Εὐριπ.)

Many other examples could be brought to show that many of the odes, especially of the Church, are fashioned exactly after many lyric and other odes of the ancients.

Rhyme, which is very common in modern Greek, is recognized by the classical poets, i. e. (Sophocles, Aj. 765, 766)

Ἔγνωκα γὰρ δὴ φωτὸς ἠπατημένη,
Καὶ τῆς παλαιᾶς χάριτος ἐκβεβλημένη.

And the following in the "Iliad" (β, 382), which is what Oekonomos calls "ὁμοιοτέλευτα εἰς τὴν τελευτὴν" : —

Εὖ μέν τις δόρυ θηξάσθω, εὖ δ' ἀσπίδα θέσθω
. . . . θηξάσθω . . . . θέσθω . . . .

Again, in the "Iliad" (ψ, 152) : —

. . . . .

Ὣς εἰπὼν ἐν χερσὶ κόμην ἑτάροιο φίλοιο
Θῆκεν, τοῖσι δὲ πᾶσιν ὑφ' ἵμερον ὦρσε γόοιο.
Καὶ νὺ κ' ὀδυρομένοισιν ἔδυ φάος Ἠελίοιο.

. ` . . .

Φίλοιο . . . . γόοιο . . . . Ἠελίοιο.

Again, in the "Iliad" (φ, 523–25) : —

. . . . .

Ἄστεος αἰθομένοιο, θεῶν δὲ ἑ μῆνις ἀνῆκεν
Πᾶσι δ' ἔθηκε πόνον, πολλοῖσι δὲ κήδε' ἐφῆκεν,
Ὣς Ἀχιλεὺς Τρώεσσι πόνον καὶ κήδε' ἔθηκεν
Ἀνῆκεν . . . . ἐφῆκεν . . . . ἔθηκεν . . . .

In the "Odyssey" we find instances of rhyme
(Od. θ, 147, 148, 111, 112, 125, 126 ; ι, 148 ; κ, 44 ;
λ, 604, etc.)   See also Herder's "Ursachen des
gesunkenen Geschmacks bey den verschiedenen
Völkern," etc., pages 278 – 290, and Sulzer's Dic-
tionary, article "Reim."

CHAPTER X.

THE ASPIRATE.

THIS is no longer sounded in modern Greek; and if it had any sound at all in ancient Greek it must have been extremely evanescent. This is evident from the fact that Aristotle says, —

Παρὰ δὲ τὴν προσωδίαν λόγοι μὲν οὐκ εἰσὶν οὔτε τῶν γεγραμμένων οὔτε τῶν λεγομένων· πλὴν εἴ τινες ὀλίγοι γένοιτ᾽ ἄν, οἷον οὗτος ὁ λόγος· ᾿Αράγέ ἐστι τὸ οὐ κατα-λύεις οἰκία ; ναί· οὐκοῦν τὸ οὐ καταλύεις τοῦ καταλύεις ἀπόφασις ; ναί· ἔφησας δὲ εἶναι τὸ οὐ καταλύεις οἰκίαν· ἡ οἰκία ἄρα ἀπόφασις. ῾Ως δὲ λυτέον δῆλον· οὐ γὰρ ταυτὸ σημαίνει τὸ μὲν ὀξύτερον τὸ δὲ βαρύτερον ῥηθέν.

It becomes evident, therefore, that in the times of Aristotle, the golden age of Grecian learning, the pronunciation of the rough οὗ (οὗ καταλύεις) differed little from the pronunciation of the smooth οὐ.

It is probable that the only difference between the rough and smooth breathing may have been that it was the custom to turn κ, π, τ into χ, φ, θ before syllables which had the rough breathing, which is still the practice of the modern Greeks,

whereas before the smooth breathing these consonants remained unaltered. But in the Ionic dialect this difference of usage did not prevail.

In modern Greek, though the rough breathing
is not heard, it affects the pronunciation of a preceding tenuis; and several compounds, as ἐφέτος
from ἐπ᾽ ἔτος, μεθαύριον for μεταύριον.

PART II.

CHAPTER I.

THE ALPHABET.

THE modern Greek letters, breathings, accents, and marks of punctuation are the same as in classical Greek.

LETTERS.

FIGURES.	NAMES.	
Α, α	῎Αλφα	*Álpha.*
Β, β	Βῆτα	*Véta.*
Γ, γ	Γάμμα	*Gháma.*
Δ, δ	Δέλτα	*Thélta.*
Ε, ε	῎Ε ψιλόν	*Epsilón.*
Ζ, ζ	Ζῆτα	*Zéta.*
Η, η	῎Ητα	*Éta.*
Θ, θ	Θῆτα	*Théta.*
Ι, ι	Ἰῶτα	*Eóta.*
Κ, κ	Κάππα	*Kápa.*
Λ, λ	Λάμβδα	*Lámvtha.*
Μ, μ	Μῦ	*Me.*
Ν, ν	Νῦ	*Ne.*
Ξ, ξ	Ξῖ	*Kse.*
Ο, ο,	῎Ο μικρόν	*Omecrón.*
Π, π	Πῖ	*Pe.*
Ρ, ρ	Ρῶ	*Rhô.*
Σ, σ	Σίγμα	*Ségma.*
Τ, τ	Ταῦ	*Taff.*
Υ, υ	῎Υ ψιλόν	*Ipsilón.*
Φ, φ	Φῖ	*Phe.*
Χ, χ	Χῖ	*He (khe).*
Ψ, ψ	Ψῖ	*Pse.*
Ω, ω	῎Ω μέγα	*Oméga.*

CHAPTER II.

SOUNDS OF THE VOWELS.

A

is pronounced like the French *a*, or like the English *a* in the words *car, far, father, calm*.

Schleicher observes that *a* was frequently represented by ε or ο. This is more especially noticed in the dialectic forms: βέρεθρον ἔρσην for βάραθρον ἄρσην. We have κλέος for κλάϝας, from *grávas*, πλέϝω or πλέω from *plávâmi*, etc. In modern Greek we have τίποτα (*tépota*) for τίποτε (*tépote*).

Geldart gives the form στροτός ὄνω ὀνεχώρησε = στρατὸς ἄνω ἀνεχώρησε (*stratós ah'no anehórese*). In modern Greek we have καταβόθρα for καταβάθρα (*katavah'thra*), ἁρμαθιά for ὁρμαθιά (*ormahtheáh*). Schleicher observes that the three terminations of contracted verbs, -άω, -έω, and όω were originally but one, viz. -αω. In modern Greek, at least in the language of the common people, -έω is always represented by -άω. We have ζητάει for ζητεῖ (*zetéē*), περιπατᾶτε for περιπατεῖτε (*peripatéēte*), and so on. Geldart states that *a* in ancient Greek is seldom weakened into υ, yet this appears to have been the case in νύξ (*nix*), ὄνυξ (*ónex*), κύκλος (*kéklos*), μύλος (*mélos*), and a few other words, as μύσταξ (*mis'tax*), which also appears in the form μάσταξ (*máhstax*) and βύθος (*véthos*), which is also written βάθος (*váhthos*). In modern Greek we get σκύφος (*sképhos*) for σκάφος (*skáhphos*) or σκάφη (*skáphē*). So, again, we have the diminutive appellation άφιον, as χωράφιον (*horáhpheon*), frequently represented by ύφιον, as ζωύφιον (*zoépheon*). The ancient Greeks prefixed *a* to many words (*a euphonicum*), as ἀβληχρός (*ahvlechrós*), ἀσταφίς (*astaphís*), ἀστεροπή (*ahsteropé*) for βληχρός (*vlechrós*), σταφίς (*staphís*), στεροπή (*steropé*). In modern Greek we have ἀβρότανον (*ahvrótanon*), ἀβράμυλον (*ahvrámelon*) for βράμυλον (*vráhmelon*), βράβυλον (*vráhvelon*).

EXAMPLES OF PRONUNCIATION.

Ἀδάμας, *ahthámas.*
Ἀδάμαστος, *ahtháhmastos.*
Ἄδος, *áhthos.*
Ἀγήρατον, *aghýraton.*
Ἀγράμματος, *ahgrámatos.*

Ἀγορανόμος, *ahghorahnómos.*
Ἁβρόβατος, *ahvróvahtos.*
Ἄβρομος, *áhvromos.*
Ἀβοήθητος, *ahvoéthetos.*

E

is intermediate between *a* and *i.* Professor Sophocles states that it requires the mouth to be moderately opened and the breath to proceed horizontally. It is approximately expressed by the English *e* in *spend, ferry,* or by the French *e.* In ancient Greek we have the forms ὀχθρός (*ochthrós*) for ἐχθρός (*ecthrós*). In modern Greek the same forms are still prevalent.

EXAMPLES OF PRONUNCIATION.

Ἐκδικάζω, *ekthekáhzo.*
Ἔκδικος, *ékthekos.*
Ἔκδημος, *ékthemos.*
Ἐκγενής, *ekghenēs.*
Ἔκδεξις, *ékthexis.*
Ἐκγράφω, *ekgráhpho.*

Ἔδαφος, *éthaphos.*
Ἐδώλιον, *ethóleon.*
Ἐκπέταμαι, *ekpétahme.*
Ἐκπέσσω, *ekpésso.*
Ἐκπηδάω, *ekpetháoh.*
Ἐκπίνω, *ekpénoh.*

H

is pronounced like the French *i*, or like the English *e* in the word *be.* The followers of Erasmus pronounce η as a long *e*, or like two *e*'s, or as *ay*, for the following reasons.

They say that in all the old inscriptions, before the letter η was introduced in the Greek alphabet, we find invariably an ε, i. e.: ΑΘΕΝ (Ἀθηνῶν), ΜΝΕΜΑ (μνῆμα), ΕΠΙ ΤΕΣ ΒΟΥΛΕΣ ΚΛΕΟΓΕΝΕΣ ΠΡΩΤΟΣ, etc.

Again, Cratinus wrote βῆ to represent the sound of the bleating of sheep. Plato says: "οὐκ ἦτα ἐχρώμεθα ἀλλὰ ε τὸ παλαιόν." Sextus says: "συσταλὲν τὸ η γίνεται ε, ἐκταθὲν δὲ τὸ ε γίνηται η." Sextus seems to regard η and ε as essentially one and the same letter. The other dialects generally express the Ionic η by ε, as, for instance, βασιλῆα, βασιλέα, etc. Finally, the Latin language also renders the Greek η by an e. These are, in short, the reasons which the followers of Erasmus bring as their justification for pronouncing the η as a long ε.

Now, in order that we may ascertain how the letter η was pronounced by the ancient Greeks, it is of the highest importance to consider, first, from what letters or sounds η has resulted.

α′) from ᾱ, especially in the Ionic dialect: νηός = νᾱός, νῆσος = νᾶσος (Doric), δευτέρη = δευτέρᾱ, etc.

β′) from αε, especially in the Doric dialect: τιμῆτε = τιμάετε, ὄρη = ὄραε, ζῆν from ζάειν, χρῆται from χράεται; ἥλιος, ἀέλιος, α-Fέλιος.

γ′) from εα: χρυσῆ, χαλκῆ, εὐγενῆ, from χρυσέα, χαλκέα, εὐγενέα.

δ′) from εε: δῆλος, ἤλπιζον, ἦλθον, from δέελος (δεFελος), ἐέλπιζον, ἔελθον, etc.

ε′) from αι, especially among the Bœotians: κῆ δεδύχθη, ἱππότη, εὐεργέτη, etc., from καὶ δεδύχθαι ἱππόται, εὐεργέταις. The letter η, a scholar says, having resulted from such letters, it is evident that it was formerly sounded both as an e (sounded as in be), which pronunciation prevails among the greater part of the modern Greeks, and like the French ê, as in fête, which pronunciation still is prevalent among not a few of the modern Greeks, as in ξηρός, κηρί(ον), σίδηρο(ν), μυρί(ον), στήκω, ἔθησα, instead of ἔθηκα, (ἐ)πόνησα, and many other words which are pronounced just as ξερός (xerós), σίδερο(ν) (sétheron), κερί(ον) (cheréon), στέκω (stécho), ἔθεσα (éthesa), (ἐ)πόνησα (epónesa). Professor Mavrophredes says, the ancient Greeks were wont to pronounce η like the French ê, as in *fête*, that is, like an *ay* ONLY in those words in which η resulted from εε. That this pronunciation was general among the Greeks we have no positive evidence, neither do we believe that it was so. Again, by the greater part of the Greeks η must have been sounded as the French *é* (*fermé*), that is, as the word κὴ = καὶ (pronounced κὲ). Now, this sound of η as an *é* has a closer resemblance to the letters αε, εα, αι, from which η has resulted, and, besides, it comes nearer to *e* (pronounced as in *be*), into which it afterwards passed among the many. This change of the sound of η into an ι seems to us to have been in use also in the Homeric times, as is evident from the words ἰδέ = ἠδέ. However, this pronunciation of η as an ι became still more prevalent about the fifth century B. C., and it must have been very common also in the common Attic dialect, because in no other way is it possible to explain the statement of Plato in Cratylus, 418, 68 a': "οἱ μὲν ἀρχαιότατοι ἱμέραν τὴν ἐμέραν ἐκάλουν, οἱ δὲ ἐμέραν· οἱ δὲ νῦν ἡμέραν." Compare also in 404: " Δημήτηρ μὲν φαίνεται κατὰ τὴν δόσιν τῆς ἐδωδῆς, διδοῦσα ὡς μήτηρ Δημήτηρ κεκλῆσθαι."

But about the second and third centuries B. C. the pronunciation of η as an ι became still more prevalent, and was generally adopted by all those speaking Greek, as is evident from the following Hebrew words: *Kithim, Levi, Charmi, Lachis, Schilo, Gilo, Dison, Sihon, Hira*, which were written in Greek by Κήτιμ, Λευή, Χαρμή, Λάχης, Σηλώ, Γηλών, Δησών, Σηών, Ἥρας, in which we plainly see that η was written for ι, and, besides, in the MS. of "Ὑπερίδου" we may often see instances in which η is interchanged with ι.

Now, many of the reasons which the followers of Erasmus bring to sustain their view of the sound of the letter η are by no means conclusive. To begin with, their argument concerning the well-known line of Cratinus,

"ὁ δ' ἠλίθιος ὥσπερ πρόβατον βῆ βῆ λέγων βαδίζει,"

is simply inadmissible, for how do we know that Cratinus

pronounced βῆ exactly after the Erasmian style? Again, even if we admit that Cratinus pronounced βῆ exactly as a follower of Erasmus would have sounded it, what scholar would be willing to accept the imaginary symbol of the in-articulate bleating of the sheep as the ground upon which to rest the decision of the question, What sound did the cul-tured nation of Greece give to the vocal elements of their language?

Again, the Latin language renders η by an ε for the simple reason that it does not have an η in its alphabet. For this reason the Latin has *crater* for κρατήρ and *poëma* for ποίη-μα, etc. Again, that η and ει were very similar in sound is rendered highly probable by the fact that they were inter-changed, e. g. κῆνος and τῆνος for κεῖνος, βούλη and βούλει. The Æolians and Dorians were wont to render by η the ει of other dialects, i. e. μναμῆον, σαμῆον, ἦχον, ἦλκοι, φιλῆτω, νοῆτω; in like manner the modern Greeks write ἀηδὼν instead of ἀειδών, ἀείδω, ἀίδω (ἄδω). The Bœotians, on the contrary, rendered by ει the η of other dialects, i. e. φίλειμι, γέλειμι, ἴστειμι, τίθειμι (Doric φίλημι, etc.), ἀγείοχα, εἰμὶ (ἠμὶ and Æolic ἔμμι and ἐσμὶ from ἐμὶ), ποειτὰς instead of ποητὰς, and so on. Numerous examples might be brought to show the similarity of sound of η, ει, and ι; for instance, in Homer we find ἠείδη, ἤδει, ἠείδει. Again, we find the same word written in three dif-ferent ways, i. e. σκεπηνὸς, σκεπεινὸς, σκεπινὸς; ἀλήτης, ἀλείτης, ἀλίτης. We have, again, ὀμβρινὸς and ὀμβρηνὸς, κεφαλῆνος and κεφαλίνος, σπαθήνης and σπαθίνης, κεμασῆνες and καμασῖνες, ἴκω and ἦκω, σκήπτω and σκίπτω, τάπης and τάπις, and so on. Now Ross thinks that the substitution of η for ε does not prove that it was sounded like an *ay*; for the Latin *e*, Geldart states, very often represented an ει, and on the other hand tended to become and therefore probably closely resembled in sound the simple ι. So we have *tristes* from *tristeis*, writ-ten *tristis*. We have also the following words written with ει instead of ε, i. e. *omneis, treis, parteis*, etc.; and not only so, but in the Byzantine period *designatus* became in Greek δισιγνάτος (*thesegnáthos*). Ross gives an inscription found at Carpathus in which ἰρώων stands for ἡρώων. Professor Mullach thinks that the very close resemblance between ι and η is evident in the parallel forms ἥκω and ἵκω, ἐπίβολος and ἐπή-βολος (where η, Geldart says, seems to be simply ι lengthened by the combined force of the accent and the ictus), γίγας and γηγενής, which two forms we have together in the Batracho-myomachia, —

Γηγενέων ἀνδρῶν μιμούμενοι ἔργα γιγάντων, —

πίδας from πηδάω, ἠδὲ and ἰδέ. Plutarch writes *Palilia*, Παλή-λια. *Quirinus* is translated Κυρήνιος, and *Scipio* into Σκηπίων.

Again, though the words κάμιλος for κάμηλος, ἐλάκτησε for ἐλάκτισε in the New Testament are no doubt errors in orthography, yet they show, as Geldart states, the early prevalence of the confusion of η with ι. Again, the scholiast on Eurip. Phœn. 685 tells us expressly that before the time of Euclides ι was used for η, ο for ω. These facts conclusively show the very early pronunciation of η as an ι.

EXAMPLES OF PRONUNCIATION.

Ἠθικός, *ethekós.*	Ἡμερονύκτιον, *emeronécteon.*
Ἦθος, *éthos.*	Ἡμέρα, *emérah.*
Ἡδύφωνος, *ethéphonos.*	Ἡσυχία, *esechéah.*
Ἡδονή, *ethoné.*	Ἡμίτμητος, *emétmetos.*
Ἠλίθιος, *elétheos.*	Ἡμίονος, *eméonos.*
Ἡμερομηνία, *emeromenéa.*	Ἡμιθαλής, *emethalés.*

Ⓘ

is pronounced unquestionably like the French *i*, or like the English *i* in the words *machine, marine.*

Liddell and Scott mention that ι was easily interchanged with ει, whence forms like εἴλω and ἴλλω. It was also interchanged with or written for η, and we have instances in the parallel forms of ἥκω and ἵκω, ἐπήβολος and ἐπίβολος. In fact

Plato, Nigidius, Quintilian, Dionysius of Halicarnassus, and others so plainly indicate the pronunciation of *ι*, that there can be no dispute in regard to it.

EXAMPLES OF PRONUNCIATION.

Ἰοδνεφής, *iothnephés.*
Ἶπος, *ipos.*
Ἰπνός, *ipnós.*
Ἴπνιος, *ipnios.*
Ἱππαστής, *ippastés.*
Ἴουλος, *ioolos* (pron. *oo* as in *moon*).
Ἱππάσιμος, *ippásimos.*
Ἰοπλόκαμυς, *ioplókamos.*

Ἴονθος, *ionthos.*
Ἱππομανής, *ippomanés.*
Ἱππομάχος, *ippomáhos.*
Ἱπποπόλος *ippopólos.*
Ἱπποδρόμιον, *ippothrómion.*
Ἱππικός, *ippikós.*
Ἵππιος, *ippios.*
Ἱππολοφία, *ippolophía.*

O and Ω

have nearly the same sound, and this sound is represented by *o* in *constant*.

That we may accurately determine the original sound of ω, we must determine from what letter or letters ω has resulted. Professor Mavrophedes remarks that ω resulted:

α´) from oo, i. e. ὠνόμαζον, ὤμοσα, etc. from ὀονόμαζον, ὀ ὄμοσα.

β´) from ā, just as o resulted from ă: i. e. φέρω, λέγω, etc. from φέρα-μι, λέγα-μι; ὠμό-ς, Sanscr. *âmà-s;* δώδεκα, Sanscr. *dvâdaçan;* πτωχό-ς (ver. πταχ-, πτακ-, πτήσσω); ὦρα, Germ. *Jahr* — " καὶ ἐν τῷ ἐπιρρηματικῷ ἐπιθέματι ὠς, ὅπερ ἐκ τοῦ ἀφαιρετικοῦ ᾶt προῆλθεν, i. e. καλῶς, κακῶς, σοφῶς, πάντως, πολλαχῶς, πῶς, τῶς, ὧς, etc.

γ´) from ao: τιμῶμεν, τιμάομεν; χρῶνται, χράονται, etc.

δ´) from oa and oη: αἰδῶ, αἰδόα; δηλῶτε, δηλόητε.

ε´) from av: i. e. ᾠόν from αὐ-ιον (whence the modern Greek αὐ-γόν, *egg*), ὠτ-ὸς from αὐ-τός (whence the modern Greek αὐ-τίον, *ear*), πῶλος (comp. τὰ παῦρος and *paulus*), ὦλαξ, Doric τῷ αὖλαξ," etc.

Now we must infer from these examples, as well as from the dialectic changes of o, ω, and ου, — such as in κοῦρος, οὖρος (Ionic), κῶρος, ὦρος (Doric), κόρος, ὅρος (Attic), and many others, — that the letter ω did not always have the sound of long *o* as in *hope*, but on the contrary a shorter sound like *o* in *constant*.

The different dialectic changes of ω, o, and ου, etc., such as κοῦρος and μοῦνος instead of κόρος and μόνος, are still common in modern Greek. We have, also, the forms τραγουδῶ for τραγωδῶ, τραγουδιστής for τραγωδιστής, etc.

EXAMPLES OF PRONUNCIATION.

Ὄζος, ózos.	*Ὠθισμός, othismós.*
Ὀζόστομος, ozóstomos.	*Ὠθέω, othéo.*
Ὄαρ, óar.	*Ὠδίς, othís.*
Ὄαρος, óahros.	*Ὠμηστής, omestés.*
Ὀβελίας, ovelías.	*Ὠμόλινον, omólinon.*
Ὄγμος, ógmos.	*Ὠλενίτης, olenítes.*
Ὄδυρμα, óthermah.	*Ὤμιλλα, ómillah.*
Ὀδυρμός, othermós.	*Ὠμίας, omías.*
Ὀδύρτης, othértes.	*Ὠλεσίκαρπος, olesíkarpos.*

Υ

is pronounced like the French *i*, or like the English *i* in *machine, marine.*

The most ancient pronunciation of υ was certainly like that of the German and Latin *u*, or like the diphthong *ou*. Afterwards it deteriorated into that of the German *ü*, or the French *u*, and at last it acquired the sound of *i*.

The old pronunciation of the letter υ as the German *ü* is preserved in numberless modern Greek words, and it is especially prevalent among the modern Athenians who pronounce τσῦρὰ instead of κυρὰ (κυρία) τσῦλίστρα = κυλίστρα, etc. In many instances, as Professor Mavrophredes states, the original pronunciation of the letter υ as ου still prevails, i. e. χρουσάφι = χρυσάφιον, κρούσταλλον = κρύσταλον, κουρκούτι = κυρκωτόν (from κυρκάω, κυκάω), etc.

Again, the forms δρίος, δρύον (Hes. Ἔργ.), μόλιβος and μολύβδαινα (Ἰλ. ω, 80), τρυφάλεια (Hom.) instead of τριφάλεια, as well as the words μυστίλλω and μιστύλλω, μίτυλος and μύτιλος, ἰλύσσω and τυλίσσω, βύβλος and βίβλος, ῥύπτω and ῥίπτω, ψιμύθιον and ψιμίθιον, πύστις and πίστις show how easily υ was exchanged with ι, and that the pronunciation of υ as an ι was not unknown to the ancients. In Asia Minor the pronunciation of υ as an ι was still more common, and about the sixth century B. C. we find in "Sappho" and "Alcæus" the forms ἴψος, ἰψηλός, ἴπερ, ἴπαρ, etc., instead of ὕψος, ὑψηλός, ὑπέρ, ὕπαρ.

Now, the pronunciation of υ as a long ι, which was so common in Asia Minor, began at an early period to spread into Greece, so that it became prevalent about the birth of Christ, as is evident from the coins of Augustus (15 A. D.), of Tiberius (37 A. D.), and Nero (69 A. D.), in which we find ΠΡΟ-ΚΡΙΤΙ ΑΦΡΟΔΥΣΙΑΣ instead of Πρόκριτοι Ἀφροδισίας. Again, Ἰουλία Σεβαστοῦ Θηγάτηρ instead of Θυγάτηρ; IMP. NERO Cæsar Aug. P. M.; ΕΥΘΙΜΙΥΣ (= Εὐθύμιος), etc. Here we may also remark the pronunciation of ει and η as an ι.

EXAMPLES OF PRONUNCIATION.

Ὕλη, *íle.*

Υἱός, *i-ós.*

Ὑετός, *i-etós.*

Ὑλακάω, *ilakáo.*

Ὑετόμαντις, *ietómantis.*

Ὑόπρωρος, *ióproros.*

Ὑοβοσκός, *iovoskós.*

Ὑμνητήριος, *imnetérios.*

Ὑλοτόμος, *ilotómos.*

CHAPTER III.

DIGRAPHS.

PROFESSOR MAVROPHREDES claims that originally they were all diphthongs, each having resulted from two different VOICES, but pronounced as "one syllable," except whenever they were purposely separated, i. e. οἴομαι, οἴω· εὖ, ἐΰ, ἀΐω, αἰών. The following vowels ι and υ had the position and force of a consonant. On this supposition, he asserts, we can easily explain the cutting off of ι and υ from εἰάν, αἰεί, αἰσύφηλος, καίω, ποιέω, Ἀλκαῖος, ἀλήθεια, ἐπισκευάζω, ἐπεσκεύασεν, εὐαμερὶς, γαύνυμαι, κραιπάλη, πολύκλειτος, εἵλωτες, from which resulted ἐὰν, ἀεί, ἀσύφηλος, κάω, ποέω (Att.), Ἄλκαος, ἀλάθεα (Æol.), ἐπισκεάζω (from ἐπισκεϜάζω), κατεσκέασεν (ἐκ τοῦ κατεσκέϜασεν), ἐαμερὶς (ἐκ τοῦ ἐϜαμερίς, Ross insc. ined. 746), γάνυμαι (from γάϜνυμαι, verb γαν, γαϜ, Latin *gaudeo*), as well as the Latin *crapula, Polycletus, Helotes*. In like manner from μεθυίω, ὀπυίω, we have μεθύω, ὀπύω. In later years the separate vowels of the diphthongs were blended, so that they came to be pronounced like the Latin or German: œ (ä), œ (ö), and ü, and finally became simple "monophthongs." But this change from "diphthongs" to "monophthongs" prevailed even in the times of Homer, because we have κοίησι, πολλῇσι, θεῇσι, etc., instead of κοίλαισι, πολλαῖσι, θεαῖσι, etc. Furthermore in the Bœotian dialect we have ἱππότη, εὐεργέτης, διακατίης, χειλίης, τῆς, κατασκευάττη, κεκόμιστη, ὀφείλετη, ἀπογράφεσθη, δεδόχθη, Θειβῆος, Ταναγρῆος, etc., instead of ἱππόται, εὐεργέταις, διακατίαις, χειλίαις, ταῖς, κατασκευάσσαι, κεκόμισται, etc., in which examples we plainly see that the diphthong αι is no longer α-ι, but has fallen into an η or é, and in later years it naturally acquired the sound of epsilon. About the third century B. C. diphthongs had entirely become monophthongs, just as they are to-day with the modern Greeks. We will now proceed to examine each DIPHTHONG separately.

CHAPTER IV.

SOUNDS OF THE DIPHTHONGS.

AI

is pronounced precisely like an epsilon, or like the English *e* in the first syllable of *example*.

1) That αι was pronounced by the ancients like an ε is evident from the fact that many words which are ordinarily written with αι, in some cases for the sake of brevity, are written with ε, e. g. αἴωρος (Plato) = ἔωρος, in Il. θ, 26:

"Δησαίμην, τὰ δὲ κ' αὖτε μετήορα πάντα γένοιτο";

in like manner we have αἰόλλω, αἴολος, in Homer and Pindar, for ἐόλλω, ἐολέω. See also Homer's "Iliad" β, 749:

"Τῇ δ''Ενιῆνες ἔποντο μενεπτόλεμοί τε Περαιβοί,"

where 'Ενιῆνες stands for Αἰνιᾶνες. Again, we have φαινίνδα for φενίνδα, φαινόλης and φενώλης, ψέκας and ψαίκας, ἀνώγαιον and ἀνώγεον, Τιθοραία and Τιθορέα (an old name of a city in Bœotia), λευκαία and λευκέα, ἀκταία and ἀκτέα, etc.

2) In prosody αι at the end of a word is short, also in scansion before a vowel. In such cases it could not have been sounded as a diphthong.

3) The translators of the Old Testament (280 B. C.) always render the long ε of the Hebrews (*tzere*) by αι, i. e. Βαιθὴλ = *Bethel*, Gen. xii.; Θαιμὰν = *Theman*, Gen. xxxvi. 11; Χαίλων = *Chelon*, Num. i. 9; Αἰνάν = *Enan*, Num. i. 15; Αἰλείμ = *Elim*, Exod. xvi. 1; etc.

4) The poet Callimachus (250 B. C.) in one of his epi-

grams distinctly represents the echo in ν-αίχι answering by
ἔχει:

    "Λυσανίη, σύγε ναίχι καλὸς, καλός · ἀλλὰ πρὶν εἰπεῖν
    Τοῦτο σαφῶς, ἠχὼ φησί τις, ἄλλος ἔχει."

5) Inscriptions of the second century B. C. bear κὲ πέζοντας,
πεζόντων, κατάκιτε, instead of καὶ παίζοντας, παιζόντων, κατάκειται.

6) Dionysius of Halicarnassus (30 B. C.) translates the
Latin *Prænestini* by Πρενεστῆνοι, and Strabo renders the
same by Πραινεστῖνοι.

7) In the Syriac translation of the Gospels αι is rendered
by the long Syriac *e* in the words Καισάρεια, Πραιτώριον, Ὑμέ-
ναιος, etc.

8) On some coins of Nero, 69 A. D. (Occo. p. 13), we find
ΠοππΕα instead of Ποππαία.

· 9) αι is rendered by *æ* in the Latin, i. e. *ægilops* = αἰγίλωψ,
ægithus = αἴγιθος, *ægophtalmus* = αἰγόφθαλμος, *ælurus* = αἴ-
λουρος, *ænigma* = αἴνιγμα, *balæna* = φαλαίνα, *hyæna* = ὕαινα.

10) In Greek inscriptions belonging to the Roman period
we find ε representing αι and *vice versâ*.

11) Plutarch indicated the true pronunciation of αι by
rendering the Latin *fenestra* by the Greek φαινέστρα, *Fenes-
tella* = Φαινεστέλλα(ς).

12) Finally, Sextus (190 A. D.) distinctly asserts that the
sound αι and ει "is simple and uniform": "Ἐπεὶ οὖν ὁ τοῦ αι
καὶ ει φθόγγος ἁπλοῦς ἐστὶ καὶ μονοειδής." So also in Sanscrit
we have *vêda* = vaida, *vêças* = vaiças, *bharaté* = bharatai =
φέρεται. In French *ai* is pronounced as an *e*, e. g. *mais,
Français, Anglais*, etc.

EXAMPLES OF PRONUNCIATION.

Ἀλάζω, eázo.	Αἰκίζω, ekízo.
Αἰανής, eanés.	Αἴλινος, élinos.
Αἵρεσις, éresis.	Αἴθω, étho.
Αἰακίδης, eakíthis.	Αἴθουσα, éthoosa.
Αἰδέομαι, ethéome.	Αἰθιοπίς, ethiopís.
Αἰδήμων, ethémon.	

AY

is pronounced like *af* or *av* according to the letter which follows it. If it is followed by θ, ξ, σ, τ, then this digraph is sounded like *af;* but before γ, δ, λ, ν, ρ, and before vowels and other digraphs it is pronounced like *av*.

1) That the pronunciation of the diphthongs αυ, ευ, and ου, in use by the modern Greeks, was the original pronunciation of the ancient Greeks is evident from the fact that the υ of these diphthongs in many instances resulted from F (*v*), or rather it occupies in many instances the place of F (*v*); e. g. αὔως (Æol. ἠώς) instead of αὔσως, from the root αϜϛ or Ϝυϛ; καίειν, λάμπειν, αὖος (*dry*) have in like manner resulted from the same root. A modern Greek scholar gives also κλαύσω = κλάϜω, ναῦος (Æol.) = ναϜός, ναός; αὐτός = ἀϜτός. The same word is also found in an inscription on the Island of Delos, ἀϜυτός. παῦρος (Lat. *parvus*) from πάρϜος = πάϜρος. In the "Iliad" (η, 86) we have χεύωσιν (the aorist subj. of χεύω), ἔχευα, χεῦαι = χέϜω, ἔχεϜα, χέϜαι; εὔκηλος = ἔϜκηλος = Ϝέκ-ηλος (from the root ναϰ, Ϝαϰ, whence Professor Mavrophredes says we get ἑκών, ἀϜέκων, ἕκητι, ἀϜέκητι, ἧκα, ἥκιστος, etc.; εὔχομαι = ἐϜχυμαι = Ϝέχομαι; εὖρος = ἔϜρος, from the root Ϝᾶ (Ϝα), whence we have also αὖρα and οὖρος, as well as οὔριος.

Again, we have βουλή (Æol. βόλλα) from the ancient βολϜα = βοϜλα, δουρός, γουνὸς from δορϜὸς = δοϜρός; γουϜὸς = γοϜνός; οὖλος (= ὅλος) from ὅλϜος = ὅϜλος (Sanscr. *sarva-s*); νοῦσος (νόσος) from νόσϜος = νόϜσος; κοῦρος and κούρη (Ionic) = κόρος, κόρη from κόρϜος, κόρϜη = κόϜρος, κόϜρη, etc.

2) The Latin language renders the diphthongs αυ and ευ by the monosyllables *av* and *ev*, i. e. *cavneas* = καυνείας; *pavo, paveo* = παύω (φάβω); *cavo* = καύω (χάω); *navis* = ναῦς, ναυός; *lavo* = λάϜω (λαύω); *favo* = φαύω; *Phavorinus* = Φαυωρῖνος (Φαβωρῖνος, Plutarch); παῦρος, by transposition *parvus* (and by another transposition *pravus*). Oekonomos gives also εὐοὶ, εὐάν = *evoe, evan, evax;* Εὔιος, *Evius;* Εὔανδρος,

Evander; Σενῆρος, Σεβῆρος, *Severus;* Δαῦος, *Davus* (Plaut., Virg., Ovid).

3) The translators of the Old Testament about the third century B. C. render the Hebrew *vav* sometimes by β, sometimes by *v*, e. g. Δαβὶδ and Δαυΐδ, Λευή = *Levi*. And, *vice versâ,* the *v* of αυ and ευ the Syriac translator of the New Testament (about the first century A. D.) renders by *vav.* Furthermore, many biblical names, such as Εὔα, Δαυΐδ, Εὐαγγέλιον, Εὐοδία, etc. are rendered in Latin *Eva, David, Evangelium, Evodia,* etc.

4) Cicero writes (Divin. 11, 40): " *Cum M. Crassus exercitum Brundisii imponeret, quidam in portu caricas Cauno advectas vendens,* CAUNEAS *clamitabat. Dicamus, si placet, monitum ab eo Crassum, caveret, ne iret: non fuisse periturum, si omini paruisset.*" Comp. Pliny (Hist. Nat. XV., 19). Professor Mavrophredes says: "Δῆλον, ὅτι τὸ ὄνομα Cauneas (e. g. καννείας ἰσχάδας) ἐν τῇ Μεγάλῃ Ἑλλάδι ὁμοφθόγγως τῇ φράσει CAV(E)NEEAS ἠχοῦν ὡς κακὸς οἰωνὸς ἐξελήφθη."

The followers of Erasmus to sustain *their* pronunciation of αυ bring forward that line of Aristophanes written to represent the barking of dogs. Now, it is curious to consider that the followers of Erasmus always call the sounds of animals to decide any points of Greek pronunciation. For instance, when they wish to settle the sound of β, they bring the well-known lines of Cratinus written to represent the bleating of the sheep; when they would fix the sound of οι, they bring that line of Aristophanes written to represent the grunting of hogs; and now, between the hogs and the sheep, they let loose the dogs to decide by their barking the sound of αυ. To what a degradation the followers of Erasmus have brought the divine language of Plato!

EXAMPLES OF PRONUNCIATION.

Before θ.

Αὐθέντης, *afthéntis.*	Αὐθήμερος, *afthémeros.*	Αὐθέψης, *afthépsis.*

Before ξ.

Αὐξάνω, afxáno.· Αὐξίτροφος, afxítrophos. Αὐξομείωσις, afxomíosis.

Before σ.

Αὐσταλέος, afstaléos. Αὐστηρία, afsteria. Αὐστηρός, afsterós.

Before τ.

Αὐτάρεσκος, aftáreskos. Αὐτάρχης, aftárhis. Αὐτερέτης, afterétis.

Before γ.

Αὐγή, avgé. Αὔγουστος, ávgoostos.

Before δ.

Αὐδή, avthé. Αὐδάζομαι, avtházome. Αὐδάτα, avtháta.

Before λ.

Αὐλός, avlós. Αὐλουρός, avlourós. Αὐλῳδία, avlothía.

Before ρ.

Αὔριον, ávrion. Αὐρίζω, avrízo. Αὐριβάτης, avrivátes.

Before Vowels.

Αὐενιών, avenión. Αὐερύω, averéo. Αὐηλός, avilós.

Before Diphthongs.

Αὐαίνω, avéno.

EY

is likewise pronounced like *ef* or *ev*. Before θ, κ, ξ, π, σ, τ, φ, χ, ψ this diphthong is sounded like *ef*. Before γ, δ, ζ, λ, μ, ν, ρ, and before vowels and diphthongs, it is pronounced like *ev*. Concerning the antiquity and genuineness of this pronunciation we spoke in detail when treating of the diphthong αυ.

EXAMPLES OF PRONUNCIATION.

Before θ.

Εὐθάλαμος, efthálamos. Εὐθάλασσος, efthálassos. Εὐθαλπής, efthalpís.

Before κ.

Εὐκάρδιος, efkárthios. Εὐκατάγνωστος, efkatágnostos.
Εὐκατάστατος, efkatástatos.

Before ξ.

Εὔξενος, *éfxenos.*   Εὔξεστος, *éfxestos.*   Εὐξήραντος, *efxírandos.*

Before π.

Εὔπεπλος, *éfpeplos.*   Εὐπένθερος, *efpéntheros.*   Εὔπεπτος, *éfpeptos.*

Before σ.

Εὐσταθής, *efstathís.*   Εὐσταλής, *efstalís.*   Εὐστέφανος, *efstéphanos.*

Before τ.

Εὐστραφής, *efstraphís.*   Εὔτρεπτος, *éftreptos.*   Εὔτρητος, *éftritos.*

Before φ.

Εὐφρόνη, *effróni.*   Εὔφωνος, *éffonos.*   Εὐφώρατος, *effóratos.*

Before χ.

Εὐχάλκωτος, *efhálkotos.*   Εὔχαρις, *éfharis.*   Εὐχαριστία, *efharistía.*

Before ψ.

Εὐψάμαθος, *efpsámathos.*   Εὐψηφίς, *efpsiphís.*

Before γ.

Εὖγε, *évge.*   Εὔγληνος, *évglenos.*   Εὐγαθής, *evgathís.*

Before δ.

Εὐδία, *evthía.*   Εὐδιάβατος, *evthiávatos.*   Εὐδιάβολος, *evthiávolos.*

Before ζ.

Εὔζηλος, *évzelos.*   Εὔζωρος, *évzoros.*   Εὔζωνος, *évzonos.*

Before λ.

Εὐλίμενος, *evlímenos.*   Εὐλόγιστος, *evlógistos.*   Εὔλογος, *évlogos.*

Before μ.

Εὐμεγέθης, *evmeyéthis.*   Εὐμενέτης, *evmenétis.*   Εὐμέλανος, *evmélanos.*

Before ν.

Εὔνια, *évnia.*   Εὔνις, *évnis.*   Εὔνημα, *évnema.*

Before ρ.

Εὐρετέος, *evretéos.*   Εὑρεσίτεχνος, *evresítechnos.*   Εὔρημα, *évrema.*

Before Vowels and Diphthongs.

Εὔαθλος, *évathlos.*   Εὐάερος, *eváeros.*   Εὖαδε, *évathe.*

Εὐαίμων, *evémon.*   Εὐαισθησία, *evesthesia.*   Εὐαίσθητος, *evésthetos.*

HY

has the sound of *if* before θ, κ, ξ, π, σ, τ, φ, χ, ψ, and *iv* before γ, δ, ζ, λ, μ, ν, ρ and before vowels and diphthongs. That ηυ and ωυ were originally pronounced exactly as they are to-day by the modern Greeks is evident from the fact that ηυ and ωυ are simply the Ionic forms of αυ and ευ: γρηῦς, νηῦς, ωὑτός θωῦμα (Ion.) = γραῦς, ναῦς, αὐτός θαῦμα, etc. It is, therefore, evident that the pronunciation of ηυ and ωυ closely resembled that of αυ, and ευ.

EXAMPLES OF PRONUNCIATION.

Γρηῦς, *gréfs.*   Νηῦς, *néfs.*

ΩΥ

is pronounced like *of* before θ, κ, ξ, π, σ, τ, φ, χ, ψ, and like *ov* before γ, δ, ζ, λ, μ, ν, ρ, also before vowels and diphthongs.

YI and YH

are pronounced exactly like the modern Greek ι or like the English *i* in *machine.* Homer almost always makes the υι in the word υἱός a short syllable, e. g. Il. ζ, 130; δ, 473; η, 47; ρ, 575. Again, the correctness of the modern Greek pronunciation of these vowel-combinations is supported by the two forms of the words μεθύω and ὀπύω, which are also written μεθυίω, ὀπυίω. Professor Mavrophredes asserts that this cannot be otherwise explained than by the assumption that the words μεθυίω, ὀπυίω, υἱός originally were pronounced μεθύjω, ὀπύjω, ὑjός; afterwards the *j* (ι) was cut out, especially between two vowels. We have many instances of this, and to this day the modern Greeks pronounce μύγα = μύjα, *méa.* Finally, in old inscriptions, as well as on coins, the noun υἱός is very often written ὑός, from which it becomes evident that υι = υ = ι.

EXAMPLES OF PRONUNCIATION.

Υἱδοῦς, *ethoõs.*   Υἱός, *eós.*   Ὑηττός, *etós.*

OY

is pronounced exactly like the French *ou* or like the English *oo* in the word *moon*.

The diphthong ου was originally a monophthong, as it is to this day with the modern Greeks, and was pronounced in some dialects like an *o* or like the Latin *u*. This is evident from the fact that in the sixth, seventh, and eighth centuries B. C. the Æolians used to render ου simply by an *o*. Again, we have many instances in which ου is rendered in different dialects by an υ, e. g. κουρίδιος (Homeric) = κυρίδιος = κύριως; κουρωθείει = κυρωθῇ; οὔδωρ = ὔδωρ; ἀσουλία = ἀσυλία.

Again, the Latin and Semitic *u* is invariably rendered in Greek by ου, e. g. Ἰούδας, Ἰουδαῖος, etc.; Ἰούνιος, Βροῦτος, Σέξτος, Ἰούλιος. Finally, the fact that ου is never written separated into two sounds (οϋ), as we occasionally find αϋ, εϋ, εϊ, οϊ, etc., is a proof, Professor Mavrophredes believes, that ου was a monophthong even in the pre-historic period of the Greek language.

EXAMPLES OF PRONUNCIATION.

Οὐσία, *oosía*.	Οὐδέποτε, *oothépote*.
Οὔτερος, *oóteros*.	Οὐδετέρως, *oothetéros*.
Οὔτησις, *oótesis*.	

OI

is pronounced like *œ* in *œconomy*, or like an English *e*. Ockonomos thinks that it was sounded in some dialects as ου = *u* Italian or like the Latin *œ*, and in some as the French *u* passing into *i*. This is highly probable from the fact that the Æolians used οι instead of ει, e. g. ὄνοιρος, ὄνειρος.

1) The Latin language renders οι by *œ*, e. g. *Œta* = Οἴτα, *Crœsus* = Κροῖσος, *Œnops* = Οἶνοψ, *Œdipus* = Οἰδίπους, *Œneus* = Οἰνεύς. Professor Mavrophredes says that the diphthong *œ* was at an early period pronounced among the ancient Romans just as the German *ö*, and consequently *œ* became, or

passed into an œ = η (é). This is highly probable from the fact that Quintilian says: "Œ *scribendum esse non proferendum, omnes edocent.*"

2) The Alexandrian, the Copt, and the Latin translators of the Bible from the third century B. C. to the third century A. D. always render the Hebrew ö by means of the Greek οι, and, *vice versâ,* they render οι by means of ö (œ). Now, that οι had also the sound of υ, which is still prevalent among the modern Greeks is highly probable from the statement of Thucyd., B. 54: "Ἐν τῷδε τῷ καιρῷ οἷα εἰκός, ἀνεμνήσθησαν καὶ τοῦδε τοῦ ἔπους φάσκοντες οἱ πρεσβύτεροι ᾄδεσθαι.

"Ἥξει δωριακὸς πόλεμος καὶ λοιμὸς ἅμ' αὐτῷ,'

ἐγένετο μὲν οὖν ἔρις τοῖς ἀνθρώποις μὴ λοιμὸν ὠνομάσθαι ἐν τῷ ἔπει ὑπὸ τῶν παλαιῶν, ἀλλὰ λιμόν· ἐνίκησε δὲ ἐπὶ τοῦ παρόντος λοιμὸν εἰρῆσθαι." So that it becomes evident that there existed between λοιμὸς and λιμὸς a SAMENESS of sound, and not an "identity of meaning." Now, of all sounds the one which has a closer resemblance to ι, or rather an identity of sound with it, is υ, judging also from the fact that Demosthenes (fourth century B. C.) writes Ἀνεμύτας instead of Ἀνεμοίτας, and from many other examples which we noticed when treating of the letter υ we must infer that the letter υ in several dialects was written instead of οι, and hence it is evident that it was equal to οι or ι (οι = υ = ι). Again, that οι at an early period had exactly the sound of a simple ι is evident from the fact that about the first century B. C. we find written on a coin of Julius Cæsar, ΙΩΝΙΣΤΗΣ for ΟΙΩΝΙΣΤΗΣ. Again, on another coin of Augustus we find ΠΡΟΚΡΙΤΙ for ΠΡΟΚΡΙΤΟΙ.

Δίων ὁ Κάσσιος relates that Nero (60 A. D.) killed two Σουλπικίους "ὅτι ποιητικοὶ ἐκ προγόνων ἐπικαλούμενοι οὐκ ἐπαύσαντο πρόσρημα τοῦτ' ἔχοντες, ἀλλ' εἰς τὰς τοῦ Νέρωνος νίκας τὰς πυθικὰς ἐκ τῆς ὁμωνυμίας ἠσέβουν." Now, we plainly see οι = υ, η = ι; also that οιη = υι = υ = ι, because confessedly υ in that period was pronounced as ι. About the second century A. D.

on some coins of "'Ἀντωνίνου τοῦ Πίου" the word εἰκοστοῦ is four times written οι, and the noun 'Ἀντωνῖνος four times is found written by ει (ΑΝΤΩΝΕΙΝΟΣ), hence it results that οι = ει = ι, etc.

Now, that ι subscriptum of the ᾳ, ῃ, ῳ was always silent is evident from the statement of Strabo (about the birth of Christ) : "Πολλοὶ χωρὶς τοῦ ι γράφουσι τὰς δοτικὰς καὶ ἐκβάλλουσί γε τὸ ἔθος φυσικὴν αἰτίαν οὐκ ἔχον," in which the "φυσικὴν αἰτίαν οὐκ ἔχον" simply means that it was unpronounced. Again, that the ι subscriptum, long before Strabo, was silent we may conclude from the way the ancient Romans rendered the words *tragœdus, comœdus, citharœdus, ode, rapsodus, prosodia, palinodia, herous, patrous,* in which the simple sound of *o* is equivalent to the Greek ῳ.

EXAMPLES OF PRONUNCIATION.

Οἴκαδε, *œ̆kathe.*   Οἰκειοπραγία, *œkeopragía.*   Οἶκος, *œ̆kos.*

EI

is pronounced like the English *i* in the words *machine, marine.* That there was a time in which ει was pronounced as ε-ι, appears from the statement of Plato, Cratyl. 402, ε: "Τὸν οὖν ἄρχοντα τῆς δυνάμεως ταύτης θεὸν ὠνόμασε Ποσειδῶνα, ὡς ποσί-δε-σμον ὄντα, τὸ δὲ ε ἔγκειται ἴσως εὐπρεπείας ἕνεκα."

However, the ει at a very early period passed into the pronunciation of a simple ι, judging from the fact that ει was rendered by *i* in the Latin language, e. g. *Nīlus* = Νεῖλος, *crocodīlus* = κροκόδειλος, *Epaminondas* = 'Επαμεινώνδας, *Chirotonia* = Χειροτονία, *spira* = σπεῖρα, *ironia* = εἰρωνεία, *elegia* = ἐλεγεία, *litania* = λιτανεία. In a Latin author we find : "*I quoque apud antiquos post E pronebatur, et EI diphthongum faciebat, quam pro omni I longa scribebant, more antiquo Grœcorum.*" Again, that ει had the same sound as ι, even among the ancient Romans, is rendered highly probable from the fact that in the very best period of the Latin language *i* was substituted for *ei*. Thus we have *idus, primus*, etc., the older forms being *eidus, preimus*, etc. The ancient Greeks, on the other hand, often rendered the *i* of the Latins by ει, e. g. Plutarch translates the words *idus, idibus* by εἰδοὺς, εἰδοῖς (older form *eidus*). The very ancient identity of the sound of ει as a simple ι is established from the fact that we find in Homer εἰδὼς, εἰδυῖα (Il. ρ, 5; ι, 128; ψ, 263; Od. α, 428, etc.), as well as ἰδυῖα (Il. σ, 380, 482; v, 12; Od. η, 92, etc.), ι short. We have ἴδυιος, ἴδυοι, as well as εἴδυοι. Again, we find the forms εἴκελος and ἴκελος, γείνομαι (Il. κ) and γίνομαι, λείχω and λίχω, ἐρείκη and ἐρίκη, στεῖβος and στίβος, δείω and δίω, πείθω and πίθω, φθείρ and φθίρ, and so on.

Plamoudes relates that Æsop (572 B. C.) pronounced σει just as συ (v = ι).

Aristophanes (450 B. C.) has a pun in διαπεινᾶμες (Bœotian, instead of διαπεινῶμεν) and διαπίνομεν. In Diogenes Laertius we find another pun on ἀλλ᾽ ἱμάτιον and ἀλειμμάτιον: "Ἰδὼν μειρακύλλιον ἱματιοκλέπτην ἐν τῷ βαλανείῳ ἔφη, ᾽ἐπ᾽ ἀλειμμάτιον ἢ ἐπ᾽ ἄλλο ἱμάτιον;᾽"

The translators of the Old Testament rendered the Hebrew *elim* by the Greek αἰλείμ, and in several other old Greek passages we find πρωτοτόκια and πρωτοτοκεῖα, παραγείνεται and παραγίνεται, Θαρσεῖς and Θαρσὶς, νεῖκος and νῖκος. Dionysius of Halicarnassus clearly regards not only ει but also αι and αυ and οι "as undivided syllables," or, in other words, considers them as simple monophthongs. Strabo renders by ει the Latin *i*, e. g. *Ligeris*, Λείρης (*Loire*), *Liris*, Λεῖρις. The Syriac translator of the Gospels renders ει by *i*, e. g. *iki* = εἰκῇ. In the New Testament we find ἐπεὶ and ἐπὶ, νήστεις and νήστις, νεῖκος and νῖκος, etc.

The writer Athenæus says of the Attic courtesan Thaïs (third century B. C.): Θαῒς πρὸς γράσωνα πορευομένη ἐραστήν, ἐπεί τις αὐτὴν ἡρώτα ποῖ πορεύεται, εἶπεν,

᾽Αἰγεῖ συνοικήσουσα τῷ Πανδίονος.᾽"

Thaïs, whilst saying Αἰγεῖ meant αἰγί (= γράσωνι); the pun is

in the similarity of sound between ει and ι, as Eustathius
says (Bas., p. 367). Plutarch translates the Latin *i* by ει, e. g.
Lusitania, Λυσιτάνεια; *Honori,* Ὀνώρει; *Pinarii,* Πεινάριοι.
On a papyrus (παρὰ Latronne) — *Fragments inédis d'an-
ciens poètes Grecs, tirés d'un papyrus appartenant au
musée royal, Paris,* 1841 — we find at times " ἐπὶφ" and at
others the same word written " ἐπείφ," thus demonstrating
the similarity of sound between ει and ι. Cicero (Epist. ad
Familiares, IX. 22) says: *"Cum loquimur* TERNI *nihil flagi-
tii dicimus; ad cum* BINI *obscenum est, græcis quidem
inquies. Nihil est ergo in verbo; quando et ego græce
scio, et tamen tibi dico,* RINI, *idque tu facis, quasi ego græce
non latine dixerim."* Hence it is evident that βίνει had the
same sound as *bini.* Nigidius says: *"Græcos non tantæ in-
scitiæ arcesso qui* OY *ex* O *et* Y *scripserunt, quantæ qui* EI
ex E *et* I; *illud enim inopia facerunt, hoc nulla re coacti."*
Finally, on coins and inscriptions words have been found
written with ει, which are also written with ι, i. e. ΤΡΙΠΟΛΕΙ-
ΤΩΝ, ΕΤΕΙΜΗΣΕΝ, ΝΕΙΚΗ, ΑΓΡΙΠΠΕΙΝΑΣ, ΤΕΙΜΗΤΗΣ,
ΣΑΒΕΙΝΟΣ, ΛΟΓΓΕΙΝΑ, ΝΕΙΚΟΣΤΡΑΤΟΣ, ΧΕΛΕΙΔΟΝΙΣ,
ΝΕΙΚΟΠΟΛΕΙΤΩΝ, etc.   Notice also the Bœotian forms
ἀνεγείρι, λαλῖς, etc., instead of ἀνεγείρει, λαλεῖς, etc.

EXAMPLES OF PRONUNCIATION.

Εἰαμενή, *eamení.*   Εἰρωνεία, *eronía.*   Εἰρκτή, *erkté.*

CHAPTER V.

THE CONSONANTS.

B

is pronounced like *v* in *vase*. The followers of Erasmus maintain that the letter β was originally pronounced like the Latin *b*. They claim that the ancient Romans rendered the β of the Greek words not by *v*, but by *b*. Again, they quote that verse of the Comedian Cratinus, —

"'Ο δ' ἠλίθιος, ὥσπερ πρόβατον, βῆ βῆ λέγων βαδίζει," —

in which (they say) it is evident that Cratinus and his fellow-citizens, the Athenians, pronounced the β as a *b*, and η as an *ê*, because the sheep in bleating say not βῆ (according to the pronunciation now prevalent in Greece), but *bee, bê*. They claim also that Cicero wrote in one of his letters that the Greek βίνει has the same sound as the Latin *bini*. These seem to me to be the only reasons which the followers of Erasmus bring to sustain their pronunciation of the letter β.

Now, the ancient Romans represented the β of many Greek words like their own *v*. Oekonomos brings the following examples: βέλω, βόλω, *volo;* βίω, βιῶ, βίϝω, *vivo;* βιοτά, *vita;* βόρω, βορὸς, *voro;* βόραξ, *vorax;* βαίνω, *venio* (perhaps this is derived from βέω, whence we have βείομαι = βάω, βαίνω, βένω); βάδω, *vado;* βία (βὶς, ϝίς, ἴς), *vis;* νὶψ νιβὸς, *nix nivis;* etc. The ancient Greeks used also to render the *v* of the Latins by β, for instance: *Valentianus*, Βαλεντιανός; *Severus*, Σεβῆρος; *Octavius*, 'Οκτάβιος; *Veturius*, Βετούριος; *Aventini*, 'Αβεντῖνοι (Plutarch). In a few instances

the *v* was rendered in Greek by ου; for instance, *Varro* =
Βάῤῥων or Οὐάῤῥων (this latter peculiarity is for the sake of
euphony, Οὐάῤῥων being more euphonic than Βάῤῥων).

From what has been said it appears probable that in the
old Latin tongue (which may be termed either the daughter
or the sister of the Æolic dialect), so long as the pronunciation of the emigrant Æolians remained unaltered, so long the
letter *b* was pronounced exactly as the modern Greeks pronounce their β. But afterwards, the Latin language being
-adopted by the other tribes of Italy, — tribes which were
barbarous and hence unacquainted with Grecian phraseology,
— the pronunciation became rather harsh and rough, as their
manner of speaking, and hence among them the Greek β
gradually degenerated into the sound of *b*. To this reason,
as a modern Greek states, must be attributed the fact of the
use of *b* instead of *v*, as is often seen in ancient inscriptions,
i. e. *bixit* instead of *vixit*, *serbus* instead of *servus*, *amabile*
and *benemeritus* instead of *amavile* and *venemeritus*. In
one of the laws of Numa which has been preserved by Fes-
tus we read *Jobis* instead of *Jovis*. Traces of the pronunciation of β are to be found in the Spanish language, i. e.
vene, *vestia*, for *bene*, *bestia;* and in French, especially among
the so-called Gascons. But Jacob Creatin, one of the most
devoted followers of Erasmus, in his "De Sono Literarum
Græcorum" admits that the ancient pronunciation of β was
not so "ἔντονος καὶ βομβηρὰ" as the present.

Liddell and Scott likewise admit that the pronunciation
was softer than our *b*, like the Spanish or modern Greek for
instance. As for Cicero's statement, no one can assure us
that the letter *b* had in his time exactly the pronunciation
now prevalent among the followers of Erasmus. Again, it is
probable that Cicero wished simply to show the similarity
which exists between these two words, as respects the length
of the syllables (in pronouncing). And, as a scholar affirms,
these two words were not pronounced by Cicero in a speech,

but simply written in a letter, whence it may result that Cicero wished simply to show the analogy in writing which exists between these two words, rather than their sound or pronunciation. As for the

"'Ο δ' ἠλίθιος ὥσπερ πρόβατον, βῆ βῆ λέγων βαδίζει,"

it is evident that Cratinus used it because he had no other letter by which he could express the sound made by a sheep. For the same reason Aristophanes, when he would represent the noise made by pigs, wrote κοΐ, κοΐ (instead of góï, góï), because the Greek language has no letter so harsh in sound as *g*. And when Aristophanes would represent the croaking of the frogs, he wrote βρεκεκέξ. Do the frogs ever say *vrekke-keks*? Or, when he would represent the cackling of hens, he wrote τιτικομπροὺ. Do the hens make such a sound? Therefore it seems to me that it is absurd to attempt to determine the sound of β by a word used to represent the bleating of sheep. For we must confess that the attempts to render the noises of animals by the articulate sounds of " μερόπων ἀνθρώπων " are very unsatisfactory.

Now, if we consider that the name of F (*vau*) was written in Greek βαῦ, that the Hebrew *bau* was rendered in the noun Δαβὶδ by β, that Strabo (p. 213, c) renders the Latin *Novum Comum*, Νοβουμκόμουμ, and that about the year 69 A. D. a coin of Nero bears the inscription OKTABIA ΣEBAΣTH, — the genuineness of the pronunciation of β as *veta* is proved beyond question.

. Finally, as a modern Greek says, the nature of the most sweetly sounding of all languages by no means admits the harsh sound of β. Just pronounce according to the Erasmian method the words βοῦν, βδάλλει, βδέλλα, βούβρωστιν, βεβρωκότα, βαβράζει, βάβαξ, βλὰξ, βεβοστρυχωμένος, βορβορόληπτος, βέμβιξ, βέβαφα, and you will acknowledge that the Grecian Minerva would never have accustomed her lips to such awkward attitudes when she would not learn to play on the flute because it compelled her to inflate her cheeks so ungracefully. The reason why so many students are unable to discover the melody so characteristic of the Greek pronunciation is to be attributed simply to the Erasmian system of pronunciation. What melody can there be in pronouncing "*bebrabeumenos*" or the word βεβοστρυχωμένος (*bebostruchoménos*)?

EXAMPLES OF PRONUNCIATION.

Βεκκεσέληνος, *vekesélenos.*

Βιβλιογράφος, *vevleográphos.*

Βίβλινος, *vévlenos.*

Βλαστάνω, *vlastáno.*

Βλάζω, *vlázo.*

Βλάπτω, *vlápto.*

Βλάβός, *vlávos.*

Βλάβη, *vlávi.*

Βλαστός, *vlastós.*

Βλασφημία, *vlasphemía.*

Βλάσφημος, *vlásphemos.*

Βλάψις, *vlápsis.*

Βίος, *víos.*

Βάλσαμον, *válsamon.*

Γ

before a, o, ω, av, ov has nearly the same sound of *ghâh*, but softer and more guttural than the *ga* of the Western nations. Before ε, ν, ι, υ, ευ, οι, γ is pronounced like *y*, and when followed by another γ, or by κ, ξ, or χ, it takes the sound of *v*.

That the letter γ was a guttural soft semivowel is evident from the fact that Homer has γ as an aspirate before some words, as αἶα for γαῖα; also in other Greek words, as ἵννος (*énnos*) for γίννος (*yénos*). In modern Greek we get λέω (*léo*) for λέγω (*légho*), πρᾶμα (*práhma*) for πρᾶγμα (*prágmah*). Professor Gandel remarks that many words in the Septuagint, especially such words as Γάζα and Γόμορρα, prove almost to a demonstration that the present pronunciation of γ by the modern Greeks must have prevailed in the time of the translators of the Septuagint√

We said that γ, when followed by another γ, κ, ξ, or χ takes the sound of *v*. This is evident from the way in which the Romans used to write such Greek words, i. e. ἄγγελος, *angelus*. Again, in very old inscriptions we find that the Greeks were wont to write γ before κ, whilst the Romans express the sound of the letter γ by ν, i. e. in a very old coin the city ΖΑΓΚΛΗ is written in Latin *ZANKLE*.

Again, in very old MS. we see that the Greeks were wont to write γ instead of ν before γ, κ, ξ, and χ not only in synthesis, but also "ἐν παραθέσει," i. e. καλὸγ κ' ἀγαθὸν, instead of καλὸν κ' ἀγαθόν; ἐγ χορὸν, instead of ἐν χορόν; ἐγ καρὸς, instead of ἐν καρὸς (ἐν καρὸς αἴση, Homer), whence resulted the synthetic noun ἔγκαρ, ἔγκαρος (just as the old grammarians were wont to read this Homeric passage). Now, many of the followers of Erasmus blame the Greek grammarians because they said that the letter ν before γ, κ, and ξ is changed in the synthetic words into γ. "What is the use," they say, "of changing ν into a γ and then pronouncing it like ν? Must not the ν always remain a ν?" We say, No! "διὰ τὴν (according to Aristotle) ἀηδῆ τῶν φθόγγων προσβολήν."

Finally, the forms γερακαραίας and γεράκων = ἱερακαρέας and ἱεράκων, and others we might enumerate show that the letter γ ought never to be sounded like the hard g of the English.

EXAMPLES OF PRONUNCIATION.

Γαλακτοποσία, ghalaktoposiah.	Γηγενής, yeyenís.
Γαλατία, ghalatéah.	Γηθαλέος, yethaléos.
Γαλάκτωσις, ghaláktosis.	Γεῦμα, yévmah.
Γόνος, ghónos.	Γεῦσις, yéfsis.
Γονοκτονέω, ghonoktonéoh.	Γευστικός, yefstikós.
Γόμφος, gómphos.	Γεῖσον, yéson.
Γωνία, ghonéah.	Γειτονία, yetoniah.
Γωλεός, gholeós.	Γοῖ, yéē.
Γωνιασμός, ghoniasmós.	Ἄγγαρος, áhngharos.
Γαῦρος, gávros.	Ἀγγεῖον, ahnghéon.
Γαύραξ, ghávrax.	Ἀγγελία, ahnghelía.
Γαυλός, ghavlós.	Ἀγκύλος, ahnghélos.
Γουννός, ghounós.	Ἄγκυρα, áhngherah.
Γούνατα, ghoúnatah.	Ἀγκυλόκωλος, ahnghelókolos.
Γουνοπαχής, ghounopahés.	Ἄγξις, áhnxis.
Γένος, yénos.	Ἀγχίτοκος, ahnchítokos.
Γεντιανή, yentiané.	Ἀγχόη, ahnchóe.
Γέννημα, yénemah.	Ἀγχόνη, ahnchóne.
Γήδιον, yéthion.	Ἀγχότατος, ahnchótatos.

Δ

is pronounced like *th* in *this, that.* The use of σδ, δδ, δ, instead of ζ, as in κωμμάδδειν, λάδδοιτο, μουσίδδει (= μυθίζει), πλαγιάδδοντες, φαιρίδδειν (σφαιρίζειν), μᾶδδαν, χρήδδεται, etc.; Σδεύς (Ζεύς), σδυγός, σδεύγλα, ὅσδος, κωμάσδω, φροντίσδω, ὀνομάσδω, εἰκάσδω, etc.; δυζόν, δυμόν, Δεύς, etc., — which forms were in use among many tribes of ancient Greece, such as the Spartans, the Megarians, the Bœotians, as well as the Æolians and Dorians, — proves most conclusively that the pronunciation of δ used by the modern Greeks was prevalent among the tribes we have enumerated, long before the time of Alexander. As ζ had a "hissing sound" (συριστικός), its dialectic substitute δ should have a similar sound (ὁμοιόφθογγος); but if δ were pronounced as a *d*, it could never be interchanged with ζ. But we cannot agree with Oekonomos that the pronunciation of δ, as pronounced by the modern Greeks, was prevalent "throughout Greece," in the very acme of the Hellenic language. On the contrary, we have reason to believe that this soft (*douce*), so to speak, pronunciation of δ was simply dialectic and not general. There are many words in modern Greek, in which δ sounds exactly as a *d*, from which it seems to us that originally the pronunciation of δ as a *d* was not uncommon among the ancient Greeks. For instance:

Δένδρον,	pronounced	*thendron.*
Ἄνδρας,	"	*ándras.*
Ἄνδρος,	"	*ándros.*
Ἀνδριώτης,	"	*andriótes.*
Ἀνδρειωμένος,	"	*andrioménos.*

Now, whenever the letter δ is preceded by a ν, the modern Greeks pronounce it as a *d*; in every other case it has its soft sound.) The different changes of the letter δ into various consonants are still prevalent in modern Greek. In ancient Greek we get the forms σάνδαλον changed into σάμβαλον; ὀδελός for ὀβελός, Δεὺς for Ζεύς, ἀρίζηλος for ἀρίδηλος, δέλω for θέλω, ἤδω for γήθω, etc. In modern Greek we get ζορκάδιον for δορκάδιον, γιερὸς for διερός, etc.

EXAMPLES OF PRONUNCIATION.

In giving these examples we thought that it might be of interest to the scholar to give a few words peculiar to the conversational style of the Greeks. Now, it must not be supposed that these words or forms are in common use in the language of literature and of educated men. The cultivated language for the most part, as Geldart affirms, preserves the grammatical forms of the age of Thucydides, avoiding most of the innovations of the later Attic dialect, as, for instance, θάλαττα for θάλασσα, or Χερρόνησος for Χερσόνησος. The scholar familiar with classical Greek, by using the modern Greek pronunciation and observing the following peculiarities chiefly noticed in the language of the common people, will find himself able to converse easily with those to whom the Greek is vernacular.

α′) Strictly speaking there are but four cases in the language of the PEOPLE. The Nominative, Genitive, Accusative, and Vocative.

β′) δόξα and words like it make in the Genitive τῆς δόξας, and are declined as follows:

S. N. V. δόξα	Μοῦσα	P. N. A. V. δόξαι(s)	Μοῦσαι(s)
G. δόξας	Μούσας	G. δοξῶν	Μουσῶν
A. δόξα(ν)	Μοῦσα(ν)⁻		

	Honor.	Opinion.
S. N. V.	Τιμή	Γνώμη
G.	Τιμῆς	Γνώμης
A.	Τιμή(ν)	Γνώμη
P. N. A. V.	Τιμαί(s)	Γνῶμαι(s)
G.	Τιμῶν	Γνωμῶν

γ′) A host of nouns belonging to different declensions are made to follow but one: thus, Ταμίας, Ἅλυς, Μάρτις or Μάρτης,

etc. are in the Singular number all declined alike; namely,
by cutting off the sign of the Nomi. ative -ς, in the Genitive
and Vocative, and changing it to ν in the Accusative. This
ν is dropped in pronunciation when the phonetic laws of the
language admit it (Geldart).

δ') All adjectives in ος have three endings: ος, η, ον. When
ος is preceded by a vowel, the Feminine ends in α. The accent of adjectives in ος always retains its original place:

S. N.	σοφός	σοφή	σοφό(ν)
G.	σοφοῦ	σοφῆς	σοφοῦ
A.	σοφό(ν)	σοφή(ν)	σοφό(ν)
V.	σοφέ		
P. N. A.	σοφοί	σοφαί(ς)	σοφά
G.	σοφῶν	σοφῶν	σοφῶν
A.	σοφούς	σοφᾶς	σοφά

S. N.	μόνος	μόνη	μόνο(ν)
G.	μόνου	μόνης	μόνου
A.	μόνο(ν)	μόνη(ν)	μόνο(ν)
P. N. V.	μόνοι	μόναι(ς)	μόνα
G.	μόνων	μόνων	μόνων
A.	μόνους	μόνας	μόνα

ε') The Plural of many words, especially of those of foreign
origin, is formed by adding -δες to the stem, as πασάδες from
πασᾶς, μαϊμοῦδες from ἡ μαϊμοῦ (*monkey*). These Plurals are
always paroxytone, whatever the accent of the word in the
Singular (Geldart).

ζ') The comparative is sometimes formed by means of
πλέον, *more*, as πλέον μεγάλος = *greater*, πλέον πλούσιος =
richer.

η') Metaplastic nouns or secondary formations are common,
as ἡ αἶγα (*the goat*), ὁ πατέρας (*father*), ὁ βασιλέας (*king*):

S. N.	πατέρας	βασιλέας
G.	πατέρα	βασιλέα
A.	πατέρα(ν)	βασιλέα(ν)
V.	πατέρα	βασιλέα

P. N. A. V. πατέρες   βασιλέες
    G. πατέρων   βασιλέων

The classical forms, however, ὁ πατήρ, πατέρος, and ὁ βασιλεύς, βασιλέως, etc., are still more prevalent.

6′) Of the pronouns ἐμὲ often appears as ἐμένα, σὲ as ἐσὲ and ἐσένα; ἡμεῖς often becomes ἐμεῖς, and in the Accusative both ἐμᾶς and μᾶς. The latter, used as an enclitic, supplies the place both of ἡμᾶς and ἡμῶν. Ὑμεῖς becomes σεῖς and ἐσεῖς, Accusative and enclitic possessive σᾶς, σας. The article, as enclitic and proclitic, is used for the personal pronoun in oblique cases (Geldart).

Personal Pronouns.

S. N. ἐγώ,	γώ.			ἐσύ.		
G. ἐμένα, '	μένα,	μοῦ.		ἐσένα,	σένα,	σοῦ.
A. ἐμένα,	μένα,	μέ.		ἐσένα,	σίνα,	σέ.
P. N. ἡμεῖς,	ἐμεῖς,	μεῖς.		ἐσεῖς,	σεῖς	
G. ἡμᾶς,	ἐμᾶς,	μᾶς.		ἐσᾶς,	σᾶς	
A. ἡμᾶς,	ἐμᾶς,	μᾶς.		ἐσᾶς,	σᾶς	

The verb εἰμί is thus conjugated :

S. εἶμαι,	εἶσαι,	εἶνε.
P. εἴμεθα,	εἶσθε,	εἶνε.

Imperfect Indicative.

S. ἤμην,	ἦσο,	ἦτο(ν).
P. ἤμεθα,	ἦστε,	ἦσαν.

Future Indicative.

S. θὰ ἦμαι,	θὰ ἦσαι,	θὰ ἦνε.
P. θὰ ἤμεθα,	θὰ ἦσθε,	θὰ ἦνε.

Also,

S. θέλω εἶσθαι,	θέλεις εἶσθαι,	θέλει εἶσθαι.
P. θέλομεν εἶσθαι,	θέλετε εἶσθαι,	θέλουν εἶσθαι.

Subjunctive.

S. ἦμαι,	ἦσαι,	ἦνε.
P. ἤμεθα,	ἦθσε,	ἦνε.

Future Subjunctive.

S. ἤθελα εἶσθαι,   ἤθελες εἶσθαι,   ἤθελεν εἶσθαι.
P. ἠθέλαμεν εἶσθαι,   ἠθέλετε εἶσθαι,   ἤθελαν εἶσθαι.

Also,

S. θὰ ἤμουν,   θὰ ἤσουν,   θὰ ἦτον.
P. θὰ ἤμεθα,   θὰ ἦσθε,   θὰ ἦσαν.

Imperative.

S. ἔσο,   ἂς ἦνε.
P.   ἂς ἦνε.

Infinitive.

Present εἶσθαι or εἶσται, only after the auxiliary θέλω.

Participle.

Present ὄντας, indeclinable.

γράφουσι becomes γράφουν; for ἔγραφον we have ἔγραφα; for ἔγραψας, ἔγραψες; for ἐγράψατε, ἐγράψετε. In the passive instead of γράφῃ or γράφει we find γράφεσαι; for γραφόμεθα, γραφόμεστε. In like manner for λεγόμεθα we find λεγόμεστε, λεγόμασταν, and various other forms down to the tragic λεγόμεσθα.

For ἐγράφθην we get ἐγράφθηκα; for ἐγράφθημεν, ἐγραφθήκαμεν; for ἐγράφθησαν, ἐγράφθηκαν.

In the present tense of contracted verbs in άω, ῶ, the third person is often uncontracted, as ἀγαπάει for ἀγαπᾶ. Τιμῶσι appears sometimes as τιμοῦν or τιμοῦνε. Τιμοῦμεν appears sometimes for τιμῶμεν.

Such are the main features of modern Greek accidence. Professor Geldart states that even with these peculiarities the modern Greek may be called the logical result of ancient Greek. "For turning to the pronouns we observe that ἐμένα and ἐσένα, for ἐμὲ and σὲ, preserve the original ν (in Sanscrit m, mâm and tvâm) of the Accusative. Ἐμεῖς is referred to by Plato (Crat. 418, c) as an older form for ἡμεῖς. As to the enclitic and proclitic use of the article it is (except for the

accent in the latter case) the same as the Homeric usage,
e. g. τὸν ἐσκότωσε, *he killed him;* ἀπεσύλησέ τους, *he spoiled
them.* Passing to the verbs we find· in λέγουν (λέγουσι) ,or
λέγουνε the traces of the old form λέγοντι (ἔχονι, Professor Geldart thinks, is quoted by Hesychius as a Cretan form). In
the passive voice the forms λέγεσαι, 2d person present, λεγό-
μαστε or λεγόμεθα, as well as λεγόμεθεν, are so plainly Archaic
forms that they need no explanation. In St. Paul's Epistle
to the Romans we have καυχᾶσαι, *thou boastest.* In the imperative aorist active λέξε for λέξον is Homeric. As to the
imperative aorist passive λέξου, I cannot but agree with Dr.
Mullach "that it is the classical middle 1st aorist imperative
of a verb in μι used as a passive, there being no middle voice
in modern Greek. Few who compare such forms as στάσο
with the corresponding modern στάσου, δέξου, etc. will be able
to doubt this." We now proceed with our examples of pronunciation :

Δείχνω (com. for δεικνύω),	*théchno.*
Δαμάσκηνον, *prune,*	*thamáskenon.*
Δενδράκι, *a small tree,*	*thendráke.*
Δέρνω, *to strike,*	*thérno.*
Δέσποινα, *mistress,*	*théspena.*
Δημοδιδάσκαλος, *a teacher of a common school,*	*themothitháskalos.*
Διάβολος, *devil,*	*theávolos.*
Διαβόητος, *famous,*	*theavóetos.*
Διαγωγὴ, *conduct,*	*theagoyé.*

Classical.

Δεξίμηλος, *thexímelos.*	Διασηκόω, *theasekóo.*
Διαπόντιος, *theapóndios.*	Διάνοια, *theánea.*
Διαπλήσσω, *theapléso.*	Διάμετρος, *theámetros.*
Διαπίμπλημι, *theapímpleme.*	Διέρχομαι, *theérchome.*
Διαρρυδᾶν, *thearrethán.*	Δίκαιος, *thékeos.*
Διασημαίνω, *theaseméno.*	Δικαιόπολις, *thekeópolis.*

Z

is pronounced like *z* or like the French *s* in the word *rose.*
Dionysius of Halicarnassus and Sextus Empiricus say that ζ

results from σδ, not δσ. Thus the forms Ἀθήναζε, Θήβαζε, θύ-
ραζε, χαμᾶζε, βύζην, evidently resulted from Ἀθήνασδε, Θήβασδε,
θύρασδε χαμάσδε, βύσδην. The followers of Erasmus maintain
that ζ results from δσ. It is quite probable that they were
misled by the supposed resemblance to the Latin z. It is
worth while, however, to consider that Quintilian remarks:
"The Latin language has no letter by which to translate the
Greek ζ, because the ζ of the Greeks sounds melodious and
sweet, but that of the Romans, rough and unmusical; and
the sweet-sounding words Ζώπυρον and Ζέφυρος, translated in
Latin *Zopyrum* and *Zephyrus*, emit but a harsh and barbarous sound."

However, the truth is that not only the Erasmians, but
Dionysius of Halicarnassus and Sextus Empiricus are alike
mistaken in their views of ζ. The letter ζ is not a double
consonant, as is evident from the following Homeric passages: Il. β, 824, οἳ δὲ Ζέλειαν; 634, οἵ τε Ζάκυνθον; δ, 103, 121,
ἄστυ Ζελείης; Od. I. 24, ὑλήεσσα Ζάκυνθος; etc., in which ζ has
the force of a *single* letter and, consequently, does not render
the syllable long by position. Nor does it seem etymolog-
ically to have resulted from δσ, because if this was true we
ought to have from the forms ἐλπίδσι, ποδσί, ἤλπιδσα, ἐκόμιδσα,
etc., ἐλπίζι, ποζί, ἤλπιζα, ἐκόμιζα, and not, as we have, ἐλπίσι,
ποσί, ἤλπισα, ἐκόμισα. Finally, Professor Mavrophredes says
that the only forms in which ζ seems to have resulted from
two letters, e. g. σδ, are simply those mentioned by Dionysius
and which we have already enumerated. Schleicher also
completely discards the notion of pronouncing ζ as δσ or σδ.

The ancient Greeks used to boast of the pretty sound of ζ
(Dion. Comp. 14, p. 172, Scäf.), and a comparison of the Greek
pronunciation with that of the Western nations will convince
anybody that the modern Greek pronunciation is by far the
softer, and consequently it distinctly verifies the statements
of both Quintilian and Dionysius. The forms νίβγω, νιβῶ,
νίζω, τρίβω, τρίβγω, τριβιῶ, τρίζω, μασδὸς, μαζός, φράδω, φράζω

are still prevalent. Again,. the θεὺς (θεὸς) and Διεὺς, Lat. *Deus*, for Ζεὺς, ἀρίζηλος for ἀρίδηλος, etc. show how easily the letter ζ passed into δ. These different changes are very common in modern Greek and we also get the forms διατάζω for διατάγω, Γαλάζιος for Γαλάγιος, etc. The change of σ into ζ, as mentioned by Liddell and Scott, is evident from the examples Ζιβίνη, Σιβύνη; Ζμύρνα, Σμύρνα; etc.

Professor Geldart says the fact that σ before μ invariably sounds as ζ in modern Greek ought to prove the identity of the sound of ζ in ancient and modern times. But Professor Geldart must certainly be mistaken, since the letter σ does not *always* sound as ζ before μ; and with the exception of the word Σμύρνη, where the sound of σ approximates that of ζ, we know of no other instance in modern Greek where the letter σ is sounded like a ζ. For instance, the words Σμῆνος (*sménos*) and Σμυρναῖος (*smernéos*) show decidedly that the letter σ is not sounded like a ζ; if there are any instances in which σ sounds like a ζ before μ, these instances are certainly dialectic and not general. On the contrary, the similarity of the changes of the letter ζ in ancient and modern Greek, and, moreover, the softness of its pronunciation by the modern Greeks, prove the identity of the sound of ζ in ancient and modern times.

EXAMPLES OF PRONUNCIATION.
Modern Greek.

Ζῶον, *animal*,	*zóön.*
Ζωντανὸς, *alive*,	*zondanós.*
Ζῦθος, *beer*,	*zéthos.*
Ζωηρὸς, *quick, lively*,	*zoërós.*
Ζήτημα, *question*; τὸ ᾿Ανατολικὸν ζήτημα, the *Eastern Question*,	*tó anatolikón zélema.*
Ζάχαρι, *sugar*,	*záhare.*
Ζεστὸς, η, ον, *warm*,	*zestós.*
Ζορκάδι (ἡ Δορκάς),	*zorkáthe.*
Ζημία, *loss, damage*,	*zemíah.*

Classical.

Ζωοστάσιον, *zoöstáseon.*	Ζοφερύς, *zopherós.*
Ζωογόνος, *zoögónos.*	Ζηλήμων, *zelémon.*
Ζωοφάγος, *zoöphágos.*	Ζηλομανής, *zelomanís.*
Ζωρός, *zorós.*	Ζηλότυπος, *zelótepos.*
Ζωστήρ, *zostér.*	

Θ

is pronounced like *th* in the words *thin, thick, think.* θ was
changed into σ in the Laconian dialect. We have, for
instance, in Aristophanes, Thucydides, and several other
authors the forms σέλει, σέτω, σηροκτόνε, σιγῆν, ἀγασός, ὀρσά,
'Ασάνα 'Ασαναῖοι, "τῶ σιῶ σύματος," Σειδέκτας, Σείπομπος, Σήριπ-
πος, instead of the forms θέλει, θέτω, θηροκτόνε, θιγῆν, ἀγαθός,
ὀρθή, 'Αθάνα, etc., τοῦ θεοῦ θύματος, Θεοδέκτας, Θεόπομπος, Θή-
ριππος.

In modern Greek we have ἀκαντσόχοιρος for ἀκανθόχοιρος,
etc.

Besides this pronunciation of *th* the letter θ must have been
also originally sounded among some tribes of ancient Greece
like τη, judging from the fact that this pronunciation of τη is
even to this day preserved in a number of words, especially
"ἐν τοῖς συνδυασμοῖς" χτ, φτ, στ, instead of χθ, φθ, σθ; for instance:

'Επλέχτηκα, *eplécteka,*	instead of	'Επλέχθην,
'Εχτές, *echtés,*	"	'Εχθές,
Φτάνω, *phtáno,*	"	Φθάνω,
'Εγράφτηκα, *egráphtekah,*	"	'Εγράφθην,
'Εγνωρίστηκα, *egnorísteka,*	"	'Εγνωρίσθην,
'Ασθενής, *astenés,*	"	'Ασθενής,
'Οχτρός, *ochtrós,*	"	'Εχθρός.

Again, in the Latin language θ is rendered by *th*, e. g. *Ther-
situs, Thyesta, Theopompus, Ægisthus.* It must be interesting to the reader to notice how faithfully the modern
Greeks have preserved the pronunciation of their ancestors,

so that traces of the various dialectic sounds of the letters are still in use.

EXAMPLES OF PRONUNCIATION.

Modern Greek.

Θεία, *aunt,*	*théa.*	Θρησκεία, *religion,*	*threskéa.*
Θάλαμος, *chamber,*	*thálamos.*	Θρόνος, *throne,*	*thrónos.*
Θόρυβος, *tumult,*	*thórevos.*	Θυμὸς, *anger,*	*themós.*
Θρῆνος, *lamentation,*	*thrénos.*		

Classical.

Θηλύγλωσσος, *theléglossos.*		Θυροκοπέω, *therokopéo.*	
Θηλυδρίας, *thelethrías.*		Θυροκόπος, *therokópos.*	
Θηλάζω, *thelázo.*		Θυρσαχθής, *thersachthís.*	
Θηκτός, *thektós.*		Θύννος, *thénos.*	

K

before α, ο, ω, αυ, ου is pronounced like *k*; but before ε, ι, υ, η, αι, ει, οι, and before liquids it becomes much softer and has a guttural sound. This letter was interchanged in ancient Greek with τ; for instance, we have Τίμων (*Tímon*) for Κίμων (*Kímon*), πόκε (*póke*) for πότε (*póte*), κίς for τίς (*tís*). So in modern Greek we have the forms σκιλβόω (*skilvóo*) for στιλβόω (*stelvóo*), φκυάριον (*phkeárion*) for φτυάριον (*phteáreon*), etc. The old Attics often changed χ into κ; thus, χνόος and κνόος, etc.; this peculiarity is still prevalent among the modern Greeks. The change of κ into β, as mentioned by Liddell and Scott, is more rare as in τήκω, Lat. *tabeo*. In a few instances π and κ are also found interchanged in ancient as well as in modern times, but these forms are comparatively rare.

EXAMPLES OF PRONUNCIATION.

Modern Greek.

Κορδέλλα, *ribbon,*	*korthéla.*
Κόρφος, *bosom,*	*kórphos.*

Κορμὶ (σῶμα), body, kormé.
Κουβαλῶ, to move furniture, koovaló.
Κόττα (ὄρνιθα), hen, kóta.
Κρεββάτι, bed, kreváte.

Classical.

Καθαρπάζω, katharpázo. Κλεψίφρων, klepsíphron.
Καθέλκω, kathélko. Κλεψίνοος, klepsínoös.
Κάθεξις, káthexis. Κλεψίρρυτος, klepsíretos.
Κάθεμα, káthema.

Λ

is pronounced like an *l*. Of the so-called liquid letters the letter ρ is both the oldest and hardest, but λ is what Professor Mavrophredes terms "μεταγενέστερος" (*more recent*) and "μαλακώτερος" (*softer*). Plato attributes *gliding* or *slipperiness* to λ. "The sweetest of semivowels," says Dionysius of Halicarnassus. "Ἡδύνει μὲν γὰρ (τὴν ἀκοὴν) τὸ λ καὶ ἔστι τῶν ἡμιφώνων γλυκύτατον· τραχύνει δὲ τὸ ρ καὶ ἔστι τῶν ὁμογενῶν γενναιότατον. (π. συνθ. ὀνομ. 14.) Compare Eusthatius, p. 1106.

The letter λ is often written instead of *ν* and ρ, e. g. ἦνθον φίντατος for ἦλθον φίλτατος, κρίβανος for κλίβανος. In some words γ and λ are interchanged, i. e. μόγις and μόλις. These changes are not uncommon in modern Greek.

That the letter λ is not as old as the letter ρ is evident from the fact that the latter is more generally used in the old languages, such as are related to the Greek and Latin, as well as from its extensive use in many hard and, so to speak, rough-sounding dialects. We are indebted to Professor Mavrophredes for the following examples which decidedly prove that instead of the Greek and Latin λανθάνω, *lateo;* φλέγω, *fulgeo;* λείπω, *linquo;* πλέκω, *plecto;* πέλεκυς, λύκος, *lupus;* ὅλος, τοῦ ὁσκικοῖ, *sollus;* πλατύς, *latus;* ἥλιος, *sol;* πολύς, πόλις, etc. we have the Sanscr. *rahâmi* (ἐγκαταλείπω), *bhragâmi, rêk'âmi, prnak'mi, paraçus, vrkas, sarvàs, prthus, sûrjas* (from *svârjas*), *parus, purî.* In like manner we get

in Greek from the one root κρυ the two words κλύω and ἀκρο-
ῶμαι (= ἀ-κ-ροϝ-α-ομαι); from the root πρα (πληροῦν) we have
πίμπλημι and πίμπρημι; from ραγ, ἀρκέω (ἀρήγω) and ἀλέξω;
from μαργ (Sanscr. mrg´) we have ἀμέργω (modern ἀρμέγω)
and ἀμέλγω; from the root ρυκ we have λύχνος and ῥύχνος
(this latter form is peculiar to the inhabitants of the island
of Chio); from γαρ we get γαρύω (γηρύω), γρῶσσα = γλῶσσα
(in the Tsakonian dialect) and γελάω, etc. These examples
show that ρ is an older and harder letter than λ.

EXAMPLES OF PRONUNCIATION.
Modern Greek.

Λάσπη, *mud*,	*láspe.*	Λερόνω, *to soil*,	*leróno.*
Λατρεία, *adoration*,	*latréa.*	Λυόνω, *to dissolve*,	*leóno.*
Λειποθυμῶ, *faint*,	*lipothemó.*	Λύπη, *sorrow*,	*lépe.*
Λεμόνι, *lemon*,	*lemóni.*		

Classical.

Λευκανία, *lephkanía.*	Λαοτρόφος, *laotróphos.*
Λέπω, *lépo.*	Λανθάνω, *lanthάno.*
Λέσβιος, *lésvios.*	Λάπη, *lápe.*
Λαπαρός, *laparós.*	Λάσανον, *lásanon.*

M

is pronounced like *m* in *man*. There is no dispute concerning the pronunciation of this letter and the same dialectic
changes which occur in ancient Greek, such as μ into π and
μ into β, i. e. βροτός, μορτός, etc., are not uncommon in modern Greek.

EXAMPLES OF PRONUNCIATION.
Modern Greek.

Μεταξὺ, *meanwhile*, etc.	*metaxí.*
Μεταφράζω, *to translate*,	*metáphrázo.*
Μεσάνυκτα, *midnight*,	*mesánecta.*
Μεταβάπτω, *to paint over*,	*metavápto.*
Μηδαμινὸς, *a man of no importance*,	*mithaminós.*
Μῆκος, *length*,	*mékos.*

Classical.

Μηνυτής, *minitis.*	Μῆτις, *mitis.*
Μήνυτρον, *mínitron.*	Μήστωρ, *mistor.*
Μήνιμα, *mínima.*	Μηρύομαι, *miríome.*
Μηνίσκος, *miniskos.*	Μήτρα, *mítra.*
Μητίομαι, *mitiome.*	Μεγάθυμος, *megáthimos.*

N

is pronounced like *n* in *now, never.* There is no difference of opinion as to the pronunciation of this letter, and the euphonic changes, such as ν into γ before the palatals γ, κ, χ, and ξ, and ν into μ before the labials β, π, φ, ψ, and ν into λ before another λ, and ν into ρ before another ρ, etc., are still prevalent in modern Greek.

EXAMPLES OF PRONUUCIATION.

Modern Greek.

Νεροχύτης, *sink,*	nerohétes.	Νύχι, *nail,*	néhi.
Νερὸν, *water,*	nerón.	Νουνὸς, *godfather,*	nounós.
Νίπτω, *to wash,*	nípto.	Νυστάζω, *to be sleepy,*	nistázo.
Νήπιος, *baby (silly),*	nípios.	Νεκρός, *a dead man,*	nechrós.

Classical.

Νάπη, *nápe.*		Ναοπόλος, *naopólos.*	
Νάρκισσος, *nárkissós.*		Ναοφύλαξ, *naophélahx.*	
Νᾶμα, *náma.*		Ναρδίτης, *narthítis.*	
Ναννιόν, *nanión.*		Νάρδος, *nárthos.*	

Ξ

The common sound of this letter is that of *x* in *axiom*, but much harder. After γ, ν, μ it generally has the sound of *gs*, e. g. τὸν ξένον (pronounced *tòn gsénon*). The pronunciation of ζ, ξ, and ψ by the modern Greeks entirely verifies the statements of Dionysius of Halicarnassus and of Phrynichus. Dionysius says: " Τριῶν δὲ ὄντων τῶν ἄλλων γραμμάτων ἃ δὴ διπλᾶ καλεῖται, τὸ μὲν ζ μᾶλλον ἡδύνει τὴν ἀκοὴν τῶν ἑτέρων · τὸ μὲν γὰρ ξ διὰ τοῦ κ, τὸ δὲ ψ διὰ τοῦ π τὸν συριγμὸν ἀποδίδωσι, ψιλῶν ὄντων ἀμφοτέρων. .... Phrynichus says: "*Nam multo molliorem sonem habet ψ quam* PS *vel* BS *sicut ergo ψ melius (mollius?) sonat, sic etiam* x *quam* GS *vel* CS. Its dialectic changes, especially transposition in the Æolic and Doric, of the consonants which form ξ, as ξίφος, ξιφύδριον, Dor. σκίφος, σκιφύδριον, are obsolete in modern Greek.

EXAMPLES OF PRONUNCIATION.

Modern Greek.

Ξερνῶ, *to vomit,*	xernó.	Ξηραίνω, *to dry,*	xiréno.
Ξηρὸς, *dry,*	xirós.	Ξεσκέπαστος, *uncovered,*	xesképahstos.
Ξοινὺς, *sower,*	xenós.	Ξεπερνῶ, *to surpass,*	xepernó.

Classical.

Ξάνθος, *xánthos.*	Ξυνός, *xinós.*
Ξανθόουλος, *xanthóoulos.*	Ξυνήων, *xiníon.*
Ξενότιμος, *xenótimos.*	Ξυλοφανής, *xilophanís.*
Ξενοτροφέω, *xenotrophéo.*	

Π

has the power of an English *p*, but when it follows μ or ν it takes the sound of *b*. In modern as in ancient Greek it is sometimes interchanged with soft β, as in πάλλω, βάλλω, and the aspirate φ, as πανός, φανός.

EXAMPLES OF PRONUNCIATION.

Modern Greek.

Παραφρονῶ, *to despise,*	paraphronó.
Παρειὰ, *cheek,*	parià.
Παρεκλήσιον, *a country-church,*	pareklésion.
Παραπόρτι, *a back-door,*	parapórti.
Παραιτῶ, *to give up,*	paretó.
Πάππος, *grandfather,*	pápos.
Παντοῦ, *everywhere,*	pandoú.
Παραβλέπω, *to neglect,*	paravlépo.
Παληκάρι, *a brave young man,*	palikári.

Παρατριβή, *paratrivé.*	Παραχορδίζω, *parahorthízo.*
Παρατύπωσις, *paratéposis.*	Παραχέω, *parahéo.*
Παρατροπή, *paratropé.*	Παρέκ, *parék.*
Παράτρητος, *parátretos.*	Πάρεκβαίνω, *parekvéno.*
Παρατρέχω, *paratrého.*	Παρέκβασις, *parékvasis.*
Παρατρέφω, *paratrépho.*	Παρεκβολή, *parekvolé.*
Παραψαλίζω, *parapsalizo.*	Παρενόχλησις, *parenóchlesis.*
Παραψάλλω, *parapsállo.*	Παρεμβολή, *paremvolé.*

P

is pronounced like the English *r,* but with more force. Plato says that in the utterance of ρ the tongue is in a state of *vibration.* Dionysius calls it a "rough letter": "Τραχύνει δὲ τὸ ρ καὶ ἔστι τῶν ὁμογενῶν γενναιότατον."

The letter ρ was always sounded *hard* at the beginning of a word, with the exception of the two words ῥάρος and ῥάριον (Ὑμνω εἰς Δημ. 450), both of which have the smooth breathing. This is evident from the fact that the letter ρ, when at the beginning of a word, always had the rough breathing, as well as from its doubling when preceded by a vowel, e. g. ῥίπτω, ῥάπτω, ῥητός, ἔρριπτον, ἔρραψα, ἄρρητος. A scholar intimates that the rough breathing received by this reduplication a certain "solidity and concentration."

Hence it becomes evident that the rule of the grammarians — "Τὸ ῥῶ ἐὰν δισσὸν γένηται ἐν μέσῃ λέξει, τὸ μὲν πρῶτον ψιλοῦται, τὸ δὲ δεύτερον δασύνεται: οἶον ἐπίρρημα, ἄρρωστος, συρράπτω, etc., ψιλοῦται δὲ τὸ μὲν πρῶτον, διότι οὐδέποτε συλλαβὴ Ἑλληνικῆς λέξεως εἰς δασὺ λήγει. Τὸ δὲ δεύτερον δασύνεται, διότι φίλαρχός ἐστιν ἡ δασεῖα!" — is not after all, as a modern Greek intimates, much of a rule. Because, whilst the letter ρ at the beginning of a word, both by its rough breathing and hard sound, renders the final vowel of a preceding word in the dactylic hexameter and the iambic trimeter of the dramatists as well as in the anapæsts long by position, as in Il. ω, 755:

"Πολλὰ ῥυστάζεσκεν ἑοῦ περὶ σῆμ' ἑτάροιο!"

it often happens that for the sake of the meter in the same word the letter ρ is not doubled though a vowel precedes it, as is evident from the Homeric ἔρεζον, ἔρεξε, ἀμφιρύτη; also in Soph. Antig. 950:

"Καὶ Ζηνὸς ταμιεύεσκε γονὰς χρυσορύτους,"

and in Aristoph. Θεσμ. 655, διάριψον, and so on.

The rough breathing of ρ at the beginning of a word has often, as Professor Mavrophredes asserts, an etymological signification; that is to say, it takes the place of some omitted consonant, e. g. ῥέπω = Sanscr. *sarpâmi*, Lat. *serpo;* ῥοφέω, Lat. *sorbeo;* ῥήγνυμι, Lat. *frango;* ῥιγέω, Lat. *frigeo;* ῥῖν(s), Sanscr. *ghrâna-m;* ῥῖπος = Lat. *scirpus;* ῥόδον, Æol. βρόδον; ῥινός = Ϝρινός; ῥέγχω = Ϝρέγχω, Lat. *rugio;* etc.

In modern Greek, although ρ is pronounced more strongly than the English *r*, the rough breathing of the letter ρ at the beginning of a word is entirely lost.

EXAMPLES OF PRONUNCIATION.

Modern Greek.

῾Ράχη, *back,*	*ráhe.*
῾Ροχαλίζω, *to snore,*	*rohalízo.*
῾Ροδάκινον, *peach,*	*rothákinon.*
῾Ρουχικὰ, *clothes,*	*roohiká.*
῾Ροπαλον, *a club* (to strike with),	*rópalon.*
῾Ράπτρια, *seamstress,*	*ráptria.*

Classical.

῾Ρᾳθυμία, *rathemía.*	῾Ράπτης, *ráptis.*
῾Ρᾴδιος, *ráthios.*	῾Ραπτός, *raptós.*
῾Ράσσω, *rásso.*	῾Ραμφή, *ramphé.*
῾Ραφιδοθήκη, *raphithothéke.*	῾Ράμνος, *rámnos.*
῾Ράσμα, *rásma.*	῾Ρέπω, *répo.*

Σ

is pronounced like *s* in *soon, see.* Plato calls σ an aspirate, and Dionysius a *hissing* and *disagreeable* letter.

A scholar says that in modern Greek the letter σ before a semivowel (β, γ, δ, ζ, λ, μ, ν, ρ) is sounded like a ζ. So also in the proclitics τούς, τάς before the same consonants; τοὺς βασιλεῖς τῆς γῆς = *touz vaselēs tez ghés*.

But this is not so. The letter σ does not sound in *modern Greek* like a ζ before the letters mentioned. The statement in "modern Greek" is too broad. This pronunciation is simply dialectic and not general. Now, the letter σ was pronounced like a ζ among some tribes of ancient Greece especially before the letters γ, δ, β, and before the liquids λ, ρ, μ. Thus, we find in many inscriptions belonging to the first century A. D. many words written with a ζ instead of a σ; e. g. Ζμάραγδος, Ζμύρνη, Ζμικρός, Ζβέσαι. The writer Lucian also in his "ἐν τῇ δίκῃ τῶν φωνηέντων" represents the letter σ as complaining of ζ and saying, "ὅτι δ' ἀνεξίκακόν εἰμι γράμμα μαρτυρεῖτέ μοι καὶ αὐτοί, μηδέποτε ἐγκαλέσαντι τῷ ζῆτα **σμάραγδον** ἀποσπάσαντι καὶ πᾶσαν ἀφελομένῳ τὴν Σμύρνην." Compare Eustathius (pp. 217, 228) and Sextus Empiricus, etc. We must not omit to mention that we have no proof that this dialectic pronunciation of σ was prevalent among the tribes of ancient Greece, and in the very best period of the Hellenic language. Now, this dialectic pronunciation of σ, which prevails in some sections of modern Greece, certainly proves that the modern Greeks have not only preserved the pronunciation of their ancestors, but even their dialectic variations.

EXAMPLES OF PRONUNCIATION.

Modern Greek.

Στρήφω, *to twist*,	strépho.	Στόλος, *a fleet*,	stólos.
Στοίχημα, *a bet*,	stéhema.	Σύγχυσις, *a confusion*,	sénhesis.
Στερῶ, *to deprive*,	sterró.		

Classical.

Σκληρός, *sklerós*.	Σκινθαρίζω, *skintharízo*.
Σκιρτάω, *skirtáo*.	Σκινδάλαμος, *skinthálamos*.
Σκιράφειον, *skiráphion*.	Σκιράς, *skirás*.

T

is pronounced like *t* in *tell, task, tin.* After *ν* it is generally sounded like a *d*, as ἔντομος = *endomos.* This pronunciation of the letter *τ* as *d* after *ν* is very old, judging from the fact that in an old Latin inscription (see Scalig. Vetust. Rom.) we find " διὰ πάντων " written *dia pandon.* Again, as regards " expression of sound " and " euphony " the reader, if he pronounces the following Homeric line:

" Πολλὰ δ' ἄναντα, κάταντα, πάραντά τε, δόχμια τ' ἦλθον,"

will observe that the sound of *τ* as a *d* after *ν* is much more " majestic " and " expressive."

EXAMPLES OF PRONUNCIATION.

Modern Greek.

Τόκος, *interest* (on money),	*tókos.*
Τίποτε, *nothing,*	*tépote.*
Τιποτένιος, *good for nothing,*	*tepoténios.*
Τιμόνι, *rudder,*	*temóni.*
Τρίζω, *grind,*	*trézo.*
Τσακόνω = ἀδράχνω, *to catch,*	*tsakóno.*

Classical.

Ταρσός, *tarsós.*	Ταράσσω, *taráso.*
Ταρσόω, *tarsóö.*	Τάραξις, *táraxis.*
Ταρβέω, *tarvéo.*	Ταριχέμπορος, *tarihémboros.*

Φ

is pronounced like *ph* in *philosopher.* In some parts of ancient Greece, especially in the Peloponnesus, the letter *φ* was often used instead of *κ*; therefore it is highly probable that the letter *φ* was originally pronounced by some as a *κ*; that is to say, like the Latin *q.* In many ancient inscriptions we find the letter *φ* used instead of *κ*, as for instance ὄρφον = ὄρκον, Μενεσιφράτους = Μενεσικράτους.

Now, this hypothesis which we advance concerning the pronunciation of φ (as a κ) is rendered highly probable from the etymology of some words. For instance the word πά-φρων, a scholar asserts, is akin to the Sanscr. *pakâmi;* in the word Λυφοδόρκος we see that the first part, λύκο-ς is akin to the Sanscr. *vṛkas,* Lat. *lupus,* which perhaps came from *lu-quus;* in this example we see plainly that φ = to the Latin *q.* Whether there are any traces of the pronunciation of φ as a κ among the modern inhabitants of Peloponnesus, we have not been able to ascertain.

EXAMPLES OF PRONUNCIATION.

Modern Greek.

Φθάσιμον, *arrival,*	*phthásimon.*	Φλόγα, *flame,*	*phlóga.*
Φθηνὰ, *cheap,*	*phthená.*	Φυλλάδιον, *pamphlet,*	*philáthion.*
Φλυτζάνι (τὸ), *cup,*	*phletzáni.*	Φωλεὰ, *nest,*	*pholeá.*

Classical.

Φιλακόλουθος, *philakóloothos.*		Φιλάρματος, *philármatos.*	
Φιλάδελφος, *philáthelphos.*		Φιλήρετμος, *philéretmos.*	
Φθόνος, *phthónos.*		Φιλοθηρία, *philotheria.*	
Φιλήμων, *philémon.*		Φιλόδουπος, *philóthoopos.*	
Φιλένθοτος, *philénthotos.*		Φιλόδαφνος, *philóthaphnos.*	
Φιλάργυρος, *philáryeros.*			

X

is pronounced like the English *h* in the word *house,* or much more like the German *h* in the word *haben.* χ and κ are often interchanged both in ancient and modern Greek, e. g. δέχομαι = δέκομαι; we also find it interchanged in modern Greek after σ, as σκίζω for σχίζω.

EXAMPLES OF PRONUNCIATION.

Modern Greek.

Χαλνῶ, *to spoil,*	*halnó.*	Χαρτὶ, *paper,*	*hartí.*
Χαμένος, *lost,*	*haménos.*	Χαψιά, *a mouthful,*	*hapsiá.*
Χαρὰ, *joy,*	*hará.*	Χαῦνος, *lazy,*	*hávnos.*

Classical.

Χοή, *hoe.* Χνόος, *hnoös.*
Χοιράς, *herás.* Χορδοτόνος, *horthotónos.*
Χνοάζω, *hnoázo.*

Ψ

is sounded like πσ, e. g.

Modern Greek.

Ψητὸς, *roasted,* *psetós.* Ψαλίδι, *scissors,* *psalíthi.*
Ψωνίζω, *purchase,* *psonízo.*

Classical.

Ψαφαρός, *psapharós.* Ψαμάθη, *psamáthi.*
Ψάω, *psáo.* Ψάλλω, *psállo.*
Ψάμαθος, *psámathos.*

CHAPTER VI.

COMBINATIONS OF CONSONANTS.

Γ

before κ, γ, ξ, χ is pronounced like ν (*ng*). For example: before κ, as in ἀγκίον, pronounced *ankéon;* before γ, as in ἄγγελος, pronounced *áng-gelos;* before ξ, as in ἄγξις, pronounced *ánxis;* before χ, as in ἀγχόνη, pronounced *anhóne.*

ΜΠ

in middle syllables is pronounced like *mb*; as ἄμπελος, pronounced *ámbelos.*

ΝΤ

occurs only in middle syllables in pure Greek words; when ν ends one word and τ begins the next, the latter takes the sound of *d*; for example: τὸν ταῦρον, pronounced *ton dávron;* τὸν τάφον, pronounced *ton dáphon.*

Κ

in the middle of a word and after γ or ν in the same word or in consecutive words partakes of the sound of γ (very soft); for example, ἐγκέφαλος, pronounced *eng-géphalos;* τὸν κῆπον, pronounced *ton ghépon.*

Π

at the beginning of a word which follows one ending with ν is sounded like a *b*; for example: τὴν πόλιν, pronounced *tèn bólen.* It likewise takes the sound of *b* after *μ* in the middle of a word; e. g. τύμπανον, *témbanon.*

(Σ (dialectic pronunciation)

before *β, δ, ρ,* is pronounced like a *z* or like the French *s* in the word *rose;* for example: before *β,* as in σβεστήρ, pronounced *zvestér;* before *δ,* as in Ἀσδρούβας, pronounced *azthroûvas;* before *ρ,* as in Ἰσραήλ, pronounced *izrael.*

CHAPTER VII.

EXAMPLES OF MODERN GREEK PRONUNCIATION.

For the purpose of connected illustration, and that the modern Greek pronunciation may be presented to the student as definitely and clearly as possible, we give here selections from ancient and modern Greek authors, putting under each word of the original text the English symbols required to represent accurately the modern Greek method:

From Xenophon's "Anabasis."

Ἔπειτα δὲ, ἀναμνήσω γὰρ ὑμᾶς καὶ τοὺς τῶν προγόνων τῶν
Épita thai, anamníso ghar emás ke toos ton proghónon ton
ἡμετέρων κινδύνους, ἵνα εἰδῆτε ὡς ἀγαθοῖς τε ὑμῖν προσήκει εἶναι
emetéron kinthínoos, éna ithétai os aghathís te emín proséki ínai
σώζονταί τε σὺν τοῖς θεοῖς καὶ ἐκ πάνυ δεινῶν οἱ ἀγαθοί. Ἐλθόντων
sózonde te sin tis theís ke ek páni thinón e aghathí. Elthóndon
μὲν γὰρ Περσῶν καὶ τῶν σὺν αὐτοῖς παμπληθεῖ στόλῳ ὡς ἀφανι-
men ghar Persón ke ton sin aftís pamplethé stólo os aphani-
ούντων τὰς Ἀθήνας, ὑποστῆναι αὐτοῖς Ἀθηναῖοι τολμήσαντες ἐνίκη-
oóndon tas Athínas, iposténe aftís Athinéi tolmísandes eníke-
σαν αὐτοὺς καὶ εὐξάμενοι τῇ Ἀρτέμιδι ὁπόσους κατακάνοιεν τῶν
san aftoós ke efxámeni te Arthémithi opósoos katakánien ton
πολεμίων τοσαύτας χιμαίρας καταθύσειν τῇ θεῷ, ἐπεὶ οὐκ εἶχον
polemíon tosáftas himéras katathísin te theó epí ook íhon
ἱκανὰς εὑρεῖν, ἔδοξεν αὐτοῖς κατ᾽ ἐνιαυτὸν πεντακοσίας θύειν, καὶ ἔτι
ekanàs evrín, éthoxen aftís kat᾽ eniaftón pendakosías thíin, ke éti
καὶ νῦν ἀποθύουσιν.
ke nin apothíoosin.

From "Πλάτωνος Ἀπολογία Σωκράτους."

Τελευτῶν οὖν ἐπὶ τοὺς χειροτέχνας ᾖα· ἐμαυτῷ γὰρ ξυνῄδειν
Teleftón oon epí toos hirotéchnas éä. emaftó ghar xiníthin
οὐδὲν ἐπισταμένῳ, ὡς ἔπος εἰπεῖν, τούτους δὲ γ' ᾔδειν ὅτι εὑρήσοι-
oothèn epistaméno, os épos ipín, tóotoos thai gh' éthin óti evrísi-
μι πολλὰ καὶ καλὰ ἐπισταμένους· καὶ τούτου μὲν οὐκ ἐψεύ-
mi pollà ke kalà epistaménoos. ke tootoo men ook epséf-
σθην, ἀλλ' ἠπίσταντο ἃ ἐγὼ οὐκ ἠπιστάμην καὶ μου ταύτῃ
sthin, al' epístando a eghó ook ipistámin ke moo táfte
σοφώτεροι ἦσαν· ἀλλ', ὦ ἄνδρες Ἀθηναῖοι, ταὐτόν μοι ἔδοξαν ἔχειν
sophóteri isan. all', o ándres Athinéï, taftón me éthoxan éhin
ἁμάρτημα, ὅπερ καὶ οἱ ποιηταί, καὶ οἱ ἀγαθοὶ δημιουργοί· διὰ τὸ
amártema óper ke e pieté, ke e aghathé themioorghé. thià te
τὴν τέχνην καλῶς ἐξεργάζεσθαι ἕκαστος ἠξίου καὶ τ' ἄλλα τὰ
tin téhnin kalós exergházesthe ékastos exíoo ke t' álla ta
μέγιστα σοφώτατος εἶναι, καὶ αὐτῶν αὕτη ἡ πλημμέλεια ἐκείνην
mégista sofótatos íne, ke aftón áfte e plimmélia ekínin
τὴν σοφίαν ἀπέκρυπτεν· ὥστ' ἐμὲ ἐμαυτὸν ἀνερωτᾶν ὑπὲρ τοῦ
tin sofían apékripten. óst' emé emaftón anerotán ipèr too
χρησμοῦ πότερα δεξαίμην ἂν οὕτως ὥσπερ ἔχω ἔχειν, μήτε τι σοφὸς
hrismoó pótera thexémin an oótos ósperého éhin, méte te sophós
ὢν τὴν ἐκείνων σοφίαν μήτε ἀμαθὴς τὴν ἀμάθιαν, ἢ ἀμφότερα ἃ
on ten ekínon sofían méte amathís ten amáthean, e amphótera a
ἐκεῖνοι· ἔχουσιν ἔχειν· ἀπεκρινάμην οὖν ἐμαυτῷ καὶ τῷ χρησμῷ, ὅτι
ekíni. éhoosin éhin. apekrinámin oon emaftó ke to hrismó, óti
μοι λυσιτελοῖ ὥσπερ ἔχω ἔχειν.
me lisiteli ósper ého éhin.

From a Greek Newspaper, October 18, 1876.

Τὸ δόγμα τῆς συνταγματικῆς θεωρίας ἀντίκειται καὶ εἰς τὴν φύσιν
To thóghma tis sintagmatikís theorías andíkete ke is ten phísin
τοῦ ἀνθρώπου καὶ εἰς τὴν φύσιν τῶν πραγμάτων. Ἡ δευτέρα μεγάλη
too anthrópoo ke is ten phísin don pragmáton. E theftéra megáli
δύναμις τῆς συνταγματικῆς θεωρίας εἶνε ἡ ἀντιπροσωπεία. Ὁ βου-
thínamis tis sentagmatikés theorías íne e •andiprosopía. O voo-

λευτὴς ἔχει ἀπόλυτον ἐξουσίαν νὰ διαθέσῃ τὴν τιμὴν τὴν περιουσίαν
leftés éhi   apóliton   exoosían na thiathése lin dimín lin   perioosían
ἑνὸς ἑκατομμυρίου καὶ πλέον ἀνθρώπων, χωρὶς νὰ ᾖ ὑποχρεωμένος νὰ
enós ekatommiríoo ke pléon anthrópon, horís na e epohreoménos na
δώσῃ περὶ τούτου λόγον. Ἐννοῦσι τοιοῦτον συμβόλαιον οἱ ἄνθρωποι
thóse perí toótoo lógon.   Ennoósi tioóton   simvóleon   e ánthrope
τοῦ δικαίου; Κυβέρνησις ἐν συνταγματικῇ πολιτείᾳ εἶνε οἱ ὑπουργοί.
too thikéoo? Kevérnisis en sindagmatiké politía éne e epoorgé.
Πρώτυπον μεγάλου πρωθυπουργοῦ ἐν Ἀγγλίᾳ ἐστι ὁ λόρδος Οὐάλ-
Prótepon megáloo   prothipoorgoó en Anklía estí o lórthos Ooál-
πωλ περὶ οὗ λέγει συγγραφεύς τις ὅ τι " ἐπὶ τῆς κυβερνήσεως τοῦ
pol perí oo léyi   singraféfs tis o ti "epí tis kiverníseos too
Οὐάλπωλ ἡ διαφθορὰ κατήντησε σύστημα διωργανισμένον," ἕτερος
Ooálpol e thiafthorá katíndise   sistema   thiorganisménon," éteros
δὲ ὅτι " οὐδεὶς κάθ' ὅλον τὸ Βασίλειον τῆς Ἀγγλίας ὑπεστήριζεν
the óti "oothís kath' ólon to Vasílion tis Anklías ipestérizen
αὐτὸν ἐκ πεποιθήσεως."
aftón ek pepithíseos."

**A Modern Greek Prayer offered before performing the Sacrament
of the Eucharist.**

Ἄρτος Ζωῆς, αἰωνιζούσης γενέσθω μοι, τὸ Σῶμά σου τὸ ἅγιον,
Ártos Zoís, eönizoósis genéstho me, to Sóma soo to ághion,
εὔσπλαγχνε Κύριε, καὶ τὸ τίμιον Αἷμα, καὶ νόσων πολυτρόπων ἀλεξη-
éfsplachne Kírie, ke to límion Éma, ke nóson politrópon alexi-
τήριον.
térion.
Βεβηλωθεὶς, ἔργοις ἀτόποις ὁ δείλαιος, τοῦ σοῦ ἀχράντου Σώμα-
Vevelothís, érghis atópis o thíleos too soo achrándoo Sóma-
τος, καὶ Θείου Αἵματος, ἀνάξιος ὑπάρχω, Χριστὲ τῆς μετουσίας, ἧς
tos, ke Thíoo Ématos, anáxios epárho, Christé tis metoosías, is
μὲ ἀξίωσυν. .... Δακρύων μοι παράσχου Χριστέ ρανίδας, τὸν ρύπον
me axíoson.   Thakríon me paráshoo Christé raníthos, ton rípon
τῆς καρδίας μου καθαιρούσας, ὡς ἂν εὐσυνειδότως κεκαθαρμένος,
·tis karthías moo katheroósas, os an efsinithótos kekatharménos

πίστει προσέρχωμαι καὶ φόβῳ Δέσποτα, ἐν τῇ μεταλήψει τῶν Θείων
písti prosérhome, ke phóvo Théspota, en te metalípsi ton Thíon
δώρων σου.
thóron soo.

Εἰς ἄφεσιν γενέσθω μοι τῶν πταισμάτων, τὸ ἄχραντόν σου Σῶμα
Is áphesin genéstho me ton ptesmáton, to áhrandón soo Sóma
καὶ Θεῖον Αἷμα, εἰς Πνεύματος Ἁγίου τε κοινωνίαν, καὶ εἰς αἰώνιον
ke Thíon Éma, is Pnévmatos Aghíoo te kinonían, ke is eónion
ζωὴν φιλάνθρωπε, καὶ παθῶν καὶ θλίψεων ἀλλοτρίωσιν.
zoín filánthrope, ke pathōn ke thlípseon allotríosin.

APPENDIX.

APPENDIX.

BREATHINGS.

THERE are two breathings. The *rough* breathing ' (*spiritus asper*) and the *smooth* breathing ' (*spiritus lenis*). They are indicated by the marks ' ' placed over the initial vowel.

Words beginning with a diphthong take their respective breathings over the second vowel: αἰδηψὸς, εἶδος, εὕδω. But in the *improper diphthongs* ι never takes the breathing, even when it stands upon the line: Ὠιδεῖον = ᾠδεῖον.

The following words have the rough breathing:

1. The initial consonant ρ: thus, ῥήτωρ; except Ῥᾶρος, *Rarus;* Ῥάριος, a, ον, *from Raros, Rarean:* esp. *the Rarian plain* near Eleusis; Ῥάρος, *a child of premature birth;* but ρρ appears in most editions ῥῥ: παλίῤῥοια.

2. All words beginning with υ: thus, ὕδωρ, ὕελος.

3. The articles ὁ, ἡ, οἱ, αἱ.

4. The relative pronouns and the relative adverbs: ὅς, ἥ, ὅ, οἷος, ὅσος, ἡλίκος, ὡς, ὅπως, ἡνίκα, etc.

5. The personal pronouns of the first and second person Plural and the third person Singular: ἡμεῖς, οὗ, οἷ, ἓ, etc.

6. The possessive pronouns which are formed from the stem of the personal pronouns ἡμέτερος. So also the reflexive pronouns of the third person ἑαυτοῦ, ἑαυτῆς.

7. The numerals εἷς, ἕξ, ἑπτὰ, ἑκατὸν, and all their derivatives, e. g. ἑνιαῖος, ἕβδομος, ἑπτακόσιοι.

REMARK 1. The following words, which are alphabetically classified, and their derivatives have also the *rough* breathing:

A.

ἄβρα, a favorite slave.

ἀβρὸς, graceful.

ἅγιος, devoted to the gods.

ἁγνὸς, holy, sacred, etc.

Ἄγνων or Ἅγνων, Hagnon (a proper name).

ἅγος, εος, reverence.

ἀγώ for ἂ ἐγώ.

ἅδε, 3 sing. aor. 2 of ἀνδάνω, Hom. inf. ἀδεῖν.

ᾅδης, the nether world.

ἅδον for ἕαδον, aor. 2 of ἀνδάνω.

ἀδρὸς, thick.

ἀδύπνοος, Dor. for ἡδύπνοος.

ἀδύς, Dor. for ἡδύς.

ἅζομαι. to stand in awe of.

αἷμα, blood.

αἵμνιον, a basin for blood.

Αἵμονες, ων, the Hæmoneans (inhabitants of Hæmonia).

Αἱμόνιος, Hæmonios (a proper name).

αἷμος or αἱμός, οῦ, prob. any scratching point, as of thorns.

Αἷμος, Hæmus (a mountain).

αἱμύλος, winning.

αἱμωδέω, to have the teeth on edge.

αἵμων, ονος, = δαίμων, knowing, skilful.

Αἵμων, Hæmon (a proper name).

αἵνω, to sift, to winnow.

αἵρεσις, a taking, conquering.

αἱρέω, to grasp, to seize.

ἅλας, salt.

ἀλεία, fishing.

ἅλεται, Ep. for ἅληται, subj. aor. 2 of ἅλλομαι, to leap.

ἀλέως, adv. from ἀλής, Hipp.

Ἅλια, a festival of the Rhodians.

Ἀλία, ας, Ion. for Ἀλίη, Halia (a Nereid).

ἀλία, Ion. ἀλίη, an assembly.

Ἀλιαί, ῶν, Haliæ (a city).

Ἀλίαρτος, Haliartus (a city).

Ἀλιάς, the territory of Haliæ.

ἀλιβδύω for ἀλιδύω, to sink in the sea.

ἀλιεὺς, a fisher.

ἀλίζω, to gather.

Ἀλιζώνιον, Halizonium (a city).

Ἀλιθέρσης, Halithersis (a proper name).

Ἀλικαρνασσὸς, Halicarnassus.

ἀλικία, Dor. for ἡλικία.

Ἀλικύαι, ῶν, Halicyæ (a city).

Ἀλίκυρνα, Halicyrna (a region of Ætolia).

Ἀλιμήδη, Halimede (a Nereid).

Ἀλιμοῦς, Halimus (a deme of the Attic tribe Leontis).

ἅλιος for ἥλιος.

ἅλιος = μάταιος, fruitless.

Ἅλιος, Halius (a proper name).

ἅλις, in heaps.

Ἀλίσαρνα, Halisarna (a city).

ἀλισγέω, ῶ, to pollute.

ἀλίσκομαι, to be taken.

Ἀλισόδημος, Halisodemus (a poet).

ἅλλομαι, to spring, leap.

ἅλμη, sea-water.

Ἅλμος, Halmus (a proper name).

ἀλουργίς, a purple robe.

ἀλουργός. dyed with sea-purple.

ἀλόω = ἀλίσκομαι.

ἅλς, a grain or lump of salt.

ἅλυσις, a chain.

Ἀλῶα, a festival of Ceres.

ἀλωεύς, one who works on a threshing-floor.

ἀλώῃ, Ep. for ἀλῷ, 3 sing. subj.
aor. 2 of ἀλίσκομαι.

ἀλώϊος = ἀλωεινός, used in a threshing-floor.

'Αλωΐς = 'Αλωάς, Theocr. 7, 155.

ἀλώκαντι, Dor. for ἑαλώκασι, 3 pl.
perf. of ἀλίσκομαι.

ἀλώμεναι, Ep. for ἀλῶναι, inf. aor. 2
of ἀλίσκομαι.

ἅλων, ωνος, ἡ, = ἅλως.

ἀλῶναι, inf. aor. of ἀλίσκομαι.

ἀλωνεύομαι, dep. to work on a
threshing floor.

ἅλως = a threshing-floor.

ἀλώω, Ep. for ἀλῶ, subj. aor. 2 of
ἀλίσκομαι.

ἅμα, adv. at once.

'Αμαδρυάς, usu. in plur., the Hama-
dryades (nymphs).

ἀμάμαξυς, a vine trained on two
poles.

ἅμαξα, a heavy wagon.

'Αμαξία, Hamaxia (a city).

ἁμαρτάνω, to miss.

ἁμαρτῆ, adv. together.

ἅμιλλα, a contest.

ἁμὶς (καὶ ἁμὶς), a ship.

ἅμμα a knot.

ἀνδάνω, to please.

ἁπαλός, tender.

ἁπάντη, everywhere.

ἁπάντοτε, always.

ἅπαξ, once.

ἁπλοῦς, simplex.

ἅπτρα, the wick of a lamp.

ἅπτω, to fasten.

ἅρκυς (ἀττικῶς), hunter's net.

ἅρμα, a chariot.

"Αρμα, Harma (a city).

"Αρματος, Harmatus (a promontory).

'Αρματοῦς, Harmatus (a city).

ἁρμόζω, to join.

'Αρμονίδης, Harmonides (a proper
name).

ἁρπάζω, to carry off.

'Αρπαλίων, Harpalion (a proper
name).

"Αρπαλος, Harpalus (a proper
name).

'Αρπάλυκος, Harpalycus (a proper
name).

ἁρπεδόνη, a rope.

ἁρπέζα, a hedge.

"Αρπινα, Harpina (a place in Elis).

'Αρποκράτης, Harpocrates (a proper
name).

'Αρποκρατίων, Harpocration (a
proper name).

"Αρπυιαι, the Harpies.

ἀψίκορος, fastidious.

ἀψίς, a tying.

E.

ἔαδα, perf 2 of ἀνδάνω.

ἑάλωκα, perf. of ἀλίσκομαι.

ἑαλώκειν for κέναι, inf. perf. of
ἀλίσκομαι.

ἑανηφόρος, a thin, light robe.

ἑανός, ή, όν, fit for wearing.

ἔαται, 3 pl. pres. from ἧμαι, Ion.
for ἧνται.

ἑαυτοῦ, ῆς, of himself.

ἐάφθη, Hom., only found in Il. ν,
543, and ξ, 419.

ἕβδομος, the seventh.

Ἕβραιος, *Hebrew.* N. T.

Ἕβρος, *the Hebrus.*

ἑδανός, epith. of oil in Hom., *pleasant.*

ἕδνα, *nuptial gifts.*

ἕδος, *stool.*

ἑδοῦμαι, fut. of ἕζομαι.

ἕδρα, *a chair.*

ἑέσσατο, 3 sing. aor. mid. Ep. of ἕννυμι.

ἕεστο, 3 sing. plpf. pass. Ep. of ἕννυμι.

ἕζομαι, *to sit.*

ἑή, fem. of ἑός, *his*, etc.

ἕηκε, Ep. for ἧκε, 3 sing. aor. 1 of ἵημι.

ἑήνδανε, Ep. for ἥνδανε, 3 sing. impf. act. from ἁνδάνω.

ἕθεν, Ep. and Att. poet. gen. for ἕο οὗ, masc. and fem. *his, her, of him, of her.*

ἕθην, aor. 1 pass. from ἵημι.

εἰανός, Ep. for ἑανός.

εἵλη, *the sun's warmth.*

εἵλιγμα, poet. for ἕλιγμα.

εἵλιγμαι, perf. pass. from ἑλίσσω.

εἱλίχατο, Ion. 3 pl. plpf. pass. from ἑλίσσω.

εἵλκυσα, aor. 1 act. of ἕλκω.

εἱλκύσθην, aor. 1 pass. of ἕλκω.

εἷλξα, less usu. aor. 1 act. from ἕλκω than εἵλκυσα.

εἷλον and εἱλόμην, aor. 2 act. and mid. of αἱρέω.

εἱλόπεδον, rarer form for θειλόπεδον, *a sunshiny place.*

εἱλύω, *to wind.*

Εἵλως, *Helot.*

εἷμα, *a dress.*

εἱμαρμένη, *fate.*

εἷμεν, 1 pl. aor. 2 opt. for εἵημεν of ἵημι.

εἱμένος, part. perf. pass. of ἕννυμι.

εἵμην, aor. 2 opt. mid. of ἵημι.

εἵνεκα, poet. for ἕνεκα.

εἷος, Ep. aor. for ἕως.

εἵργνυμι, *to shut in.*

εἱρκτή, *prison.*

εἷς, μία, ἕν, *one.*

εἷς, part. abr. 2 of ἵημι.

εἷσα, *I put, placed.*

εἱσάμην, aor. mid. of εἷσα, Att.

εἷτο, 3 sing. aor. 2 ind. (also opt.) mid. of ἵημι.

εἵως, Ep. for ἕως, *constantly.*

Ἑκάβη, *Hecuba.*

Ἑκάλη, *Hecale* (an Attic borough).

Ἑκαμήδη, *Hecamede* (a proper name).

ἑκὰς, *afar.*

ἕκαστος, *every one.*

ἑκάτερος, *each of two.*

ἑκατόν, *a hundred.*

ἕκητι, *by means of.*

ἑκκαίδεκα, *sixteen.*

Ἕκτωρ, *Hector* (a proper name).

ἑκών, *willing.*

ἕλειαι, *meadow-nymphs.*

Ἑλειοι, *the Helei* (a people of Arabia; Strabo).

ἑλειός, *the dormouse.*

Ἑλένη, *Helen.*

Ἕλενος, *Helenus.*

ἑλέσθαι, inf. aor. 2 mid. of αἱρέω.

ἕλη, *the heat.*

ἕλῃ, 3 subj. aor. 2 of αἱρέω.

ἕλῃαι, Ion for ἕλῃ.

Ἑλίκη, *Helice* (a proper name).

Ἑλικών, *Helicon.*

ἐλινύω, *to rest.*

ἕλιξ, *anything twisted.*

ἑλίσσω, *to turn round.*

ἕλκος, *a wound.*

ἑλκύω, *to draw.*

Ἑλλάς, *Greece.*

ἐλλέβορος, *hellebore.*

Ἕλλην, *a Greek.*

Ἑλλήσποντος, *the Hellespont.*

ἕλμινς, *a worm.*

ἑλοίμι, ἑλοίμην, opt. aor. 2 act. and mid. of αἱρέω.

Ἕλος, *Helos* (a city).

ἕλος, *wet, low ground.*

ἔμεν and ἔμεναι, poet. for εἶναι, inf. aor. 2 from ἵημι.

ἔμενος, part. aor. 2 mid. of ἵημι.

ἕνος (καὶ ἔνος), *a year old.*

ἑνότης, *unity.*

ἕννυμι, *to clothe one's self in.*

ἕξ, *six.*

ἑξῆς, *in order.*

ἕο, Ep. gen. of the pers. pron. 3 pers. for οὗ.

ἑοῖ, Ep. dat. sing. of pers. pron. οὗ for οἷ.

ἑοῖο, Ep. gen. from ἑός for ἑοῦ.

ἑοῖς, dat. pl. from ἑός.

ἑορτὴ, *a feast.*

ἑός, ἑή, ἑόν, Ion. and Ep. for ὅς, ἥ, ὄν, *his, her own.*

ἕπευ, Ion. imp. from ἕπομαι.

ἕπομαι, *to follow.*

ἑπτά, *seven.*

ἕρκος, *a fence.*

ἕρμα, *a prop, support.*

ἑρμηνεύω, *to interpret.*

Ἑρμῆς, *Hermes.*

ἕρπω, *to creep.*

ἕρση (καὶ ἔρση), *dew.*

ἕς, imp. aor. 2 from ἵημι.

ἔσμα, *a stalk.*

ἑσμός, *anything let loose,* esp. a swarm of bees.

ἑσπέρα, *evening.*

Ἕσπερος, *Hesperus* (a proper name).

ἕσσων, Ion. for ἥσσων.

ἕσταα, pf. 2 of ἵστημι.

ἕστακα, transit. perf. of ἵστημι.

ἑστάμεν, ἑστάμεναι, Ep. for ἑστάναι, inf. perf. syncop. from ἵστημι.

ἕσταμεν, 1 pl. perf. syncop. of ἵστημι.

ἑσταότες, pl. from ἑσταώς.

ἕστασαν, 3 pl. plpf. syncop. of ἵστημι.

ἑστᾶσι, 3 pl. perf. syncop. of ἵστημι.

ἕστατε, 2 pl. perf. syncop. of ἵστημι.

ἕστηκα, perf. act. from ἵστημι.

ἑστήξω, inf. fut. from ἵστημι.

ἑστία, *the hearth.*

ἑστιῶ, *to entertain hospitably.*

ἕστο, 3 sing. plpf. pass. of ἕννυμι.

ἕστωρ, *a peg.*

ἑταῖρος, *a comrade.*

ἕτερος, *the other.*

ἑτοῖμος, *at hand, ready.*

εὑρίσκω, *to find.*

ἑφθὸς, *boiled, dressed.*

ἕψω, *to boil.*

ἕω, gen. and acc. sing. from ἕως, *the dawn.*

ἕω, Ion. subj. aor. 2 of ἵημι.

ἑῷ, dat. from ἑός, Hom.

ἔωλος, a day old.

ἑώρα, 3 sing. imp. act. from ὁράω.

ἑώρακα, perf. act. from ὁράω.

ἕως, so long as.

H.

ἡβάσκω, Lat. pubescere.

ἥβη, manhood.

ἡβὸς, ripe.

Ἡγήμων, Hegemon (a proper name).

Ἡγησαῖος, Hegesæus (a proper name).

Ἡγησανδρίδας, Hegesandridas (a proper name).

Ἡγησιάναξ, Hegesianax (a proper name).

Ἡγησίας, Hegesias (a proper name).

Ἡγησικλέης, Hegesicles (a proper name).

Ἡγησίνους, Hegesinus (a proper name).

Ἡγήσιππος, Hegesippus (a proper name).

ἡγοῦμαι, to go before.

ἥδε, fem. from ὅδε.

ἥδομαι, to delight.

Ἡδύλειον, Mt. Hedylius (in Phocis).

ἡδύς, ἡδεῖα, ἡδύ, sweet.

ἧκα, aor. 1 of ἵημι.

ἥκιστος, the least.

ἥκω, I am come.

ἡλικία, age.

ἡλίκος, as big as.

ἧλιξ, in the prime of life.

ἥλιος, the sun.

ἡλίσκος, dim. from ἧλος, a little nail.

ἧλος, a nail.

ἧμαι, to be set.

ἡμέρα, day.

ἥμερος, tamed.

ἤμην, impf. from ἧμαι.

ἡμίονος, a half-ass, i. e. a mule.

ἥμισυς, a half.

ἧμμαι, perf. pass. from ἅπτω.

ἡμωδία, Ion. for αἱμωδία.

ἥμων, a darter.

ἥν, acc. sing. fem. from relat. pron. ὅς.

ἡνία, ίων, τά, the reins.

ἡνία, as, ἡ, the bitted bridle.

ἡνίκα, adv. when.

ἧπαρ, the liver.

Ἥρα, Juno.

Ἡρακλῆς, Hercules.

Ἡράκων, Heracon (a proper name).

Ἡρέας, Hereas (a proper name).

Ἡρόδικος, Herodicus (a proper name).

Ἡρόδοτος, Herodotus (a proper name).

Ἡρώδης, Herodes (a proper name).

ἥρως, a hero.

ᾖσα, aor. 1 from ᾔδω.

ᾖσαι, 2 sing. from ἧμαι.

Ἡσαΐας, Iesaias.

ᾔσατο, Ep. 3 sing. aor. 1 from ἥδομαι.

ᾔσειν, inf. fut. of ἵημι.

ᾖσθαι, inf. from ἧμαι.

Ἡσίοδος, Hesiod.

ᾖσο, 2 sing. imper. from ἧμαι, Hom.

ἡσσάομαι, to be worsted.

ἥσσων, to be less.

ᾖσται, 3 sing. from ἧμαι.

ᾖστο, 3 sing. impf. of ἧμαι.

ἥσυχος, calm.

ᾔσω, fut. of ἵημι.

Ἥφαιστος, Hephaistos.

I.

ἰᾶσι, 3 pl. pres. from ἵημι for ἱέασι.

ἰβίσκος, Lat. hibiscus, a kind of marsh-mallow.

ἱδρόω, to sweat.

ἱδρύω, to seat.

ἱδρῶ, acc. from ἱδρώς for ἱδρῶτα.

ἵδρωα, pustules.

ἱδρώς, sweat.

ἵει, 3 sing. impf. Ion. and Att. of ἵημι.

ἱείς, ἱεῖσα, ἱέν, pres. part. from ἵημι.

ἵεμαι, pres. pass. and mid. from ἵημι.

ἱέμεν, ἱέμεναι, Ep. pres. inf. from ἵημι for ἱέναι.

ἵεν, Æol. for ἵεσαν, 3 pl. impf. from ἵημι.

Ἱερά (νῆσος), Hiera, one of the Lipari islands.

ἱέραξ, a hawk.

ἱερός, sacred.

ἱζάνω (ἵζω), to make to sit, seat.

ἵημι, to set agoing.

ἱκανός, able.

ἱκάνω, to come, to arrive.

ἱκέτης, a suppliant.

ἵκηαι, 2 sing. subj. aor. 2 from ἱκνέομαι.

ἱκνοῦμαι, to arrive.

ἵκω, to come.

ἵλαος (Att. ἵλεως), soothed.

ἱλάρια, a festival of mirth.

ἱλαρός, cheerful.

ἱλάσθητι, aor. pass. imp. of ἱλάσκομαι.

ἱλάσκομαι, to appease, soothe.

ἱλήκω, to be gracious.

ἱμάς, a leathern strap.

ἱμάτιον, a piece of dress.

ἵμερος, longing.

ἵνα, in order that.

Ἱππίας, Hippias.

Ἱπποκόων, Hippocoön.

Ἱπποκράτης, Hippocrates.

Ἱππόλεω ἄκρη, promontory of Hippolaus.

Ἱππόλοχος, Hippolochus.

Ἱππολύτη, Hippolyte.

ἵππος, horse.

ἵπταμαι, to fly.

ἵστημι, to stand.

Ἱστιαία, Histiæa.

Ἱστιαῖος, Histiæus.

ἱστιάτωρ, the chief offerer.

ἱστίον, a sail.

ἱστορία, history.

ἱστός, a ship's mast.

O.

ὅγε, ἥγε, τόγε, the demonstr. pron. he, she, it.

ὅδε, ἥδε, τόδε, the demonstr. pron. Lat. hicce, hæcce, hocce.

ὁδηγός, a guide.

ὁδοιπόρος, a traveller.

ὁδός, street.

ὅθεν, whence.

οἷον, neut. from οἷος.

οἱονανεί, for οἷον ἄν εἰ, just as if.

οἷος, α, ον, such as.

ὁλκάς, merchantman.

ὁλκέω, to draw.

ὅλμος, a round, smooth stone.

ὁλοκαυτέω, to bring a burnt-offering.

ὅλος, whole, entire.

ὅλωσις, a making whole.

ὅμαδος, a noise.

ὁμαλὸς, *level, smooth.*
ὁμάριον, *temple of Jupiter.*
ὁμαρτέω, *to meet.*
ὁμαρτῆ, adv. *together.*
ὁμάς, *the whole.*
ὁμήγυρις, *an assembly.*
ὁμῆλιξ, *of the same age.*
Ὅμηρος, *Homer.*
ὅμηρος, *hostage.*
ὅμιλος, *a throng* of people.
ὁμίχλη, *fog.*
ὅμοιας, *similar.*
ὁμοκλέω, *to call out.*
ὁμός, *one and the same, common.*
ὁμοῦ, *together.*
ὁμῶς, *equally.*
ὅμως, *nevertheless.*
ὁπλὴ, *a hoof.*
ὅπλον, *implement.*
ὁπόθεν, *whence.*
ὅποι, adv. *whither.*
ὁποῖος, *of what sort.*
ὁπόσος, η, ον, *as many.*
ὁπόταν, *whensoever.*
ὁπότερος, *which of two.*
ὅπου, *where.*
ὅπως, *in what manner.*
ὁράω, *to see.*
ὅρηαι or ὁρῆαι, 2 sing. pres. mid. of
  ὁράω.
ὅρημι, Æol. and Dor. for ὁράω,
  hence inf. ὁρῆν.

ὅρητο or ὁρῆτο, 3 sing. impf. mid.
  of ὁράω.
ὁρίζω, *to divide* (as a border).
ὅρκος, *the witness* of an oath.
ὁρμάω, *to set in motion, urge.*
ὁρμέατο, Ion. for ὥρμηντο, 3 pl.
  perf. pass. of ὁρμάω.
ὁρμέω, *to lie at anchor.*
ὁρμή, *attack, violent pressure.*
ὁρμίζω, *to bring to a safe anchorage.*
ὅρμος, *a necklace.*
ὅρος, *a boundary, limit.*
ὅς, ἥ, ὅ, *who,* etc.
ὁσημέραι, *daily.*
ὅσιος, *hallowed.*
ὅσος, *as great as.*
ὁσῶραι, *every hour.*
ὅστις, *whosoever.*
ὅταν, adv. *whenever.*
ὅτε, *when.*
ὅτι, *for that, because.*

Ω.

ὧδε, Att. ὡδί, from ὅδε, *in this wise.*
ὤμιλλα, *a kind of game.*
ὥρα, *hour, season.*
ὡραῖος, *beautiful,* etc.
ὥριος, *timely.*
ὡς, adv. *thus, so,* etc.
ὥσπερ, adv. *even as, just as.*
ὥστε, adv. *for, so that, in order.*

REMARK 2. When two words have the same form, but are of different meanings, the ancient Greeks often indicated the difference by placing a breathing over the vowel or ρ in the middle of a word; thus, ἐσῆλατο (aorist of εἰσάλλομαι, ἐσάλλομαι), but ἐσῆλατο (aorist of σάλλομαι), κοτυλλήῤῥυτος (κοτύλη ῥέω), but κοτυλήῤυτος (κοτύλη ἀρύω).

ACCENT.

THE accents are three. The acute ´, the grave `, and the circumflex ˆ. The acute can stand only on one of the last three syllables of a word; the circumflex, on one of the last two; and the grave, only on the last syllable.

In case of a diphthong, the accent stands over the *second* vowel; thus, παύσω, ταῦτα, ἐκείνους, ἐκεῖ, etc.

The acute may stand either on a long or a short syllable; thus, τρέχω, λόγους, ἐκείνους. The *acute* only can stand on a long penultima, followed by a long ultima: μήκους, γλώσσης. When the Nominative and Accusative of uncontracted nouns are accented on the ultima, said cases are oxytone: ἡ τιμή, τὴν τιμήν, ἡ χαρά, τὴν χαράν, ὁ αἰών, ὁ καρπός. When a word is accented on the *antepenult*, said syllable is always proparoxytone: βασιλεύοντος.

Words ending in ευ and ου, when accented on the ultima, are perispomena; thus, εὖ, ποῦ · except ἰδού, ἰού, and οὔ.

When the Vocative of nouns in ευς and ω of the third declension ends in ευ and οι, said case must be perispomenon if accented on the ultima: ὦ βασιλεῦ, ὦ αἰδοῖ, ὦ σαπφοῖ.

When the Genitive and Dative of nouns end with a long syllable, said cases must be perispomena if accented on the ultima: τῆς τιμῆς, τῇ τιμῇ, τοῦ καρποῦ, τῷ καρπῷ, τῶν τιμῶν, τοῖς καρποῖς.

A contract ultima is always perispomenon, if the acute stood on the penultima before contraction: τιμῶ (τιμάω), πλακοῦς (πλακόεις). Adverbs in ως, if accented on the ultima, are perispomena: καλῶς, εὐσεβῶς.

REMARK 1. The circumflex stands on the Nominative and Accusative of many monosyllabic words; thus, γραῦς, ναῦς, βοῦς, χοῦς, μῦς, δρῦς, σῦς, οὖς, πῦρ, σκῶρ, εἷς, πᾶς, πᾶν, etc.

REMARK 2. The circumflex stands also on many monosyllabic adverbs and conjunctions; thus, εὖ, φεῦ, ὦ, αὖ, νῦν, οὖν, γοῦν, ἦ, μῶν, πῇ, ποῖ, ποῦ, πῶς, etc.

In accenting a word, a syllable *long* by *position* is treated as short; thus, λέξις, τάξις (but πρᾶξις, πρᾶγμα, because the letter a in these words is long not by position, but by nature). Final αι and οι have the effect of *short* vowels on the accent of the penult and antepenult: λύονται, ἄνθρωποι, πολῖται, νῆσοι, etc.

Not so, however, in the optative mode: παιδεύοι and the adverb οἴκοι, *at home.*

When the *ultima* is long, the antepenult is not accented: ἀνθρώπου, ἀνθρώπῳ. The Genitives Singular and Plural of some nouns of the third declension are exceptions, e. g. πόλεως, πόλεων, πήχεως, πήχεων.

Primitive words accent the syllable belonging to the root; thus, φίλος. Derivative words accent the syllable which specifies or defines; thus, φιλικός, ἄφιλος. Hence we have the following rules:

Whenever a new syllable is prefixed to a word, the accent is thrown back if the ultima permits it; thus, λύω, ἔλυον.

When a new syllable is affixed to a word, the accent is thrown forward if the ultima requires it; e. g. παράδειγμα, παραδείγματος, παραδειγμάτων, φῶς, φωτίζω, φωτιζόμενος, φωτιζομένη. Final ξ and ψ, after a short vowel, exclude the acute from the antepenult, but not the circumflex from the penult; thus we have ἧλιξ, but νυκτοφύλαξ instead of νυκτόφυλαξ.

SPECIAL RULES (FIRST DECLENSION).

Endings.

The following Masculine nouns in ης are of the first declension:

1. Proper patronymic nouns in δης; thus, Ἀτρείδης, *son of Atreus ;* Νεστορίδης, *son of Nestor.*

2. Common nouns in της; thus, πολίτης, *a citizen ;* λῃστής, *a robber.*

3. Nouns (common or proper) compounded with verbs;

thus, γεωμέτρης, *a geometer ;* βιβλιοπώλης, *a book-seller.* Except nouns compounded with φαίνομαι, *to appear ;* thus, 'Αριστοφάνης, *Aristophanes ;* Λεξιφάνης, *Lexiphanes ;* and a few foreign nouns.

4. Nouns compounded with Feminine nouns of the first declension; thus, 'Ολυμπιονίκης (νίκη), *a conqueror in the Olympic games ;* 'Αρχιδίκης (δίκη), *chief judge.*

Accent.

1. Nouns of this declension form the Genitive Plural per-ispomenon.

Three masculines have an irregular accent in the Gen. Pl.: χρήστης, *usurer,* Gen. Pl. χρήστων (but χρηστῶν, Gen. Pl. of the adjective χρηστός, *good*), χλούνης, *living* or *feeding alone,* Gen. Pl. χλούνων (but χλουνῶν, Gen. Pl. of the adjective χλουνος, epith. of gold in Hesychius (Lexicographus), and ἐτησίαι, *annual winds,* Gen. Pl. ἐτησίων. So also the Feminine ἀφύη, *anchovy,* Gen. Pl. ἀφύων (but ἀφυῶν, Gen. Pl. of the adjective ἀφυής, *dull*).

2. Adjectives whose Masculine is of the third declension have the Genitive Plural Feminine perispomenon; thus, ὁ τυφθείς, ἡ τυφθεῖσα, τῶν τυφθεισῶν. Adjectives whose Masculine is of the second declension accent the Genitive Plural Feminine regularly (rule 1st): ὁ ἅγιος, οἱ ἅγιοι, τῶν ἁγίων, ἡ ἁγία, αἱ ἅγιαι, τῶν ἁγιῶν.

Case-Endings.

1. Nouns ending in α *pure* or ρα and a few proper nouns like Λήδα, *Leda,* Γέλα, *Gela,* Φιλομήλα, *Philomela,* 'Ανδρομέδα, *Andromeda,* and contract substantives and adjectives in α retain the α in all the cases of the Singular number.

2. Masculine nouns in ας, with the exception of the Genitive Singular, follow the same rule.

3. Masculine nouns of this declension form the Accusative Singular by changing σ of the Nominative to ν. The Feminines by affixing ν to the Nominative Singular.

4. Masculine words in ης form the Vocative Singular in η. But nouns in της and πης and names of nations and words compounded with πωλῶ, *to sell*, τρίβω, *to rub*, μετρῶ, *to measure*, ἄρχω, *to be first*, ὠνοῦμαι, *to purchase*, and λατρεύω, *to serve*, form the Vocative Singular in a short; thus, πολῖτα (Nom. πολίτης, *a citizen*); γεωμέτρα (Nom. γεωμέτρης, *a geometer*); βιβλιοπῶλα (Nom. βιβλιοπώλης, *a book-seller*); etc.

5. A few Doric nouns in ας form their Genitive Singular in a by omitting the termination ο; thus, Πυθαγόρας τοῦ Πυθαγόρα, ὁ Λεωνίδας τοῦ Λεωνίδα (from the Doric Gen. Πυθαγόραο, Λεωνίδαο). In the same way many proper foreign nouns and many nouns of the Hellenistic Greek form their Genitive Singular; thus, τοῦ Ἀννίβα, τοῦ Ὀρόντα.

Quantity of Final α.

The following Feminine words in a have the final a of the Nominative Singular long:

1. Adjectives whose Masculine is of the second declension; thus, ἅγιος, *sacred*, ἁγία. Except πέπειρος, πέπειρα, Lat. *maturus*, and nouns which suffer contraction in the penultima; thus, δῖϊος, δῖος, δῖα (of Jupiter), *holy*, *pure;* Χίϊος, Χῖος, Χῖα (of or from Chios), *Chian.*

2. Paroxytone nouns in ια; thus, κακία, *wickedness;* σοφία, *wisdom.*

3. Dissyllabic nouns in εια and nouns in εια derived from verbs ending in ευω; thus, μνεία, *memory;* βασιλεία, *kingdom* (βασιλεύω).

4. All oxytone nouns; thus, χαρά, *joy;* λαλιά, *speech.*

5. Dissyllabic nouns in ρα which have a vowel in the penultima; thus, ὥρα, *hour;* θήρα, *the chase.* Except πρῶρα, *a ship's prow;* χύτρα, *an earthen pot;* σφῦρα, *a hammer.*

6. Paroxytone nouns in οα and εα; thus, χρόα, *the skin;* πόα, *grass;* μηλέα, *an apple-tree;* Τεγέα, *Tegea.*

7. Nouns of more than *two* syllables in αια; thus, ἐλαία, *the olive-tree;* κεραία, *a horn.* Except the names of a few cities; thus, Φώκαια, *Phocæa;* Πλάταια, *Platæa.*

The following words have the α short:

1. Feminine adjectives whose Masculine is of the third declension; thus, πᾶς, πᾶσα, every (whole).

2. All disyllabic nouns in αια; thus, μαῖα, good mother; γραῖα, an old woman.

3. Common nouns in εια which are derived from common nouns in ευς; thus, ἱερεύς, ἱέρεια, a priestess; Ἀλεξανδρεύς, Ἀλεξάνδρεια, Alexandria.

4. Abstract nouns in εια which are derived from adjectives in ης of the third declension; thus, εὐγενής, εὐγένεια, nobility.

5. Abstract nouns in οια derived from adjectives in οος, ους; thus, εὔνοος, εὔνους, εὔνοια, good will.

6. Substantives in υια; thus, μυῖα, a fly. So also the oxytone nouns ὀργυιά, strictly the length of the outstretched arms; ἀγυιά, a way.

7. All nouns which in the Genitive Singular change α into η; thus, Μοῦσα, Muse; γλῶσσα, a tongue.

8. Dissyllabic nouns in ρα which have a diphthong in the penultima; thus, σφαῖρα, a sphere; πεῖρα, a trial. Except αἴθρᾱ, a clear (bright) sky; Φαίδρᾱ, Phædra; αὔρᾱ, breeze; λαύρᾱ, an alley; σαύρᾱ, a lizard.

9. Nouns in τρια and τειρα derived from nouns in της and τηρ τρια and all proparoxytone nouns; thus, ποιητής, ποιήτριᾰ, a poetess; σωτήρ, σώτειρα, frequ. an epith. of protecting goddesses; τράπεζα.

SPECIAL⤚RULES (SECOND DECLENSION).

Accent.

1. Nouns compounded with νόος and πλόος, even when contracted, are paroxytone; thus, περίπλοος, περίπλους, περιπλόου, περίπλου, a sailing round; εὔνοος, εὔνους, εὐνόου, εὔνου, kind-hearted. The termination οα, however, always remains uncontracted: εὔνοα, εὔπλοα.

REMARK. Ὄγδοος, the eighth, and λιθοξόος, a stone-mason, áre never contracted; but ἀντίξοος, hostile, δορυξόος, spear-polishing, and πρόχοος, *a pitcher*, are contracted; thus, ἀντίξοος, ἀντίξους, ἀντιξόου, ἀντίξου, προχόου, πρόχου. These nouns, however, sometimes drop *o* of the stem; thus, ἄντιξος, δόρυξος.

Peculiarities of Gender.

1. Many nouns in changing their gender change their signification, e. g. ὁ ζυγός, *the yoke*, ἡ ζυγός, *the scale*; ὁ ἵππος, *a horse*, ἡ ἵππος, *a mare*.

2. Many nouns of the Masculine or Feminine gender in the Singular are Neuter in the Plural; thus, ὁ δεσμός, τὰ δεσμά, *fetters*; ἡ κέλευθος, τὰ κέλευθα, *a road (ways)*; "ὑγρὰ καὶ ἰχθυόεντα κέλευθα."

SPECIAL RULES (THIRD DECLENSION).

Accent.

1. Monosyllabic substantives are oxytone, e. g. μήν, *a month*; θήρ, *a wild beast*; χείρ, *a hand*. Nouns, however, which have lengthened their stem-vowels, or whose Nominatives are contracted from barytone or oxytone nouns, are perispomena; thus, μυός, μῦς, *a mouse*; πυρός, πῦρ, *fire*; (ὄσατος, ὦς), οὖς, *the ear*. Two nouns, τὸ φῶς (from φωΐς, *a man*) and δᾴς (from δαΐς, *a fire-brand*), are oxytone.

REMARK. The vowel which results from contraction, if accented, must be perispomenon; thus, γέα-γῆ, *earth*. Except, (a) when the vowel stands before a long *ultima*; (b) when it stands before the antepenult; and (c) when the second of the contracted vowels is oxytone, e. g. ἑσταώς, ἑστώς.

2. Monosyllabic words of this declension accent the Genitive and Dative of all numbers on the case-ending; the other cases are accented on the stem. Except,

(*a*) Participles of one syllable, which always accent the stem, e. g. θείς, θέντος, θέντι, θέντα.

(*b*) The Genitive Plural of the following nouns: παῖς *a boy, girl*, παίδων; ἡ δάς, *torch*, δάδων; ἡ φώς, *blister*, φώδων; κράς, *the head* (Nom. obsolete), κράτων; οὖς, *ear*, ὤτων; δμώς, *a slave*; Τρώς, *a Trojan*, Τρώων; τὸ φῶς, *light*, φώτων; θώς, *the jackal,* θώων; ὁ σής, *moth,* σέων. The word φωτῶν (*of men*) has for its Nom. Sing. φώς, Gen. Sing. φωτός.

(*c*) Some words which have been contracted from disyllabic stems, e. g. ἔαρ, *spring,* Gen. ἔαρος or ἦρος, Dat. ἔαρι or ἦρι.

4. Nouns whose final stem-letter is δ are oxytone; thus, ἐλπίς, *hope,* ἐλπίδος. Except the noun ἔρις, *strife,* ἔριδος, and Feminine common nouns in τις, whose Masculine ends in της; thus, ὁ προφήτης, *prophet,* ἡ προφῆτις.

Adjectives.

Adjectives are either of three endings, of two, or of one. The following adjectives in ος are of three endings:

(*a*) Verbal in τος and τεος; thus, λεκτός, ή, όν, *chosen.*

(*b*) Adjectives in ικος, λος, νος, ρος, and λέος, e. g. νομικός, ική, ικόν, *a lawyer;* σιγηλός, λή, λόν, *silent;* δεινός, νή, νόν, *fearful;* αἰσχρός, ρά, ρόν, *causing shame;* etc.

(*c*) Comparatives and superlatives; thus, λυπηρότερος, οτέρα, ότερον; λυπηρότατος, οτάτη, ότατον, from λυπηρός, *sorrowful.* Except a few superlatives which are found of two terminations among poets and Attic writers; thus, δυσεκβολώτατος ἡ λοκρίς (Thuc. ε΄ 101), τὴν ὕπατον ἀρχήν (Dion. Hal. Ῥυμ. ἀρχ. ϛ΄ 1), ὀλοώτατος ὀδμή (Od. δ, 442).

The following adjectives in ος are of two endings:

(*a*) Compounds and those which are derived from verbs already compounded; thus, ὁ καὶ ἡ ἄσκοπος τὸ ἄσκοπον, *imprudent.*

(*b*) Positive and comparative adjectives in ων: ὁ καὶ ἡ εὐδαίμων τὸ εὔδαιμον, *happy, prosperous.*

(*c*) Many adjectives compounded from substantives in ις, υς, and ους; thus, ὁ καὶ ἡ εὔχαρις, τὸ εὔχαρι, *charming;* ὁ καὶ ἡ πολύπους, τὸ πολύπουν, *many-footed.*

(*d*) Words compounded with γέλως and κέρας, which are also declined according to the second Attic declension; thus, ὁ καὶ ἡ πολύγελως, τὸ πολύγελων, τοῦ πολύγελω καὶ πολυγέλωτος, *laughing much.*

The following adjectives are of one ending:

(*a*) Adjectives which have been compounded with substantives keep the latter unchanged even after composition; thus, ὁ καὶ ἡ ἄπαις, *childless;* μακρόχειρ, *long-armed.*

REMARK. The Genitive and Dative Plural of these adjectives are found among the poets in the Neuter gender also.

Feminine Endings of Adjectives in ος.

The following adjectives. in ος of three endings form their Feminine:

(*a*) In η, if there is no vowel or ρ before the termination; thus, ἀγαθός, ἀγαθή, *kind.*

(*b*) In α, if they end in α pure or in ρος, ροος, and ρεος;, thus, ἅγιος, ἁγία, *holy;* καθαρός, καθαρά, *proper, clean.*

Neuter Endings.

Adjectives in ος form their neuter in ον; thus καλός, καλή, καλόν, *good.* The following form their neuter in ο:

(*a*) ἄλλος, ἄλλη, ἄλλο, *another;* ὅς, ἥ, ὅ, *who, which;* αὐτός, αὐτή, αὐτό, *self* (Lat. *ipse*); ἐκεῖνος, ἐκείνη, ἐκεῖνο, *there* (Lat. *ille*); οὗτος, αὕτη, τοῦτο, *this, that.*

Demonstratives of quality, quantity, and age form their neuter in the following manner: τοσοῦτος, τοσαύτη, τοσοῦτο(ν), *such* (in quantity or number); τοιοῦτος, τοιαύτη, τοιοῦτο(ν), *such* (in quality); τηλικοῦτος, τηλικαύτη, τηλικοῦτο(ν), *such* (in age or size).

Cambridge: Electrotyped and Printed by Welch, Bigelow, & Co.